A to Z Ready for K

A to Z Ready for K

A Complete 35-Week Preschool Curriculum

SUSAN EHRHARDT

ILLUSTRATIONS BY JANICE STENTZ

Redleaf Press®
www.redleafpress.org
800-423-8309

Published by Redleaf Press
10 Yorkton Court
St. Paul, MN 55117
www.redleafpress.org

First edition 2018
Cover design by Jim Handrigan
Cover photographs by Robert Kneschke – stock.adobe.com (top); © bst2012 – stock.adobe.com (center); © junce11 – stock.adobe.com (bottom)
Interior design and illustrations by Janice Stentz
Typeset in Frutiger LT
Printed in the United States of America
24 23 22 21 20 19 18 17 1 2 3 4 5 6 7 8

Library of Congress Cataloging-in-Publication Data
CIP data is on file with the Library of Congress

Printed on acid-free paper

Dedication

Thank you to all the children I have taught over the years.
You have given me great joy and inspired my creativity.
Even though I was your teacher and you were my students,
I learned far more from you than you will ever know.

~ Mrs. Ehrhardt

TABLE OF CONTENTS

ACKNOWLEDGMENTS

Thank you to Scot and Dana Ehrhardt—my son and daughter-in-law, the teachers—for reviewing my book. You were always willing to answer my questions about structure and grammar.

Thank you to my friend and graphic artist, Janice Stentz. You were so patient when I asked you to redo the artwork and layout over and over and over.

And thank you to Kara Lomen, my editor. You always listened to my ideas and to what I thought was important. Your editing expertise made what felt like an overwhelming project come to fruition.

INTRODUCTION

A to Z Ready for K is a hands-on, easy to use curriculum resource. The title seems to suggest that the book moves through the alphabet beginning with the letter *Aa* and ending with *Zz*. But not so! This is a new, creative approach. Take a peek at the Table of Contents to see the order of the alphabet and the themes surrounding each letter. However, before starting the alphabet letters, the year begins with two introductory weeks. First, the children learn about themselves and their families and second, they learn about colors. The first two weeks will give you the opportunity to begin to get to know the children in your class and assess where they are academically, socially, and emotionally. When the alphabet does begin, we start simply. The letter *Oo* comes first. It is an easy letter to print. The upper and lower case look the same. The children begin with an "I can" attitude!

Along with a chapter for each letter of the alphabet, there are some additional chapters: Simple Machines, Thanksgiving, Snow Week, Five Senses, Spring Week, Artist Week, and Ready for Kindergarten. These chapters give a break in the routine. For instance, Simple Machines is taught between *Rr* and *Dd* Week. The Snow Week chapter creates a break during the long winter months. Artist Week is my favorite week. It is a study of the artists: Leonardo da Vinci, Michelangelo, Vincent Van Gogh, Paul Gauguin, Georges Seurat, Henri Matisse, Alexander Calder, Pablo Picasso, Marcel Duchamp, and Jackson Pollock. The children look at examples of their work and, at the preschool level, try to imitate their techniques. This comes at the end of the school year so all of their beautiful artwork can be displayed to create a Pre-K art gallery. Family and friends view the children's masterpieces when they come to an End-of-the-Year program.

Creativity creates interest, but routine and repetition create stability. This is important for young children to feel comfortable and secure. Therefore, each chapter is structured the same. Each weekly chapter includes the following:

- Early childhood standards
- Weekly themes
- Dramatic play and prop suggestions
- Listening activities and songs
- Stories
- Interactive charts and props
- Circle-time activities
- Table work
- Writing center activities
- Board games
- Sensory table suggestions
- Workbench activities
- Art and craft activities
- Lesson plan template

To make this curriculum even easier, reproducibles, craft, and project patterns are included. Wherever you see an asterisk, there is a reproducible available on the Redleaf Press website at redleafpress.org/atoz. *

A to Z Ready for K is for anyone looking for new ideas or for a curriculum to use lesson by lesson, every day. It is a result of my more than twenty-five years of preschool teaching experience. After years of planning, writing, and rewriting, my hope is that you will find this curriculum resource to be a useful and helpful tool in preparing young children for kindergarten.

Note: The dramatic play illustration above is Vacation and Travel used during *Kk* Week.

Welcome!

Before the children arrive, let me show you around the classroom

Dramatic Play Area

Dramatic play creates the atmosphere of the classroom. Most often, it is confined to one area of the classroom, but that is not always best. For instance, a grocery store dramatic play space with grocery carts may be more interesting spread throughout the classroom.

There are suggestions for dramatic play in each chapter of this curriculum.

The themes include the following:

- pet store
- construction zone
- pizza parlor
- farm with harvest market
- racecar pit stop
- simple machines
- nature/camping
- kitchen
- five food groups grocery store
- fitness center with yoga
- snow indoors
- friendship card factory
- laundry room
- zoo hospital
- ice cream parlor
- vacation and travel
- space travel
- spring
- baseball and bowling
- art studio
- gardening/flower shop

TIP Collect props for dramatic play themes at garage sales and flea markets whenever you see them. Setting up is easy if you store materials in prop boxes for each dramatic play theme.

Class Rules

The following are some examples of classroom rules:

- We must keep everyone safe.
- Be helpful to each other.
- Listen to one another.
- We speak one at a time.
- Use only kind words.

Teacher's Mailbox

Purchase a mailbox from a home improvement store. Use the mailbox for notes from parents and gifts of artwork from the children.

TIP Be sure to clean the mailbox out every day!

Chore Chart

The chore chart identifies the child helpers, which are Line Leader, Calendar Keeper, Weather Reporter, and Teacher's Helper.

TIP Rotate names weekly on the chart. A variety of chore charts are available at your local school supply store.

Calendar and Weather

The Calendar Keeper and Weather Reporter are two of the child's chores that are completed during CIRCLE TIME.

TIP Encourage children to use complete sentences for the calendar and the weather report.

Letter of the Week Display

A set of alphabet letters and American Sign Language cards can be purchased. Display these cards with pictures of animals or other things that begin with the letter of the week.

TIP For every chapter that focuses on a letter of the alphabet, the CIRCLE TIME ACTIVITY on the first day of the week is to introduce the letter of the week. See *Oo* Week on page 26 for a full explanation.

Bulletin Board

Use this space to display the children's work.

It can reflect the theme or season. Shown above is an example from *Zz* Week when the zoo hospital is in the DRAMATIC PLAY area. Have the children draw an animal they have seen at the zoo. String black yarn up and down the bulletin board to resemble a cage and tuck the children's drawings behind the yarn so the animals look like they are in the cage.

Hooks for Art Projects

Art projects are made at CRAFT TIME. I have a morning and afternoon class, so there are two rows of hooks—one hook for each child. The hooks are permanently attached to a board which is then attached to the wall. Each week I add the child's project to an *O* ring. At the end of the school year, each child takes the ring of their projects home. They are so proud to show them to their families!

Magnetic Dry-Erase Board

Use it for magnetic letters, numbers, pictures, etc. Write on the dry-erase board to demonstrate letter and number formation for TABLE WORK. The board can also be used to display the interactive charts at CIRCLE TIME. The children learn how the interactive chart works and often play with it again at FREE CHOICE PLAY.

TIP When an interactive chart is introduced at CIRCLE TIME, always give each child a turn. This develops communication skills and helps the children begin feeling comfortable speaking in front of a group.

Interactive Charts and Props

Interactive charts and teaching props aid the visual learner. Interactive charts can be made easily with poster board, pictures, and sentence strips.

TIP A bucket of tiny wooden ginger-bread people labeled with each child's name is a great way to choose children randomly for an activity!

TIP If there are two classes, put a label on each side of the ginger-bread person using two different colors for the morning and afternoon.

Circle Rug

Use it for CIRCLE TIME. The rug should be large enough to seat all the children comfortably and within view of the chore chart. Also, it should be accessible to the calendar and weather chart and close to the magnetic dry-erase board in order to use interactive charts.

Place a comfortable chair and small shelf for a few books to use this space for story time. Finally, use it as the area for block building at FREE CHOICE PLAY.

Crafts

Our shelves contain the following:

- four toolboxes (one for each table), each containing glue, scissors, and pencils for every child
- crayons and markers
- paper for drawing
- box of usable scraps of construction paper
- envelopes
- old magazines for cutting pictures
- tape, staplers, hole punchers
- empty space for craft supplies that change weekly

Board Games and Puzzles

Board games are suggested in each chapter of the curriculum. Make sure games are simple so children can play without adult supervision. A good time to rotate board games and puzzles is when you change DRAMATIC PLAY themes. Add a small table with chairs nearby for two-player board games.

TIP Challenge the children with more difficult puzzles. Designate a table or flat surface to store a partially completed puzzle so it can be finished the next day.

Sensory Table

Each chapter has sensory table suggestions.

Fill the sensory table with water, uncooked rice, beans, moldable sand, playdough, snow, flour, potting soil, beads for making necklaces, and so forth. Look for more suggestions in each chapter. The sensory table can also become part of the DRAMATIC PLAY area.

Workbench

There are various suggestions in the weekly chapters for activities at the workbench. One week a handsaw is suggested. In order to use a handsaw safely, there will need to be a vice firmly attached to one side of the workbench.

The workbench should be used under adult supervision.

TIP Always display the workbench safety rules:

- Wear safety goggles at all times
- Only two children working at a time
- Always keep both hands on the handle of the saw

Easel and Dry Rack

The easel should be close to the dry rack, and the dry rack should be at a height low enough to allow the children to hang their own papers without dripping too much on the floor. Change the art medium and the tools at the easel frequently.

Listening Center

Put out two floor pillows and use two headphones to listen to music or a book on tape. Be sure to locate the listening center near an electrical outlet if needed. Musical instruments can also be displayed in this area.

Writing Table

The writing table is used primarily for a weekly activity done in conjunction with the letter of the alphabet we are studying that week. The children copy the assigned words for the week in their journals. The work is done anytime during FREE CHOICE PLAY and is to be completed before the last day of the week. The writing table can also be used by children to explore print and writing materials.

TIP The weekly journal is an excellent way for a child to begin learning personal time management.

The following are supplies used at the writing table:

- journal for each child
- set of rubber alphabet stamps which have 2–3 picture stamps for each letter of the alphabet (for example, for the letter *Aa* there is an airplane, apple, and ant)
- ink pad
- pencils and crayons
- clipboards
- different sizes and shapes of paper
- placemats (to add color and define the number of children that can work at the writing table at one time)

NOTE: The writing journals are used for two things:

1. **Copying the weekly words at the writing table**
2. **Journal work done for TABLE WORK**

Block Shelf

The circle rug gives a defined boundary for building with blocks. A theme-based manipulative can be added to the block area to encourage creativity. For example, during *Zz* Week add zoo animals to the block shelf.

The children are arriving and the day begins . . .

My Pre-K Daily Schedule

Beginning Circle

- *Teacher's Helper* passes out musical instruments
- Sing "Hello Song"
- *Calendar Keeper* tells the day of the week and marks the calendar
- *Weather Reporter* gives the weather
- CIRCLE TIME ACTIVITY

Before moving to TABLE WORK, take time to stand and stretch.

TABLE WORK

FREE CHOICE PLAY

Cleanup

Story

Ending Circle

- CIRCLE TIME ACTIVITY
- Song
- "Good-bye Song" or "Good-bye Poem"
  The "Good-bye Song" is used the first half of the year, and the "Good-bye Poem" is used after winter break. The *Line Leader* takes the class outside to play or to the inside large-motor space.

Large-Motor Activity

Circle Time Activities

Each chapter has a list of suggestions for CIRCLE TIME ACTIVITIES. CIRCLE TIME ACTIVITIES are used at the **Beginning Circle** and **Ending Circle.**

"Hello Song"
(to the tune of "Skip to My Lou")

Hello, how are you?
Hello, how are you?
Hello, how are you?
How are you today? Hey!

(remaining verses use all the children's names, three at a time)

Hello [*child's name*], how are you?
Hello [*another child's name*], how are you?
Hello [*another child's name*], how are you?
How are you today? Hey!

—Original author unknown

Use the chore chart to determine the Line Leader, Calendar Keeper, Weather Reporter, and Teacher's Helper.

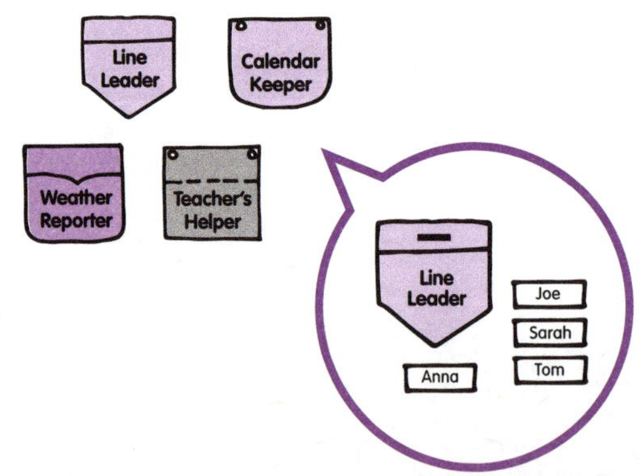

Listening Activities and Songs
Songs are listed for quick reference. The words to the songs created to the tune of traditional songs are in the appropriate chapters. Daily instructional and transitional songs and poems are listed as they are introduced in each chapter. Use as needed throughout the year.

Table Work

A series of reproducibles for TABLE WORK accompany the curriculum resource.

TIP All reproducibles marked with a * can be found on the Redleaf Press website at www.redleafpress.org/atoz. Click on the Web Components tab.

Free Choice Play

"Cleanup Song"
(to the tune of "The More We Get Together")

Oh we can work together, together, together;
Oh we can work together to clean up our room.
Pick this up and that up and this up and that up.
Oh we can work together to clean up our room.

TIP At the end of FREE CHOICE PLAY use a simple song or soft instrumental music for cleanup.

Stories

Stories are listed by title and author for quick reference. There are more stories suggested than needed.

These stories promote self-esteem:

- *Hurray for Pre-K!* by Ellen B. Senisi
- *It's Hard to be Five: Learning How to Work My Control Panel* by Jamie Lee Curtis and Laura Cornell
- *What I Do Best!* by Allia Zobel Nolan
- *Hooray for You!* by Marianne Richmond
- *You're Wonderful* by Debbie Clement (includes a CD of the song)

"Good-bye Song"
(to the tune of "*Frére Jacques*")

Teacher sings: Good-bye, children.
Children sing: Good-bye, teacher.
Teacher: It was a good day!
Children: It was a good day!
Teacher: We'll meet again on [*day of the week*].
Children: We'll meet again on [*day of the week*].
Teacher: Go-ood-bye!
Children: Go-ood-bye!

Another line can be added for a special project or field trip. For example,

Teacher: We're going to the library!
Children: We're going to the library!

"Good-bye Poem"

Good-bye, my friends.
See you later, alligator.
Toodle-loo, honeydew.
After a while, crocodile.
Ta-ta, mama llama.
Give a hug, little bug.
Take care, panda bear.
See you soon, macaroon.
No cryin', little lion.
Out the door, with a ROAR!

Adapted by Susan Ehrhardt

Notes

WEEK 1

Learning About Living Things

Learning About Myself

Dramatic Play

Pet Store

Learning Objectives

Physical and Motor

- Copies and draws simple shapes and letters
- Uses scissors
- Uses small muscles in hands to color, cut, paste, and paint

Cognitive

- Identifies and names body parts
- Writes own name

Communication and Language

- Sings simple repetitive songs
- Uses sentences with seven words or more

Social and Emotional

- Engages in pretend play
- Makes simple choices

Approaches to Learning

- Purposefully explores new things or ideas

Listening Activities and Songs

- Song: "B-I-N-G-O" ("There was a farmer had a dog and Bingo was his name-o") (Traditional)
- Song: "Parts of the Body Song" (teacher makes up the words)

"Parts of the Body Song"
To the tune of "Where Is Thumbkin?"
(Make it up as you go along.)

Where are your eyes?
Where are your eyes?
Blink them now.
Blink them now.
Say: [*child's name*] show us
your eyes.

Where are your knees?
Where are your knees?
Bend them now.
Bend them now.
Say: [*next child*] show us
your knees.

(Continue naming all parts of the body that you want the children to learn)

Stories

- *Sharing How Kindness Grows* by Fran Shaw
- *Chrysanthemum* by Kevin Henkes
- *Socrates* by Rascal and Gert Bogaerts
- *Arthur's Pet Business* by Marc Brown
- *My Big Dog* by Janet Stevens and Susan Stevens Crummel
- *Who Wants Arthur?* by Amanda Graham
- *The Colors of Us* by Karen Katz
- *We Both Read About Pets* by Sindy McKay
- *The One and Only Special Me* by Rozanne Lanczak Williams

WEEK 1

CIRCLE TIME

Interactive Charts and Props

- Create your own Parts of the Body chart (parts to be learned are listed below)
- Create your own Find My Dog House chart.
- Animal reproducibles to make stencils

Body Parts To Learn

The body parts that should be learned are the following:

mouth	eyes	nose
feet	hair	tongue
teeth	hands	ears
head	legs	arms
fingers	thumbs	toes
neck	stomach	chest
back	knees	chin
fingernails	heels	elbows
shoulders	ankles	jaw
hips	wrists	waist

TIP Make stencils of the traced animals for cutting practice so they can be used at the easel in week 2.

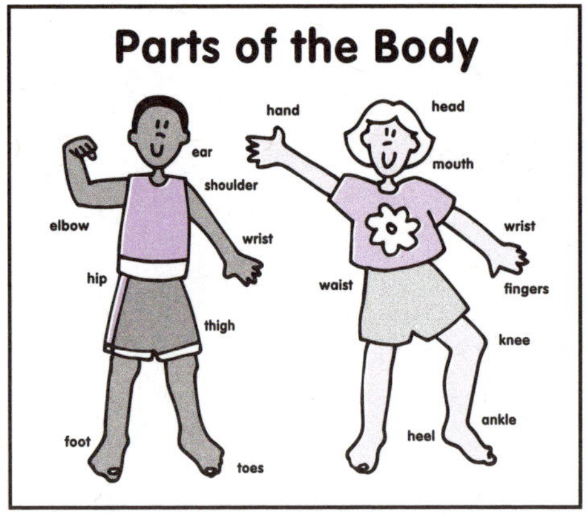

Circle Time Activities

- Discuss living things vs. nonliving things (living things grow, need food, sometimes move, etc.).
- Discuss how living things grow and change. (What can babies do? What can pre-K children do?)
- Review parts of the body with a **Parts of the Body chart**. Sing: **"Parts of the Body Song"**
- Read the Big Book ***The One and Only Special Me*** by Rozanne Lanczak Williams.
- Have children look in a mirror to find their eye and hair color, then talk about how they are alike and different.
- Take inventory of the pets in the DRAMATIC PLAY pet store. Also use this activity to give expectations for daily cleanup.
- Discuss how animals help people (guide dogs, canine unit in police department, horses for transportation and farm work, etc.).

TABLE WORK

WEEK 1

- Use the **Find My Dog House interactive chart.** Match the size and shape of dog to the correct dog house.

TIP To practice verbal skills, have the children answer in a complete sentence. For example, "The dog is short so it lives in a small doghouse."

- Sing **"B-I-N-G-O"**

- CIRCLE TIME is a great opportunity to teach the children how to play a board game (see board game suggestions on page 16).

- Reproducible: "This is me on my first day in Preschool." Have a name card available if needed for children to practice writing their names. (Teacher glues this paper in the front of children's writing journal.)

- Use the animal stencils to trace animals on construction paper. Children can practice cutting out the animals.

- Reproducible: Dog and Cat Match

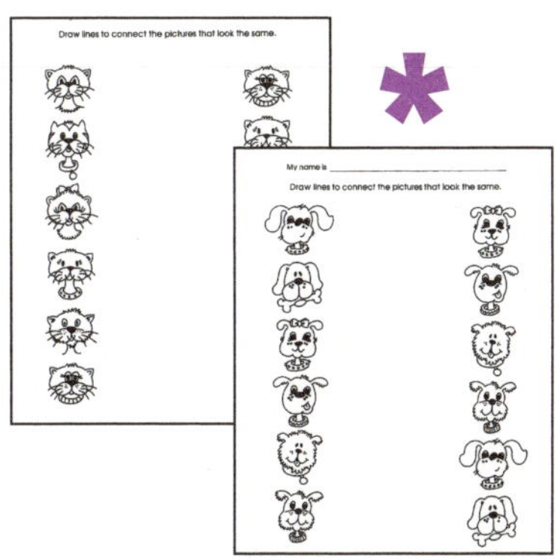

- Reproducible: Match the number of dogs or dinosaurs to the correct number of bones.

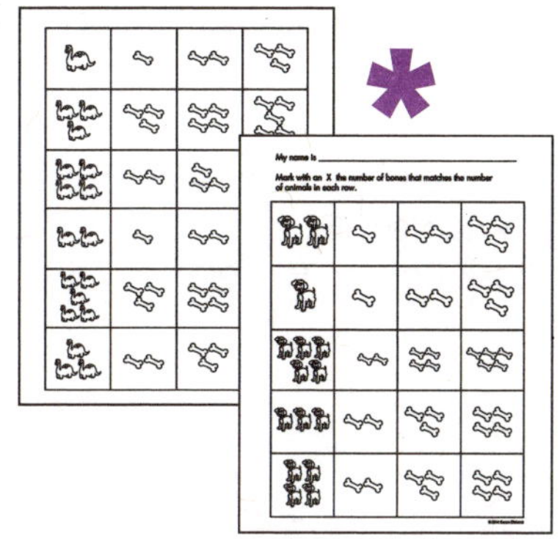

- **Journal** Write: *pet*
  Ask the children to draw a pet they have at home or would like to have some day. You can write the pet's name or the type of pet by the drawing.

TIP All reproducibles marked with a * can be found on the Redleaf Press website at www.redleafpress.org/atoz.

FREE CHOICE PLAY

Writing Center

Have the children practice writing their names this week.

TIP Store children's name cards at the WRITING CENTER. Often they will ask how to write a friend's name.

Board Games

- Honeybee Tree by International Playthings
- Feed the Kitty by Gamewright
- Copy Cats by TREND Enterprises
- Pet Hunt by Binary Arts
- Feed the Dog by Lakeshore Learning

Sensory Table: Water

Plastic or play fish, nets, fishbowl, wire rack, press-to-close bags (children learn to seal bags)

Workbench

Place the correct number of dog biscuits in the dog bowls numbered 1–10.

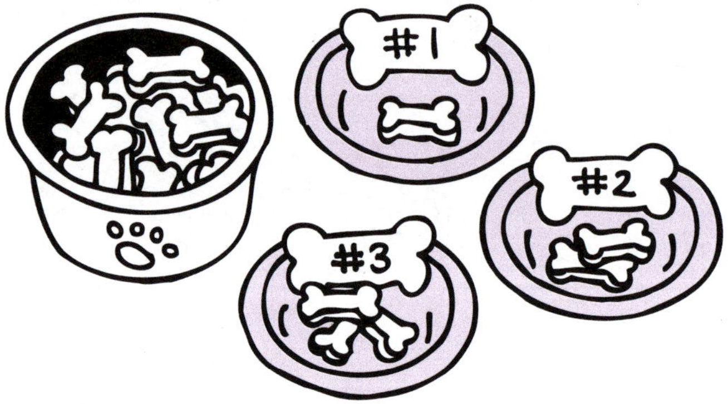

Easel Art

Primary and secondary colors of washable tempera paint.

Crafts

- Cookie cutters as stencils.

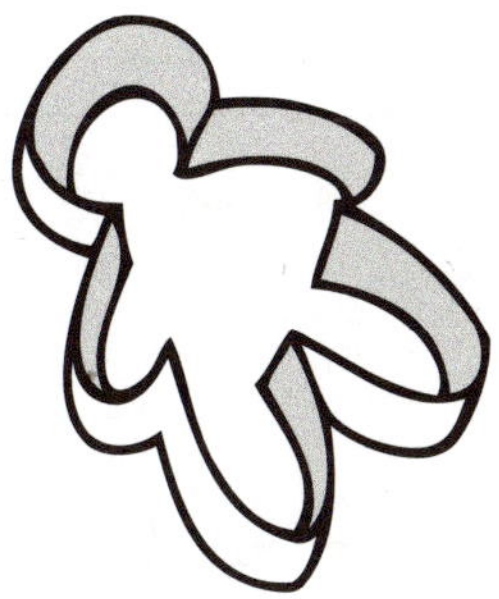

- Trace cookie cutters on contruction paper. Children cut the shapes out and decorate them.

- Paper cutouts of children can be made to sit on a shelf if bent at the waist and the knees. Children can decorate them with faces and clothes.

- Small squares of dogs, cats, fish, and bones to decorate, cut, and glue.

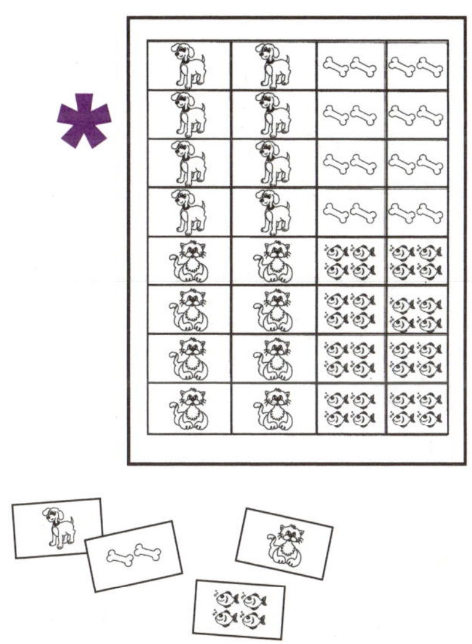

Notes & Evaluations

	Circle Time	Table Work	Free Choice Play	Crafts
Monday	Beginning: Ending:			
	Story:			
Tuesday	Beginning: Ending:			
	Story:			
Wednesday	Beginning: Ending:			
	Story:			
Thursday	Beginning: Ending:			
	Story:			
Friday	Beginning: Ending:			
	Story:			

WEEK 2

Colors

Dramatic Play

Pet Store

Add play money, stickers for prices, and playdough to make pet food.

Learning Objectives

Physical and Motor

- Copies and draws simple shapes and letters
- Uses scissors

Cognitive

- Matches objects
- Sorts and organizes

Communication and Language

- Sings simple repetitive songs
- Follows 2–3-step directions

Social and Emotional

- Plays with other children
- Takes turns

Approaches to Learning

- Reflects on past experiences and applies information to new situations

"Color Match" Poem

Take a color, say its name
Look for the match
that is the same
We call that the Color Game

Listening Activities and Songs

- Song: "B-I-N-G-O" (Traditional)
- *Oh Where, Oh Where Has My Little Dog Gone* by Iza Trapani
- "Color Match" poem
- Introduce "Good-bye Song" (used every day)

"Good-Bye Song"
Sung to the tune of "*Frére Jacques*"

Teacher: Good-bye, children.
Children: Good-bye, teacher.

Teacher: It was a good day!
Children: It was a good day!

Teacher: We'll meet again on [*day of the week*].
Children: We'll meet again on [*day of the week*].

Teacher: Go-ood-bye!
Children: Go-ood-bye!

Stories

- *Mix It Up* by Herve Tullet
- *A Color of His Own* by Leo Lionni
- *Little Blue and Little Yellow* by Leo Lionni
- *Mouse Paint* by Ellen Stoll Walsh
- *The Day the Crayons Quit* by Drew Daywalt
- *My Many Colored Days* by Dr. Seuss

OR Read 2–3 chapters each day from *The Canary Caper* by Ron Roy and John Gurney

RECIPE: Cooked Playdough

2 cups flour
1 cup salt
4 teaspoons cream of tartar
2 tablespoons oil
2 cups water

Mix all ingredients together and cook over medium heat, stirring constantly. When the mixture comes to a boil and thickens, turn it out of the pan onto a wooden cutting board, wait for it to cool to the touch, and knead the dough for 20 seconds. Store the playdough in an airtight container. It keeps up to two weeks or until it becomes crumbly.

CIRCLE TIME

Interactive Charts and Props

- Create your own Color Is All Around Us interactive chart.
- Create your own Color Match Game chart with color cards.
- Create your own Color Bears on a Stick (painted wood or construction paper bears, glued or taped on a popsicle stick).

Colors to Learn

Children should learn the following colors:

red	blue	green	yellow
orange	purple	brown	black
pink	gray	white	

Circle Time Activities

- Take turns using the **Color Is All Around Us interactive chart.** Invite the children to find examples of color samples to place on the chart during FREE CHOICE PLAY.
- Give each child a **Color Bear on a Stick**. Find the matching color in the classroom (for example, a green bear next to a green leaf). Take a photo of each child and make a class color book.

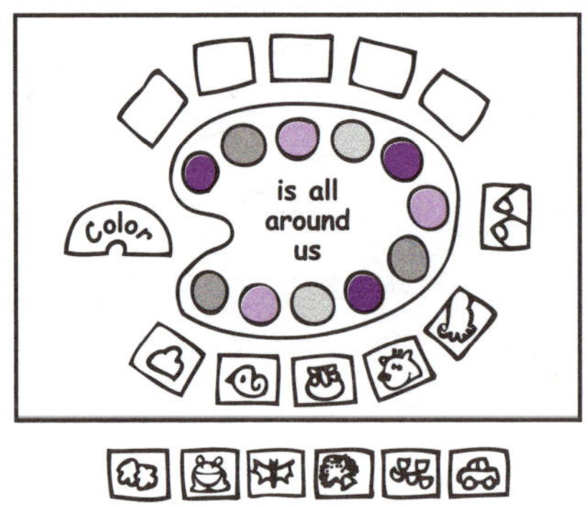

- To practice color recognition, use the **Color Match Game interactive chart** along with the **"Color Match" poem**.
- Read the book ***Mouse Paint*** by Ellen Walsh.
- Add shaving cream to washable tempera paint, then demonstrate mixing primary colors to form secondary colors.
- Prepare ahead of time red, yellow, and blue ice cubes made with food coloring and water. Place two different-colored ice cubes in a clear glass bowl and set them out for the children to observe as they melt and mix into a secondary color.
- Demonstrate the color spinner made at TABLE WORK.
- Ask each child her favorite color. Write it on an index card. Use the cards to make a color graph. Use the index cards for the journal writing activity this week.
- Teach the children to play **The Color Bears Game** (see FREE CHOICE PLAY for instructions).

TABLE WORK

- Make a color wheel. Give each child a teaspoon of washable tempera paint in each primary color on the appropriate place on the color wheel. One step at a time, instruct them to mix two primary colors to create a secondary color until the color wheel is complete.

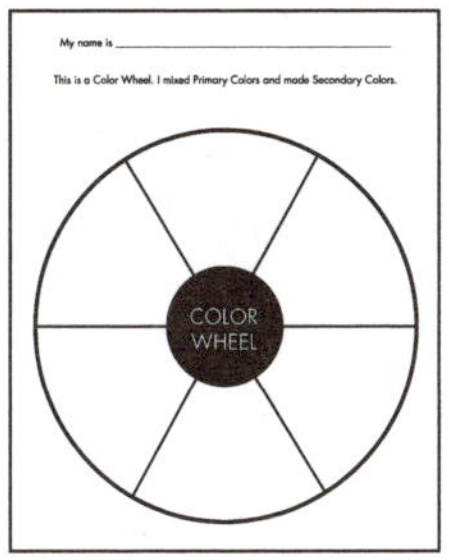

*

- Reproducible: Pet Graphing

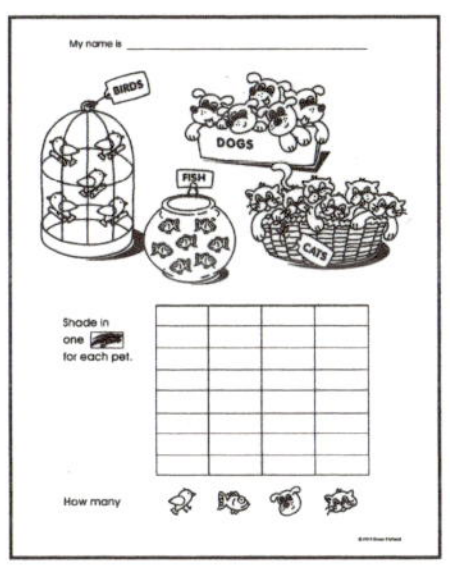

*

- Make a color spinner (see instructions below).

- Provide color bears traced on construction paper. Children will cut out bears and tape them to popsicle sticks. Make 3 or 4 at TABLE WORK. Encourage them to complete the set during FREE CHOICE PLAY.

- **Journal:** Have children copy their favorite color from the index card (CIRCLE TIME ACTIVITY). Decorate the page with the appropriate color.

TIP Use only crayons to color in the journal. Coloring with markers can bleed through the page.

HOW TO: Make a Color Spinner

You will need:

- A sheet of card stock, large enough to cut out a 5" circle.
- A pencil with a point.

Teacher, trace a 5" circle for each child on card stock, then draw two lines to divide the circle into four equal parts. (1) Have the children color the circle with two primary colors—coloring each of the two sections across from each other the same color. (2) Then cut out the circle. (3) Carefully punch a hole in the center. (4) Poke a short pencil through the hole and spin it like a top. The two colors will visually mix together, creating a secondary color (for example, blue and yellow will appear green while the disk is spinning).

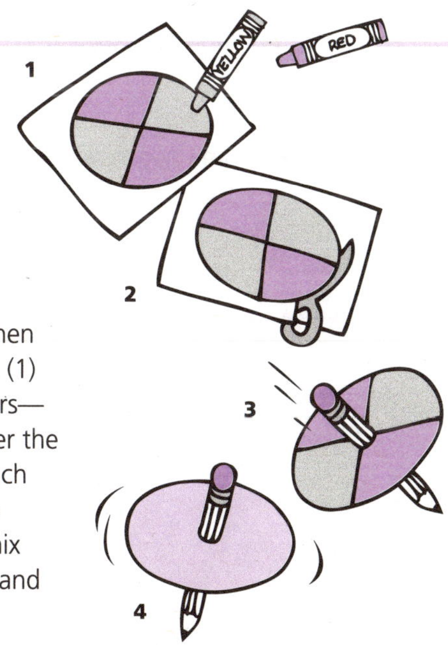

FREE CHOICE PLAY

Writing Center

Trace over the words "Be kind to your pets" and the animals in the picture.

Board Games

- Keep the same board games from previous week.
- The Color Bears Game (see instructions on page 23)

Sensory Table

Use the sensory table for color-mixing activities and melting the colored ice cubes.

Workbench

Make the workbench the playdough center.

Easel Art

Add brown, black, tan, gray, and white paint to the colors from previous week. Spray animal stencils with a small amount of spray adhesive. Stick stencils on the easel paper and paint inside stencils. Wipe stencils frequently.

Crafts

- Cut out pictures from magazines to add to the **Colors Are All Around Us chart.**
- Make available traced construction-paper bears to cut out, popsicle sticks, and masking tape. Encourage the children to make a complete set of Color Bears for practice at home.
- Put the leftover primary colors mixed with shaving cream in airtight containers so children can continue to experiment with color mixing along with brushes and paper for painting.

Notes & Evaluations

HOW TO: Play the Color Bears Game

You need the following:

- A die numbered 1–6
- Colored plastic bowls (or 6 colored construction-paper circles—red, blue, green, yellow, orange, and purple)
- Small colored bears for counting—6 of each color to match the bowls (6 green bears, 6 yellow bears, etc.—36 bears total)
- 2–6 players

The object of the game is to get one bear of each color in your bowl.

- To begin, each player chooses a colored bowl and places 6 bears of the same color in their bowl.
- Even if there are only two players, finish putting the six bears in the remaining matching colored bowls. An unattended bowl is still used to play the game.
- The first player rolls the dice.
- Whatever number is rolled, there are only two rules:

  1. You may take bears from only one bowl.
  2. You can never make a bowl empty. (If a six is rolled on the first turn, nothing can be done because there are only six bears in each bowl, so it's the next child's turn.)

Let's play a couple of turns (there are three players in this example).

- The first player has the **red bowl** with six red bears in it. She rolls a two. She takes two bears from the green bowl.
- The second player has the **blue bowl.** He still has six blue bears. He rolls a four. He takes the two green bears and two red bears from the red bowl. He now has three different-colored bears in his bowl!
- The third player has the **yellow bowl.** She rolls a six. She may not take from the purple or orange bowls because those bowls have only six bears and would become empty. She chooses to take bears from the **blue bowl.** She takes one red bear, one green bear and four blue bears. She now has four different-colored bears in her bowl. As long as she takes six bears, she can choose any combination of colors.

Player number two was lucky—the third player left some different colors still in his bowl.

- Back to the first player with the **red bowl.** She has four red bears left in her bowl. She rolls a three and chooses to take three bears from the **yellow bowl.** Did she choose wisely and take one yellow bear, one red bear, and one green bear and leave the **yellow bowl** only two different-colored bears? If so, she now has four different-colored bears! (Children will begin to learn strategy the more they play.)

The winner is the first player to have at least one bear of each color in his bowl.

TIP Remind children often that the object of the game is not to have a lot of bears but to have one bear of each color—then you win!

	Circle Time	Table Work	Free Choice Play	Crafts
Monday	Beginning: Ending:			
	Story:			
Tuesday	Beginning: Ending:			
	Story:			
Wednesday	Beginning: Ending:			
	Story:			
Thursday	Beginning: Ending:			
	Story:			
Friday	Beginning: Ending:			
	Story:			

Oo WEEK

Shapes

Our State

The Letter *Oo*

Dramatic Play

Construction Zone

Include the workbench, construction hats, vests, and gloves. Use construction vehicles in the block area.

Learning Objectives

Physical and Motor

- Uses left or right hand predominantly
- Uses small muscles in hands to color, cut, paste, and paint
- Builds and stacks with several small blocks

Cognitive

- Follows 2–3-step directions
- Names simple shapes

Communication and Language

- Enjoys books
- Asks questions and seeks answers

Social and Emotional

- Shows independence
- Plays simple games with rules

Approaches to Learning

- Works at tasks despite distractions and interruptions

Listening Activities and Songs

- Song: "London Bridge Is Falling Down" (Traditional)
- Musical instruments: round drums, cymbals, finger cymbals, triangles, rectangle blocks, etc.
- Listen to opera music.

"London Bridge Is Falling Down"

London Bridge is falling down,
Falling down, falling down.
London Bridge is falling down,
My fair lady.

(Continue the song with these verses.)

Build it up with iron bars . . .

Iron bars will bend and break . . .

Build it up with silver and gold . . .

Now the bridge is all built up . . .

Stories

- *Iggy Peck, Architect* by Andrea Beaty
- *The 50 States: Explore the U.S.A. with 50 Fact-Filled Maps* by Gabrielle Balkan
- *Our 50 States: A Family Adventure Across America* by Lynne Cheney
- *Building a House* by Byron Barton
- *Round Is a Tortilla: A Book of Shapes* by Roseanne Thong
- *The Giving Tree* by Shel Silverstein
- *The Missing Piece* by Shel Silverstein
- *The Missing Piece Meets the Big O* by Shel Silverstein
- *Shape by Shape* by Suse MacDonald

TIP **Story Time Added Activity**

Read the book: *The Missing Piece* by Shel Silverstein. Tell the children this author has written many books. Read another book by him the next day, allowing the children to choose either *The Missing Piece Meets the Big O* or *The Giving Tree.* (Photocopy the cover of each book and have the children make a choice by signing their name to vote for the book they would like read the next day.)

CIRCLE TIME

Interactive Charts and Props

- Create your own Shape Block interactive chart.
- Create your own Name the Shapes chart (make a poster using pictures of items that are different shapes).
- Provide a USA map or USA puzzle map.
- Provide a picture of your state flag.

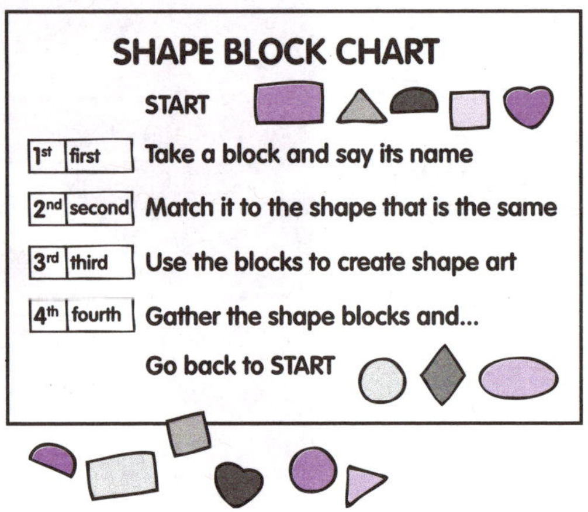

Circle Time Activities

- Introduce the letter *Oo*.

For every chapter on a letter of the alphabet, the CIRCLE TIME ACTIVITY on the first day of the week is to introduce the *letter of the week*. Follow these steps:

1. Look at the printed letter. Ask, "Do the upper and lower case look the same or different?"
2. Listen to the sounds the letter makes. Practice the sounds together.
3. Ask, "Does anyone's name begin with the letter? A family member or a friend?"
4. Think of words that begin with the letter.
5. Read a short story that emphasizes the letter.

There are many series of books from which to choose. ***Alpha Tales*** by Scholastic provides a book for each letter of the alphabet, with accompanying sequence cards. The cards help the children retell the story and look for words that begin with the letter of the week.

TIP Have the Teacher's Helper put the sequence cards in order.

TIP See the optional American Sign Language activity on page 32.

- Because *Oo* is the first letter of the alphabet studied, take time to show the children what is expected at the WRITING CENTER. (See the full explanation of the WRITING CENTER in the FREE CHOICE PLAY section.)
- Use the **Shape Block interactive chart.**
  1. Take a shape block and say its name.
  2. Match the shape block with a shape on the chart that is the same.
  3. Use the shape blocks to create your own "shape art."
  4. To finish, gather the shape blocks and go back to START. (This chart practices shape identification and subtly introduces ordinal numbers.)
- Use the **Name the Shapes interactive chart** to explain that shapes are all around us, just like colors. Give each child a shape block from the **Shape Block interactive chart.** Have them find an object with the same shape in the classroom. For example, the door is a rectangle. Take a photo of the child holding the shape block by the door. Make a Shape Book like the Color Book.

- Make shapes with "yarn loops." (Use 18-inch lengths of yarn and tie the ends together to form a loop.) Give each child a yarn loop. Lay the yarn loops on the floor, then ask children to push and pull with their fingertips to create shapes.

- Place wooden or plastic shapes in a cloth bag. Reach inside and feel to guess the shape.
- Sing **"London Bridge Is Falling Down"** using the musical instruments. Use different instruments for each verse. The children love to end playing all the instruments together!
- The WORKBENCH is used in the CONSTRUCTION ZONE in DRAMATIC PLAY as a workbench with real tools. Take time to discuss the safety rules for the workbench. (See FREE CHOICE PLAY for Workbench Safety Rules.)

- Locate your state on a USA map. Tell the children there is a state flag, state bird, drink, flower, and so forth. As a group, think of places families can visit in your state.
- Set up an obstacle course as a large-motor activity. Show the children how a stopwatch works. Have them compete against their own best time, never against one another!
- Introduce opposites.
- Before the first show-and-tell week, role play taking home a bag and bringing back an item the next day, emphasizing *show* and *tell*. Be very deliberate to *show* the item and then *tell* about it.

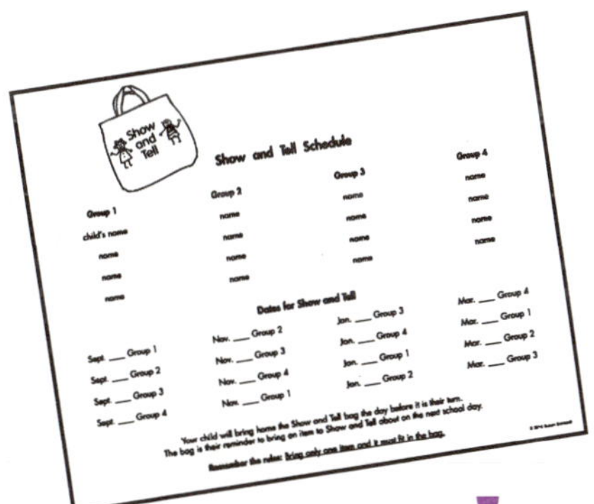

Show and Tell Schedule

Group 1	Group 2	Group 3	Group 4
child's name	name	name	name
name	name	name	name
name	name	name	name
name	name	name	name

Dates for Show and Tell

Sept. ___ Group 1	Nov. ___ Group 2	Jan. ___ Group 3	Mar. ___ Group 4
Sept. ___ Group 2	Nov. ___ Group 3	Jan. ___ Group 4	Mar. ___ Group 1
Sept. ___ Group 3	Nov. ___ Group 4	Jan. ___ Group 1	Mar. ___ Group 2
Sept. ___ Group 4	Nov. ___ Group 1	Jan. ___ Group 2	Mar. ___ Group 3

Your child will bring home the Show and Tell bag the day before it is their turn.
The bag is their reminder to bring an item to Show and Tell about on the next school day.
Remember the rules: bring only one item and it must fit in the bag.

HOW TO: Prepare for Show-and-Tell

Show-and-tell is a valuable tool for improving children's self-confidence when speaking to a group. Purchase a 13-by-15-inch canvas bag and decorate it with fabric paint. You may want a few extra just in case a child is absent or forgets to return the bag.

Rules for Show-and-Tell

1. When you receive a bag, it is your turn the next school day to show-and-tell.
2. Bring only one item.
3. It must fit in the bag.

Oo
WEEK

TABLE WORK

Practice writing the letter of the week.

- Practice writing the letter *Oo*.

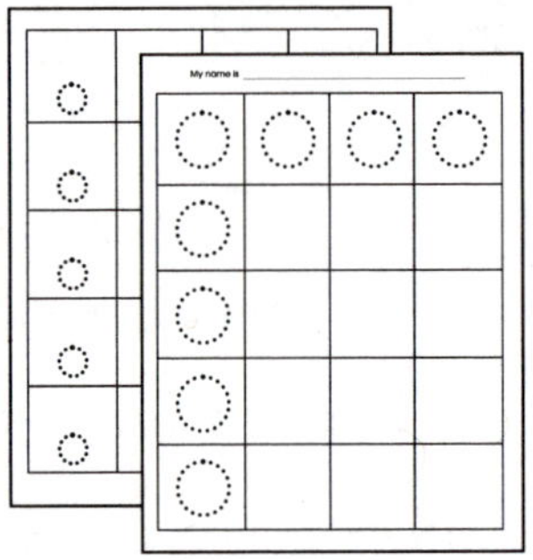

*

Each week there is a Phonics Sheet. The children identify the pictures that begin with the letter of the week.

TIP Phonics Sheets will begin next week. Preschoolers may have a hard time recognizing vowels as beginning sounds.

Trace, then draw shapes (rectangle, oval, triangle).

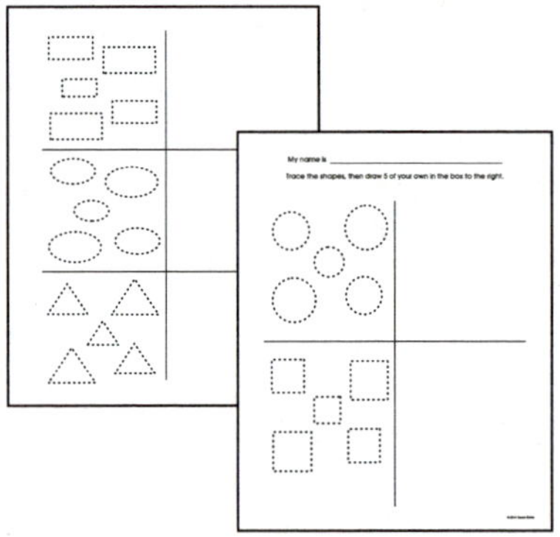

*

Journal work is primarily a writing assignment, so words are always written before an activity or illustration. Some children have difficulty copying a word from a chart or board across the classroom. Keep words on index cards at the writing table so children can place them next to their journals as they write.

Journal

1. Have the children cut apart the reproducible (see example below) on the dotted line so the word "shapes" is a separate piece of paper. They can refer to this for STEP 2.
2. Tell the children to copy the word *shapes* into their journals.
3. First, the children trace the shapes for practice. Second, the children draw the shape next to the tracing on their own.
4. Glue the Shapes reproducible in the journal.

Shapes Around the House Project

This project is started at TABLE WORK and completed at home.

Cut out and glue each traced shape from the reproducible on a separate paper for the "Shapes Around the House" take-home project.

Prepare a front and back cover for the project. When the glue is dry on the shape pages, staple them together with the covers to send home with the note below.

TIP When making the cover for the book, use the house for the front cover and save the frame to use in *Vv* Week.

Send home this note:

Dear families,
The class is making a Shapes Around the House Book. Your child has glued five shapes, each on a separate paper. Please help your child find one example around your home for each shape. This will help your child understand the application of shapes in their environment. First, have your child draw a picture of the example. Then either you or your child should label it. Just one example for each shape is needed.

Oo
WEEK

FREE CHOICE PLAY

Writing Center

Oo picture stamps and corresponding words to copy.

The WRITING CENTER is used primarily for a weekly activity done in conjunction with the letter of the alphabet that week. The children copy the assigned words for the week in their journals. The work is done anytime during FREE CHOICE PLAY and is to be completed before the last day of the week. Remind children the day before the journal words are due.

TIP At the start of the year it may be less overwhelming to begin with just two words at the WRITING CENTER.

TIP Prepare the entire set of cards for the alphabet ahead of time.

TIP This weekly writing goal is an excellent way for a child to begin learning personal time management.

Board Games

- Perfection by Milton Bradley
- Colorama by Kaplan
- Any memory cards (just use cards with shapes and colors)
- Colors & Shapes BINGO by TREND (or any color/shape lotto)

Sensory Table

Tape shape cards to the inside of the SENSORY TABLE. Use straws, cut in half, and balls of clay to create shapes. The shapes become three dimensional!

SAFETY RULES FOR THE WORKBENCH

- Wear safety goggles at all times.
- Only two children working at a time.
- Keep two hands on the handle of the saw. (Have a vice to hold the wood. A handsaw is added to the CONSTRUCTION ZONE the second week.)

Workbench

Safety goggles, hammers, nails, soft pine wood, and screwdrivers, wood screws, corrugated cardboard, and work aprons used in the DRAMATIC PLAY area. (See Workbench Safety Rules above.)

Easel Art

Using shape stencils, trace shapes with a crayon. Paint with a watercolor wash. The crayon resists the watercolor and the shapes stand out!

Crafts

- Construction paper octopus

HOW TO: Make An Octopus

Copy the octopuses onto a 9-by-12-inch sheet of construction paper (each sheet makes two).

This activity teaches three things:

1. How to round off a corner to create a curved edge.
2. How to cut the center out of the letter *O*. Tell the children to fold the *O* in half loosely, then make a small snip. Stick the point of the scissors into the opening and say "nibble out the middle."
3. Cut the straight lines to make eight arms. Roll each arm around a pencil, then hold and count to ten to curl. Note: octopuses do not have tentacles or legs. They have four sets of arms.

TIP Before curling the arms, draw *O*'s on them. An octopus has many small suction cups on each arm to keep the arms from getting tangled or stuck to each other.

- Record player circles

HOW TO: Make Record Player Circles

If you can find an old record player, this project is lots of fun!

Trace circles the same size as the turntable of the record player. Mark a small *x* in the middle, which will be punched out in order to place the circles on the turntable. A cardboard circle must be placed under each cutout circle for stability. Set the turntable to rotate slowly. Turn the record player on. Touch a marker or crayon lightly to the spinning circle—change colors for a unique design!

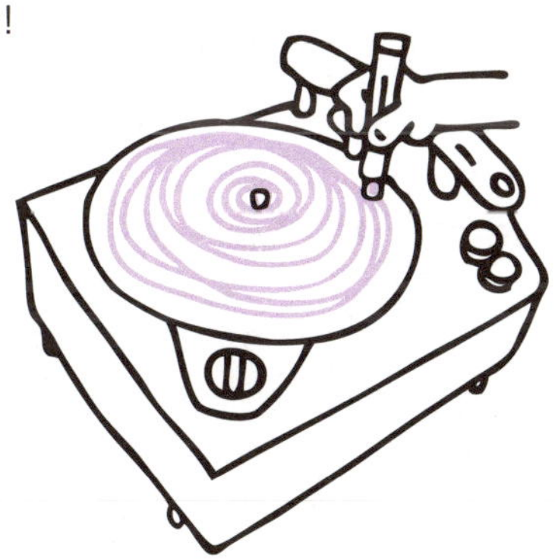

TIP Teach the children to punch the center by placing their cut-out circle on a thick piece of corrugated cardboard and punching it with the point of a scissors or the tip of a pencil.

- Reproducible: Cut out the construction tools and glue them on the pegboard.

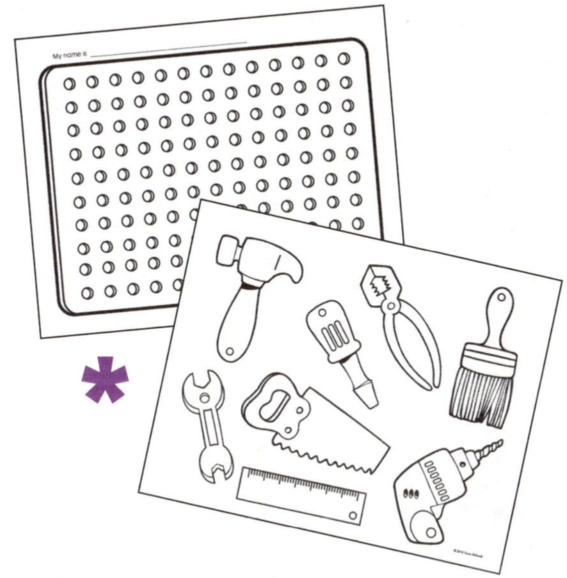

- Cut pictures from magazines to add to the **Name the Shapes chart**.

OPTIONAL TEACHING CIRCLE ACTIVITY

American Sign Language

When each letter is introduced at CIRCLE TIME, show the children the ASL sign for the letter of the alphabet.

Also show the children there are ASL signs that mean a whole word or phrase. For example, *hello*, *family*, *thank you*, and *dog* are all expressed using only one sign.

Another fun activity is singing songs using American Sign Language. To simplify, there is no need to sign every word.

TIP This CIRCLE TIME ACTIVITY is completely optional.

There are many sign language reference books. Here are a few:

- From the Beginning Sign Language series published by Garlic Press: *Signing at School; Songs in Sign; Foods; Fruits and Vegetables*
- *Sign Language: My First 100 Words* by Michiyo Nelson
- *Sign to Learn: American Sign Language in the Early Childhood Classroom* by Kristen Dennis and Tressa Azpiri
- *Li'l Pick Me Up! Fun Songs for Learning ASL Signs* by Sign2Me Early Learning
- *The Kid's Guide to Sign Language* by Kathryn Clay
- *The Handmade Alphabet* by Laura Rankin
- *Sign Language for Kids: A Fun and Easy Guide to American Sign Language* by Lora Heller

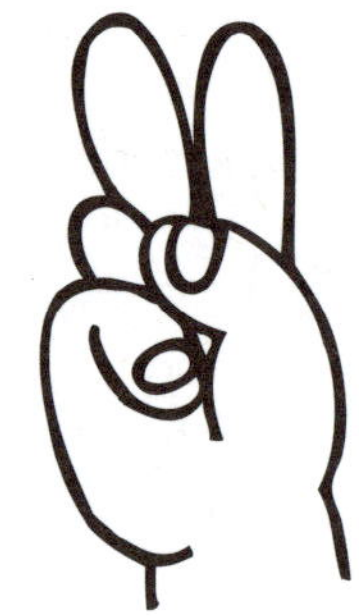

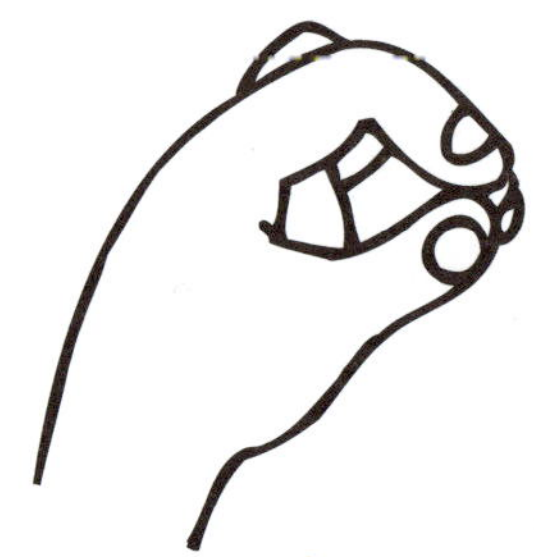

Notes & Evaluations

A Note from the Author

As this curriculum continues and you study each chapter, you will see there is repetition and routine. Each letter of the alphabet is introduced the same way. There is some type of journal writing activity done every week. The children become comfortable as they learn to expect what they will do each day of the week.

	Circle Time	Table Work	Free Choice Play	Crafts
Monday	Beginning: Ending:			
	Story:			
Tuesday	Beginning: Ending:			
	Story:			
Wednesday	Beginning: Ending:			
	Story:			
Thursday	Beginning: Ending:			
	Story:			
Friday	Beginning: Ending:			
	Story:			

Tt WEEK

Tangrams and More Shapes

Dramatic Play

Continue Construction Zone. This week add a handsaw to the workbench. Use adult supervision.

Learning Objectives

Physical and Motor

- Uses large muscles to throw, climb, skip, hop, jump, catch, turn somersaults, and bounce
- Puts puzzles together
- Throws a ball to a target overhand and underhand

Cognitive

- Can stay with the same activity for five to ten minutes (increasing concentration)
- Uses reason to solve problems

Communication and Language

- Likes to learn new words
- Listens for details

Social and Emotional

- Enjoys helping with household tasks
- Engages in group play

Approaches to Learning

- Invents new purposes for objects

Listening Activities and Songs

- Triangle trio (three sizes of triangle instruments)
- Songs and poems from the previous week

Stories

- *Grandfather Tang's Story* by Ann Tompert
- *The Greedy Triangle* by Marilyn Burns
- *Show & Tell Day* by Anne Rockwell
- *Seaweed Soup* by Stuart J. Murphy
- *Thunder Cake* by Patricia Polacco
- *The Tower* by Richard Paul Evans
- *Too Many Toys* by David Shannon
- *Tikki Tikki Tembo* by Arlene Mosel

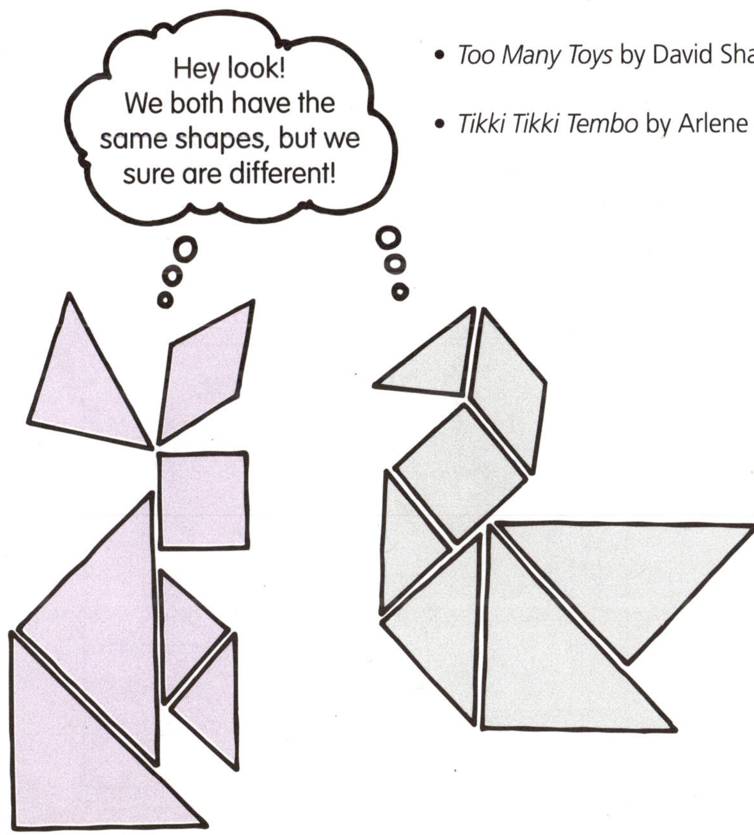

CIRCLE TIME

Interactive Charts and Props

- Create your own chart with the seven tangram pictures shown below.
- Individual copies of each of the tangram puzzles from the seven tangram pictures for a craft activity
- Four-to-six sets of tangrams (plastic)
- Other books of tangram pictures found at the library, etc.
- Placemat that shows how to set the table
- Placemats and items needed to practice setting the table

*

Circle Time Activities

- Introduce the letter *Tt*.
- Pass out the show-and-tell bags to Group 1. Remind the children of the rules for show-and-tell.

TIP The show-and-tell bags are passed on to Group 2 the following day. Continue until all children have had a turn.

- Remind children of the Workbench Safety Rules.
- Add the following rules for the handsaw:
  1. Always put the wood in the vice.
  2. Always keep two hands on the handle of the saw.
  3. Make sure you have adult supervision.

- Read the book ***Grandfather Tang's Story*** by Ann Tompert. Demonstrate the tangram designs from the story.
- Demonstrate how to spray-paint over a tangram design to get a negative art piece (EASEL ART for this week).
- Review shapes learned the previous week. Name the shapes used in the tangram. Put plastic tangram shapes in the cloth bag. Have children take turns reaching into the bag to feel and guess the shapes.
- Look together at the completed "Shapes Around the House" assignment. Have each child share her examples of the shapes she found at home.
- Review with the children how to play tic-tac-toe. Teach them to draw the crisscross lines to begin the game.
- Teach the children to play **Trouble** by Milton Bradley.
- Toss beanbags to tunes. Play music and have the children toss beanbags, first alone, then with a partner, until the music stops.
- Discuss eating healthy food for a healthy body and healthy teeth. Show the children the large tooth reproducible. Look in magazines to find healthy foods. Cut them out and glue them on the tooth during FREE CHOICE PLAY.

TABLE WORK

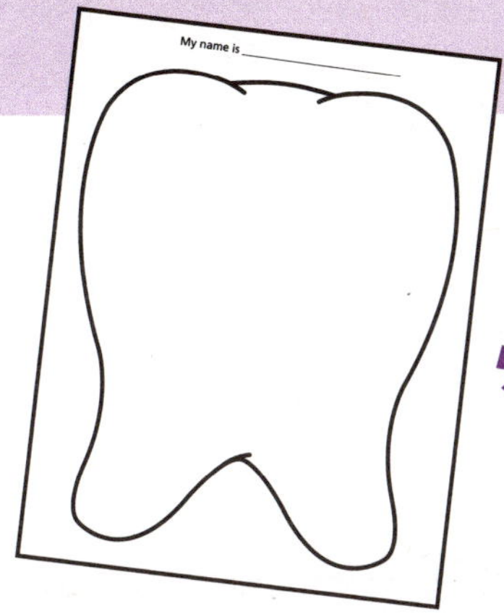

- Learn to set the table so they can help their family at home. Read the story ***Seaweed Soup*** by Stuart J. Murphy and teach the children to set the table. Use the placemats that show how to set the table as a guide. Next, use plain placemats and give each child a piece of a place setting to add until the table is set. For example, for sixteen children you will use three plain placemats and you will need three cups, three plates, three knives, three forks, three spoons, and three napkins. Give each child one of the items. There will be two extra items so the teacher can ask for extra help to finish the last table setting.

- Have children make the sound of a thunderstorm. First, they rub their hands together quickly, back and forth, palms together, which sounds like drizzling rain. Second, they snap their fingers, which sounds like a steady rain. Third, they pat their knees with open hands, which sounds like pouring rain. And finally, a few children at a time begin clapping loudly until all are clapping, which sounds like a thunderstorm! (To make the thunderstorm stop, do the steps in reverse.)

- Practice writing the letter of the week. Practice writing the letter *Tt*.

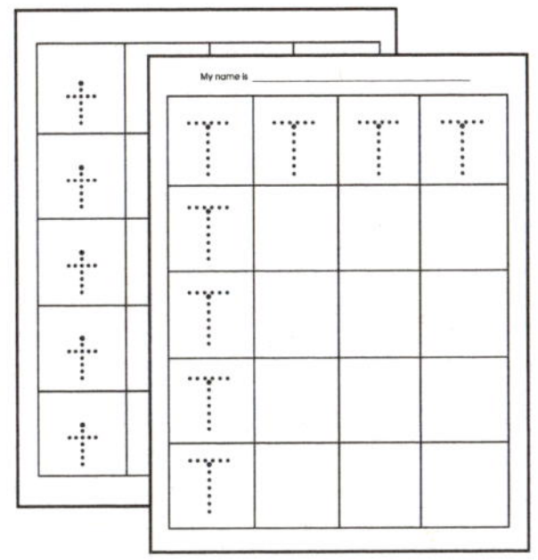

- Phonics Sheet for the letter *Tt*. Children identify pictures that begin with the letter *Tt*.

- Trace and draw using the Shape Reproducible (semicircle, diamond, heart).

- **Journal** Write: *tangram*
(Have a "tangram square" traced for each child.) Children cut the tangram into the seven shapes and put them together to create a picture, then glue it in their journals.

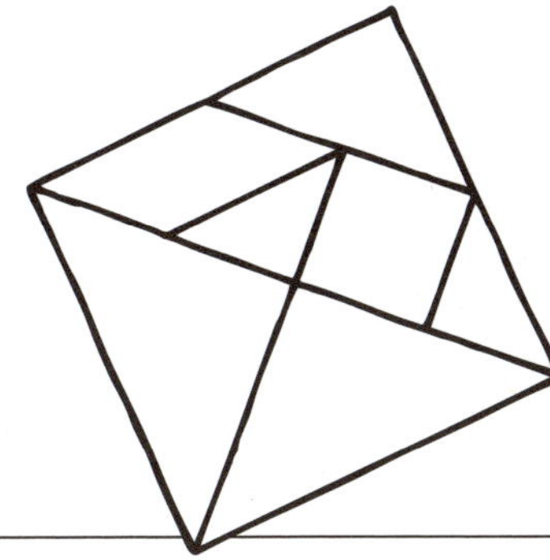

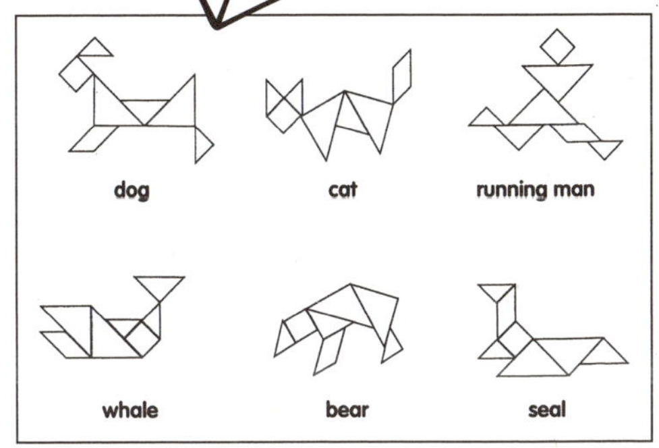

FREE CHOICE PLAY

Writing Center

Tt picture stamps and corresponding word cards to copy in journal.

Board Games

- Continue using games from the previous week.
- Add Trouble by Milton Bradley.
- Have paper and pencils out for tic-tac-toe.

Sensory Table

In the empty sensory table, spin small wooden or plastic tops.

Or

Fill the table with uncooked rice. Add at least eight lengths (six to twelve inches each) of clear plastic tubing with small scoops and large bolts used as stoppers. Funnels are also fun if the tubes have a large diameter.

Workbench

Add the handsaw to the other workbench tools. (Remind the children again of the safety rules.)

SAFETY RULES FOR THE HANDSAW:

- Always put the wood in the vice.
- Always keep two hands on the handle of the saw.

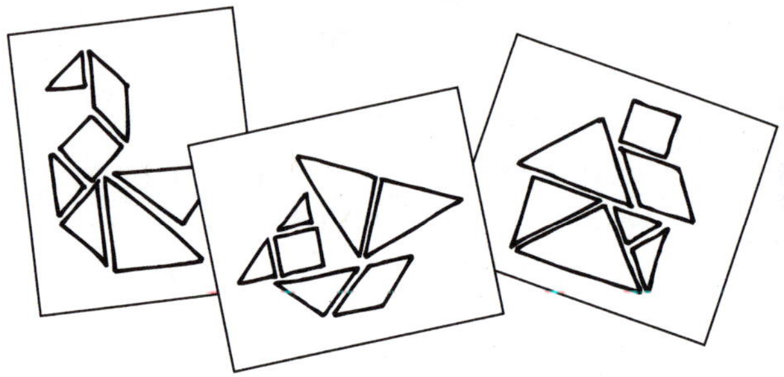

Notes & Evaluations

Easel Art

Make a spray-bottle-painted tangram picture. To keep the spray contained at the easel, turn a large box on its side and clip the box to the easel.

Have tangram squares traced on construction paper.

Have children cut the tangram square into the seven shapes. Using the shapes, create a picture on manila paper. Secure the shapes with rolled masking tape. Tape the paper inside the box. Spray lightly with colored water. The children will be able to peel off the tangram shapes and discard them. When the shapes are removed, the picture remains!

TIP Make little masking tape rolls ahead of time and stick them on a tray for the children to use. Just refill the tray as needed.

Crafts

- Glue popsicle sticks together to make a tic-tac-toe game. Cut various-shaped game pieces out of art foam.
- Provide different sizes of triangle stencils for children to trace then cut. (Triangles need a lot of practice because diagonal lines are difficult for children.)
- Cut and glue the two-part turtle.

- In addition to the **Chart of Tangram Puzzles**, have the tangram pictures available from the book ***Grandfather Tang's Story*** by Ann Tompert along with traced tangram squares so the Journal Writing Activity can be repeated as a craft.
- As introduced in CIRCLE TIME, cut out healthy foods from magazines and glue them on the large tooth reproducible.

	Circle Time	Table Work	Free Choice Play	Crafts
Monday	Beginning: Ending:			
	Story:			
Tuesday	Beginning: Ending:			
	Story:			
Wednesday	Beginning: Ending:			
	Story:			
Thursday	Beginning: Ending:			
	Story:			
Friday	Beginning: Ending:			
	Story:			

LI WEEK

Leaves

Listening

Light

Fall Harvest

Dramatic Play

Pizza Parlor

Just "carry-out" pizza the first week

Learning Objectives

Physical and Motor

- Makes marks or strokes with drawing tools
- Uses small muscles in hands to color, cut, paste, and paint
- Copies and draws simple shapes and letters

Cognitive

- Uses positional terms (*under*, *over*, *through*, *next*)
- Develops elaborate play themes

Communication and Language

- Tells stories without prompting
- Uses language socially (pragmatics)

Social and Emotional

- Shares
- Likes to be silly and make others laugh

Approaches to Learning

- Creates stories, imagining and describing things or situations that do not exist

Listening Activities and Songs

- Shadow Puppet Story: "Great Lion and Tiny Mouse" (see CIRCLE TIME ACTIVITIES)
- Song: "All the Leaves Are Falling Down" (tune of "London Bridge")
- Song from the book *Mary Had a Little Lamb* by Iza Trapani
- Song: "The Farmer in the Field" (to the tune of "The Farmer in the Dell")

"All The Leaves Are Falling Down"
(to the tune of "London Bridge")

All the leaves are falling down,
falling down, falling down
All the leaves are falling down
In the autumn

Red and yellow, orange and brown,
. . . In the autumn

Take the rake and rake them up,
. . . In the autumn

Scoop them up into a pile,
. . . In the autumn

See the children run and jump
. . . In the autumn

Stories

- *Red Leaf, Yellow Leaf* by Lois Ehlert
- *Autumn Leaves* by Ken Robbins
- *The Falling Leaves* by Steve Metzger
- *Apple Trouble!* by Ragnhild Scamell
- "Great Lion and Tiny Mouse" in the book *Tell It Again! 2* by Shirley C. Raines and Rebecca Isbell
- *What Makes a Shadow?* by Clyde Robert Bulla

"The Farmer in the Field"
(to the tune of "The Farmer in the Dell")

The farmer in the field
The farmer in the field
Hi ho the derry-o
The farmer in the field

The farmer plants the corn . . .

The crows eat all the corn . . .

The scarecrow's in the field . . .

To scare away the crows . . .

The farmer gathers corn . . .

To feed his family . . .

CIRCLE TIME

Interactive Charts and Props

- Create your own Parts of a Plant poster.
- Create your own Let's Have Pizza interactive chart.
- Create your own Pizza Order Form (and menu for dramatic play).
- Create a Shadow Puppet Stage (see instructions on this page).
- Leaf Rubbing Plates by Roylco
- A dollhouse to play the game "Where is the Scarecrow?"
- Streamers or scarves (optional)

HOW TO: Make a Shadow Puppet Stage

To make the shadow puppet stage, cut an opening in a large piece of cardboard (for example, a refrigerator box from an appliance store). Insert white paper in the opening and adhere it with masking tape. The paper must be thin enough for light to shine through.

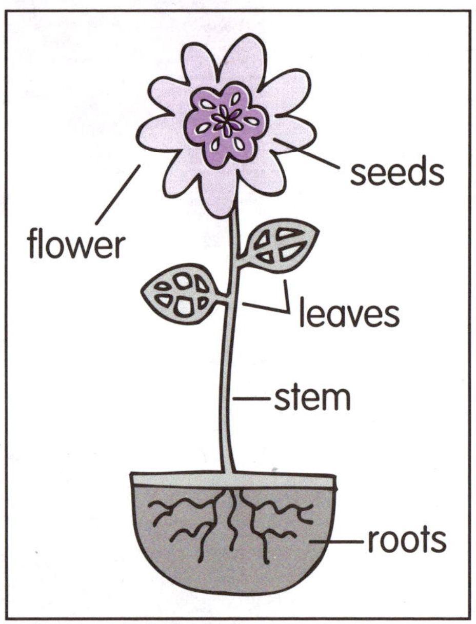

Circle Time Activities

- Introduce the letter *Ll*.
- Demonstrate how to use the **Pizza Order form** (used in the DRAMATIC PLAY area). Take turns using the **Let's Have Pizza interactive chart.**
- Discuss how to listen. Look at the person speaking. Keep hands and feet still.
- Discuss and teach the **parts of a plant** using the poster.
- Discuss the concept of light and how it can create shadows. Show the children the **Shadow Puppet Stage** and shadow puppet props. (The teacher makes the shadow puppet props ahead of time and tapes them to popsicle sticks.)
- Read the story **"Great Lion and Tiny Mouse."** Allow each child a turn to be a character. (The story may need to be read twice.)

Fall Harvest Show

Each fall the class puts on a show. This week begins the preparation for the Fall Harvest Show. Each part of the show will be introduced in the upcoming weeks.

- Read the book ***Why Do Leaves Change Color?*** by Betsy Maestro.
- Sing **"All The Leaves Are Falling Down"** using colored streamers or scarves.

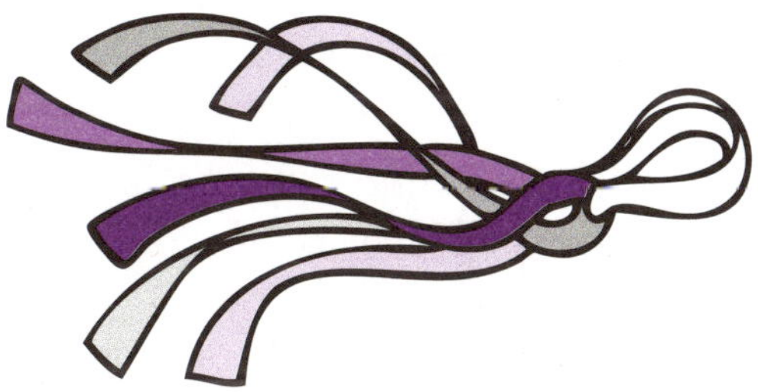

- Play the game "Where Is Scarecrow?" Make a miniature scarecrow puppet ahead of time like the one the children make at FREE CHOICE PLAY. Using a dollhouse, ask the question, "Where is Scarecrow?" Hold the puppet in different places in the dollhouse (for example, under the chair, behind the door, in front of the window, etc.). After you demonstrate with the dollhouse the children can hide their scarecrow puppets somewhere in the classroom, ask each child, "Where is your Scarecrow?" The child answers, "My Scarecrow is under the shelf, behind the story chair, etc." **Remember, every child takes a turn.**
- Teach the children the board game **Pizza Math** by TREND Enterprises.
- Teach the children the board game **Pizza Party** by Parker Brothers.

Notes & Evaluations

TABLE WORK

- Practice writing the letter of the week. Practice writing the letter *Ll*.

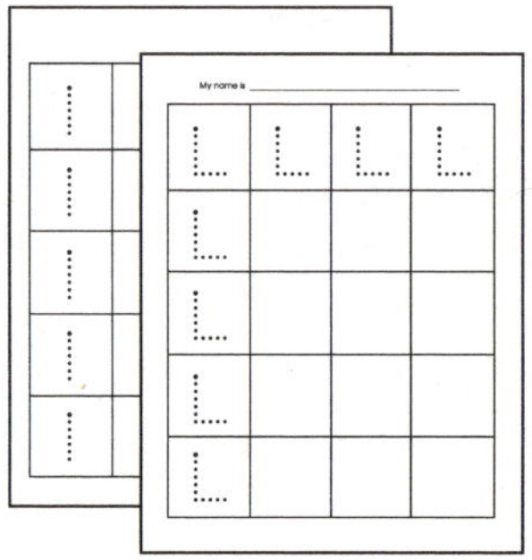

- Phonics Sheet for the letter *Ll*. Children identify pictures that begin with the letter *Ll*.

- Listening Sheets. Children listen and follow directions.

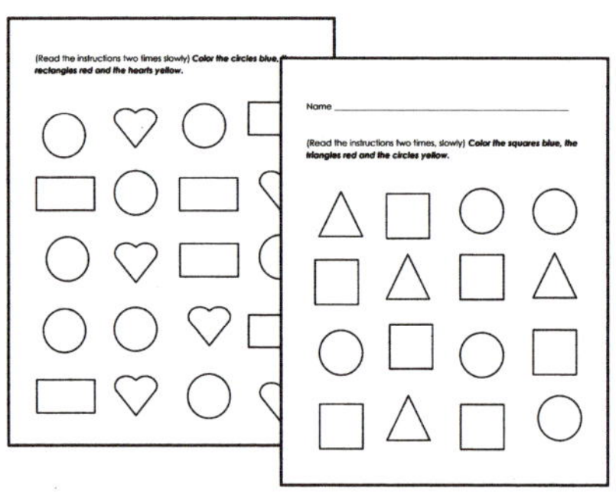

- **Journal:** Each child picks a different leaf plate (Leaf Rubbing Plates by Roylco **or** use a real leaf). Instruct the children to write the name of the leaf in their journals, then make a leaf rub. If possible, use a tree book (such as the *National Audubon Society First Field Guide Trees* by Brian Cassie) to identify each leaf.

TIP Teach the children that each tree has its own type of leaf.

Writing Center

- *Ll* picture stamps and word cards.
- This center can also be incorporated into DRAMATIC PLAY for the **Pizza Order Forms.**

Board Games

- Any listening lotto game
- Pizza Math by TREND Enterprises
- Pizza Party by Parker Brothers.

Sensory Table

Use the table for lacing (sewing) cards. It could also be used in the pizza parlor. Tape a small, medium, and large cardboard circle to the inside/bottom of the table to make each size pizza.

Workbench

Children write "I love you" or any message on a sheet of paper. To decorate, make leaf rubs with the Leaf Rubbing Plates by Roylco.

TIP Teacher can write "I love you" on a paper for the children to copy.

FREE CHOICE PLAY

Crafts

- Scarecrow puppet

TIP Strongly encourage each child to make a scarecrow puppet, which will be used at the Fall Harvest Show.

- Marble paint spider webs: Cut a black construction paper circle. Lay it in a box then add a squirt of white tempera paint and a marble. Either close the box and shake it or cut off the box lid and let the children tilt the box slightly and watch as the marble rolls through the paint and makes white spider webs.

- Trace small, medium, and large pizza dough circles. Each child chooses one size and cuts it out. Teacher mixes white glue and red washable tempera paint to make "sauce." Paint the sauce on the pizza dough. Cut out ingredients to place on the pizza. Cut strips of yellow "cheese" to sprinkle on top.

- Black cat with wallpaper mask.

Easel Art

Cut leaf shapes from coffee filters. Use a glue stick to adhere the leaf to manila art paper. Paint with watercolors. When the project is dry there are two art pieces: a colored leaf and a leaf picture on manila!

Notes & Evaluations

	Circle Time	Table Work	Free Choice Play	Crafts
Monday	Beginning: Ending:			
	Story:			
Tuesday	Beginning: Ending:			
	Story:			
Wednesday	Beginning: Ending:			
	Story:			
Thursday	Beginning: Ending:			
	Story:			
Friday	Beginning: Ending:			
	Story:			

Pp WEEK

Pumpkins

(small, medium, large)

Patterns

Fractions

(pieces of pizza)

Dramatic Play

Pizza Parlor

Add playdough for pizza dough and table and chairs for an eat-in restaurant.

Learning Objectives

Physical and Motor

- Balances well
- Puts puzzles together
- Catches a ball when thrown or bounced

Cognitive

- Engages in fantasy play, making up plots
- Uses props to symbolize real objects

Communication and Language

- Answers questions about familiar stories
- Sings songs, finger plays, and rhymes with increasing accuracy

Social and Emotional

- Plays with peers, sharing ideas and toys
- Follows and makes simple rules

Approaches to Learning

- Approaches new situations with increasing flexibility

Listening Activities and Songs

- Book on tape: *The Pumpkin Book* by Gail Gibbons
- Chant: "Pumpkins grow in a pumpkin patch; count how many you can catch"
- Song: "The Pumpkin Goes Around" (to the tune of "The Farmer in the Dell")
- Other fall songs

"The Pumpkin Goes Around"
(to the tune of "The Farmer in the Dell")

The pumkin goes around,
The pumpkin goes around,
All the things that you will see
Begin with the letter *P*.

Now stop and reach inside,
Now stop and reach inside,
Take one out and look and see
what begins with the letter *P*.

Stories

- *Too Many Pumpkins* by Linda White
- *The Biggest Pumpkin Surprise Ever* by Steven Kroll
- *From Seed to Pumpkin* by Wendy Pfeffer
- *Pattern Bugs* by Trudy Harris
- *Whole-y Cow!* by Taryn Souders
- *Pinduli* by Janell Cannon
- *Sylvester and the Magic Pebble* by William Steig
- *Don't Let the Pigeon Drive the Bus!* by Mo Willems
- *Give Me Half!* by Stuart J. Murphy
- *All the Colors We Are* by Katie Kissinger

RECIPE: Cooked Playdough

(See page 19 for recipe.)

CIRCLE TIME

Interactive Charts and Props

- Pizza Order Form/Menu for the restaurant from previous week
- Three real pumpkins (small, medium, and large)
- Pairs of socks (one pair per child) in a laundry basket
- Two kinds of musical instruments to make patterns with sound (for example, drums and bells)
- Pass the pumpkin treat bucket or bag with items that begin with the letter *P*. Suggested items are pencil, paperclip, pine cone, picture, postcard, potholder, etc.

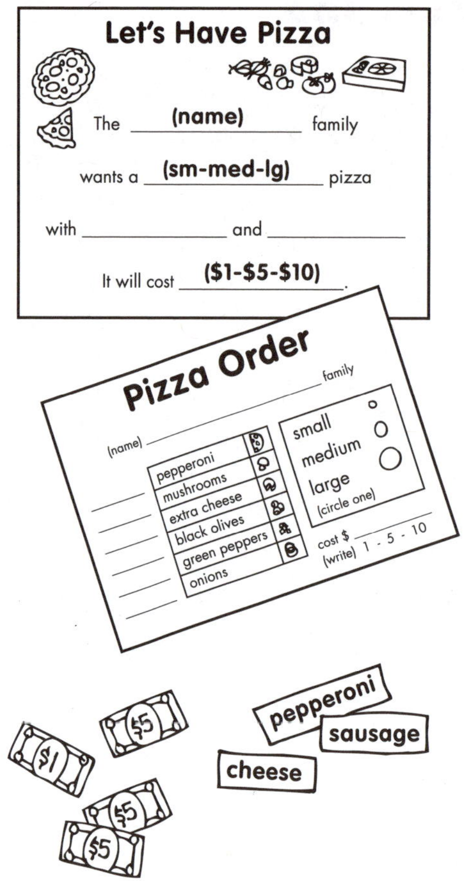

Circle Time Activities

- Introduce the letter *Pp*.
- Review the **Pizza Order Form.** Remind the children to complete an order before making a pizza. Explain how to use the playdough to roll out a small, medium, or large pizza.
- Read the book ***From Seed to Pumpkin*** by Wendy Pfeffer and discuss how pumpkins grow.
- Discuss the concept of small, medium, and large. Display three real pumpkins.
- Sing **"The Pumpkin Goes Around."** Use a plastic pumpkin treat bucket or bag full of items that begin with the letter *Pp* (at least one per child).
- Talk about pairs. Say to the children, "Think of your body. What do you have a pair of? What other things come in pairs?" Give a sock to each child and put the other sock into a laundry basket. Have each child take a turn to find the match. Teach children to fold the socks so they can help their family at home.

TIP Looking at things that match prepares the children for the next concept of patterns, in which things are different.

TABLE WORK

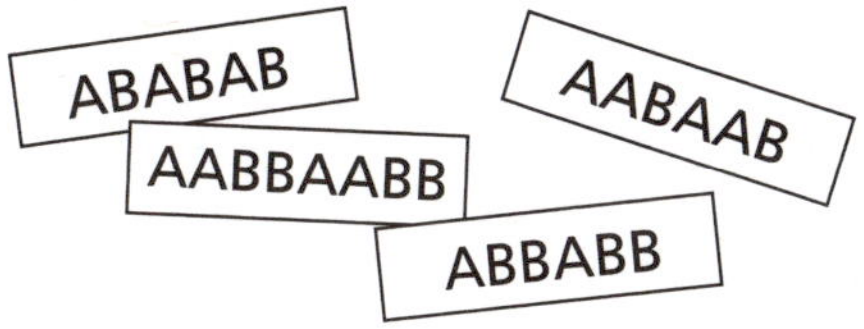

- Teach the patterns ABABAB, AABBAABB, AABAAB, and ABBABBA. Use small manipulatives to sort and create patterns. Make "people patterns" with the children: girl/boy/girl/boy, etc. Also make "sound patterns" using two different instruments like drums and bells.

- Read the book ***Give Me Half*** by Stuart J. Murphy. Teach the concepts *whole*, *half*, *one-third*, and *one-fourth* using a paper pizza cut into pieces.

- Teach the game **Frog Pond Fractions Game** by TREND Enterprises.

- Chant "Pumpkins grow in a pumpkin patch; count how many you can catch." While chanting, the children toss beanbags first by themselves, then with a partner.

- Practice the **Shadow Puppet Story**, giving each child a turn to be a character (use for Fall Harvest Show).

- Practice writing the letter of the week. Practice writing the letter *Pp*.

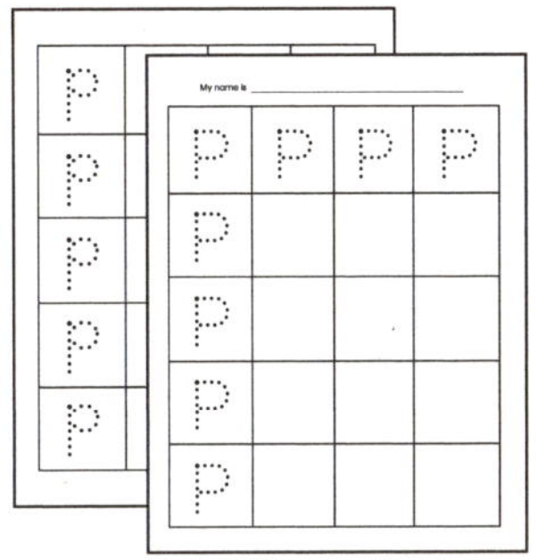

- Phonics Sheet for letter *Pp*. Children identify pictures that begin with the letter *Pp*.

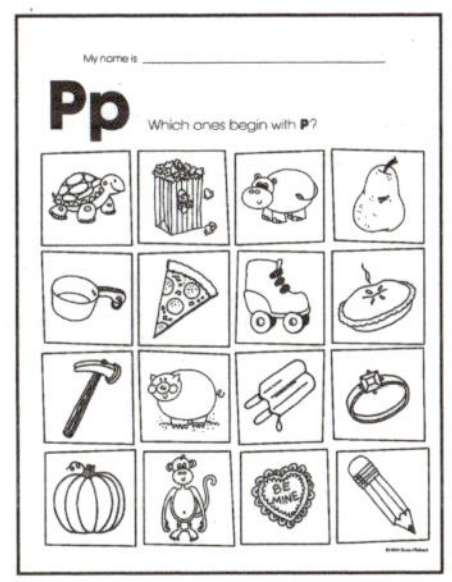

- Pattern Reproducible: Give the children ministickers to create patterns.

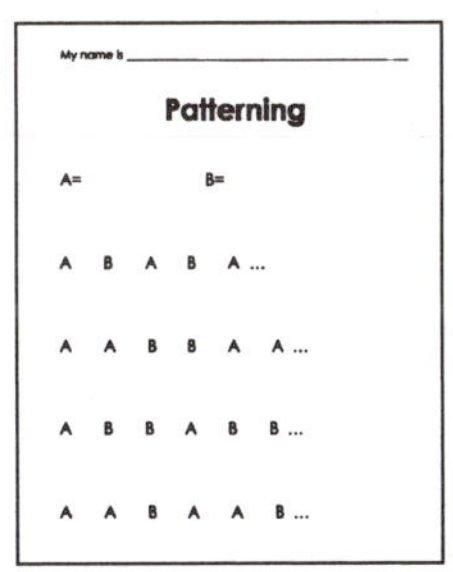

- Color the snake in a pattern using two colors (allow child to chose the pattern—ABABAB, AABBAABB, AABAAB, ABBABBA).

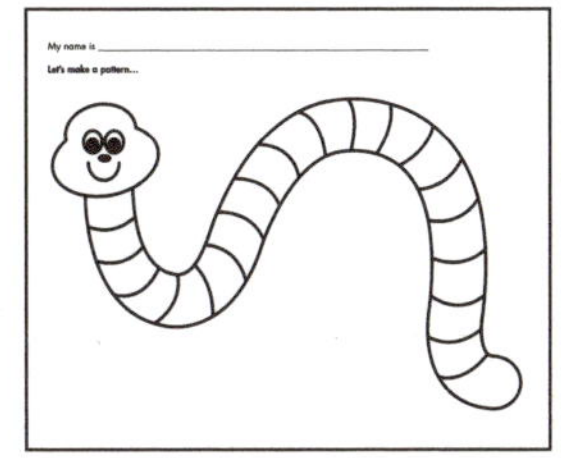

- Small, Medium, Large Reproducible

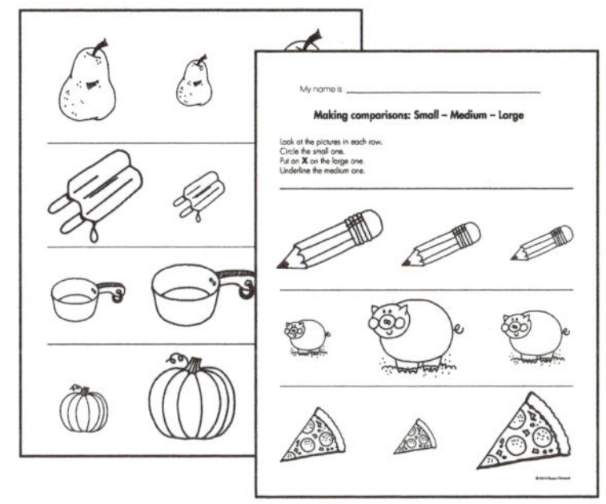

- **Journal** Write: *pumpkin puzzle*
  Color and cut out the pumpkin into no more than four or five pieces. Glue it back together in the journal to make a pumpkin puzzle.

FREE CHOICE PLAY

Writing Center

- *Pp* alphabet stamps and corresponding word cards to copy in journal

Board Games

- Spin-a-Slice Pizza Matching Game by Melissa & Doug
- Pizza Math by TREND Enterprises
- Frog Pond Fractions Game by TREND Enterprises

Sensory Table

Use the table in the pizza parlor to roll the play dough into small, medium, and large pizza crusts by taping a small, medium, and large circle to the inside of the SENSORY TABLE.

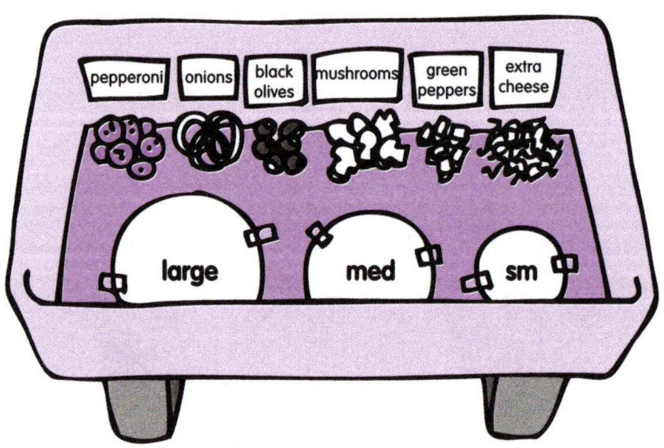

Workbench

Trace a small, medium, and large pumpkin on construction paper. Lay two indoor/outdoor carpet squares on the workbench. Place the pumpkin paper on the carpet square. Punch around the small, medium, and large pumpkins with corn cob holders. Children can use the corn cob holder to punch a face or decorate the pumpkin. Hang the pumpkin in a window and the light will shine through.

TIP Place small, medium, and large baskets near the workbench to sort the pumpkins.

Easel Art

Paint "Pizza to Go." Fill out a **Pizza Order Form.** (Glue is added to red tempera paint to make the sauce.) Paint a paper plate with the "sauce." Use construction paper cut out ingredients from the pizza parlor. Tape the **Pizza Order Form** to the back of the Pizza to Go and allow it to dry.

Crafts

- Sock puppets (see instructions on page 51)
- Pumpkin parachute (see instructions below)
- Pumpkin balls (see instructions on page 51)
- Use the extra ministickers to make more patterns (display the pattern cards near the craft area).
- Paper to draw and color pictures to be cut into four to five pieces to make "picture puzzles" (provide envelopes to bring them home)

HOW TO: Make a Pumpkin Parachute

To make a pumpkin parachute, fold a sheet of orange construction paper in half and trace a pumpkin, touching the bottom to the folded edge of the paper. Each parachute needs four strings twelve inches long and a square of plastic sheeting or a cloth handkerchief (try using plastic table covering). Have the strings tied to each corner of the square ahead of time. Tell children to cut the pumpkin, open it, and tape a penny inside for weight. Fold the pumpkin together and punch a hole on either side of the top of the pumpkin; tie two strings to each hole. Drop the parachute from a climber at outdoor playtime!

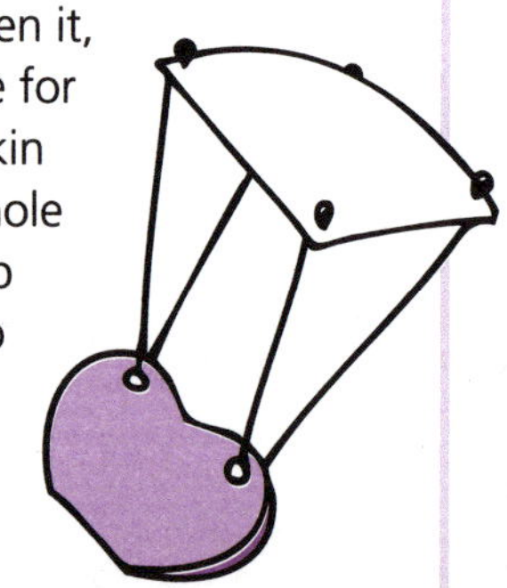

Notes & Evaluations

HOW TO: Make a Sock Puppet

To make sock puppets, you will need child-size sport/tube socks; felt cutout eyes, noses, and mouths; and yarn for hair. Stretch the sock over a soda pop can. Ask the child, "What color are your eyes and hair?" Dot fabric glue on the sock, and let the child press on the felt pieces. Allow children to cut yarn pieces the length of their hair. Put a generous amount of fabric glue on top of the head. The children lay pieces in place. Small pieces can be used as bangs in front (puppets can be embellished with ribbons, buttons and bows, and so forth).

HOW TO: Make Pumpkin Balls

To make pumpkin balls, have orange construction paper cut into strips approximately 1¼ inches wide the short length of the construction paper (strips will be 9 x 1¼ inches). Trace green stems for the top. Each pumpkin uses eight orange strips, one stem, and two paper fasteners. Children punch a hole in the top and bottom of each strip and on one edge of the green stem. Lay one paper fastener on the table with the point up. First place the stem on the paper fastener, then carefully place each of the eight orange strips using one of the punched holes. Spread the paper fastener to hold the strips and stem together. Pick up the flat strips and insert the second paper fastener into each hole at the other end of the orange strips and spread it. Using your fingertips, gently spread the strips apart, forming them into a ball. Bend the stem up and it's a pumpkin! Fold it flat to take it home.

	Circle Time	Table Work	Free Choice Play	Crafts
Monday	Beginning: Ending:			
	Story:			
Tuesday	Beginning: Ending:			
	Story:			
Wednesday	Beginning: Ending:			
	Story:			
Thursday	Beginning: Ending:			
	Story:			
Friday	Beginning: Ending:			
	Story:			

Xx WEEK

Skeleton

X-ray

Parts of the Body

Dramatic Play

Farm with a Harvest Market

Use barns with farm animals. Dress up in flannel shirts and straw hats.

Learning Objectives

Physical and Motor

- Uses left or right hand predominantly
- Copies and draws simple shapes and letters

Cognitive

- Recognizes own name in print
- Recognizes rhyming sounds in words

Communication and Language

- Speaks when spoken to
- Knows and says first and last names

Social and Emotional

- Is self-directed
- Has an increasing attention span

Approaches to Learning

- Offers ideas and suggestions

Listening Activities and Songs

- Xylophone (learn to play "Mary Had a Little Lamb"/"Skeleton Song")

"Skeleton Song"
(to the tune of "Mary Had a Little Lamb")

Our skeleton is made of bones,
made of bones, made of bones.
Our skeleton is made of bones.
See them on an X-ray.

How many bones do we have, do
we have, do we have?
How many bones do we have?
We have two hundred six.
See them on an X-ray.

RECIPE: Bounce Putty

1 cup white glue
1 cup liquid starch
Food coloring

In a bowl, slowly add 1 cup white glue to 1 cup liquid starch, stirring constantly. Food coloring can be added for color. Store in a plastic ziplock bag in the refrigerator. It lasts one to two weeks.

Stories

- *The Little Old Lady Who Was Not Afraid of Anything* by Linda Williams **(use for the Fall Harvest Show)**
- *The Skeleton Inside You* by Philip Balestrino
- *Inside Your Outside: All about the Human Body* by Tish Rabe
- *Hidden World Human Body* by Claude Delafosse
- *Jessica's X-ray* by Pat Zonta
- *My Little Blue Robot* by Stephen T. Johnson
- *Boy + Bot* by Ame Dyckman
- *Parts* by Tedd Arnold
- *Go Away, Big Green Monster!* by Ed Emberley

CIRCLE TIME

Interactive Charts and Props

- Create your own large Hangman Chart, newsprint, or chalkboard with a set of alphabet letters and skeleton to "hang."

TIP Use the skeleton in CRAFTS. Place a magnet on each piece to "hang."

- Real X-ray photos for display
- Costumes and props for the story ***The Little Old Lady Who Was Not Afraid of Anything*** by Linda Williams

TIP For props, put a flannel shirt on a hanger and a pair of jeans on a pants hanger. An old pair of men's shoes will "clomp" well on a board.

Circle Time Activities

- Introduce the letter *Xx*.
- Make homemade **Bounce Putty.** Use it in the SENSORY TABLE.
- Teach the children to sort things into sets. Create sets of items where one thing does not belong. Lay a large construction paper *X* on the item that does not belong. (For example, with four different buttons and one penny, you would lay the *X* on the penny. With three construction vehicles and one boat, you would lay the *X* on the boat.)
- Weigh and measure each child.
- Review the parts of the body. A fun way is to use a large sheet of paper to draw a "silly person." Give each child a card with the name of a body part. Then, each child draws the part listed on their card. Start with the head, then the body, continuing until every child takes a turn.
- Explain the Body/Robot project. This project could be done for TABLE WORK, if there is enough space for all the children to spread out with their Body/Robot, or during FREE CHOICE PLAY with a few children at a time.
- Continue to practice songs and the **Shadow Puppet Story** to prepare for the **Fall Harvest Show.**
- Read the story ***The Little Old Lady Who Was Not Afraid of Anything*** by Linda Williams. Act it out with props and costumes **(use for Fall Harvest Show)**.
- Teach the children to play the game **Count Your Chickens** by Peaceable Kingdom.
- Play the game **Hangman** at CIRCLE TIME each day. Use the children's first names for guessing. The props needed are a **Hangman Chart,** a skeleton to build, a set of magnetic alphabet letters to hang, and the children's name cards displayed to help them guess. Don't forget you will need extra alphabet letters if any names have repeated letters. For example, *Tommy* needs two *M*s. Be sure to guess each child's name!

TABLE WORK

- Practice writing the letter of the week. Practice writing the letter *Xx*.

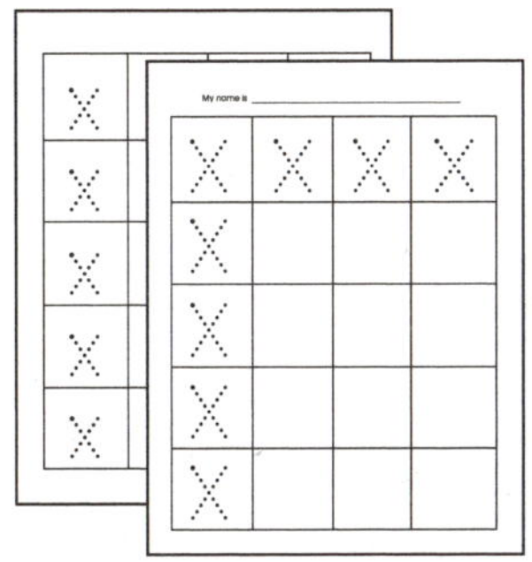

- Phonics Sheet for letter *Xx*

- *X* the Picture That Does Not Belong Worksheet

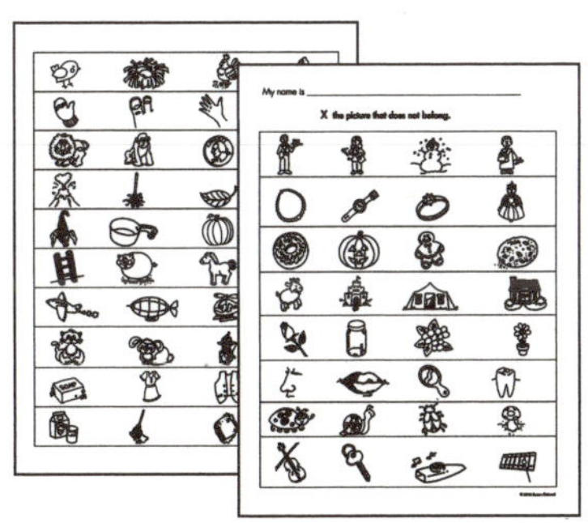

- Weigh and Measure Reproducible (save for end of the year)

- **Journal** Write: *my X-ray*
  Have a body traced on black construction paper for each child. Tell the children to cut them out. Using a small dish of white paint and toothpicks, children draw bones on the body (a white crayon would be less messy). Glue the X-ray body in their journals when it is dry.

FREE CHOICE PLAY

Writing Center

Xx Alphabet Stamps and corresponding word cards to copy in journal

Board Games

- Tic-tac-toe
- 1–2–3 Farmyard! by TREND Enterprises
- Chicken Coop Domino Game by Ideal
- Barnyard Bingo by Fisher-Price
- Count Your Chickens! by Peaceable Kingdom

Sensory Table

Bounce putty, small plastic skeletons, measuring cups and spoons

Workbench

Provide any construction manipulative that would be suitable for building a robot.

Easel Art

Cut large easel paper into the shape of a barn. Use easel paint with fall and farm animal stamps. Demonstrate how to brush paint on the stamp instead of using a stamp pad.

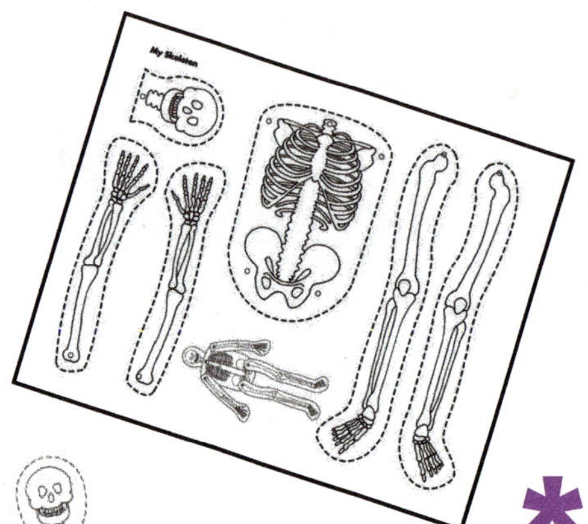

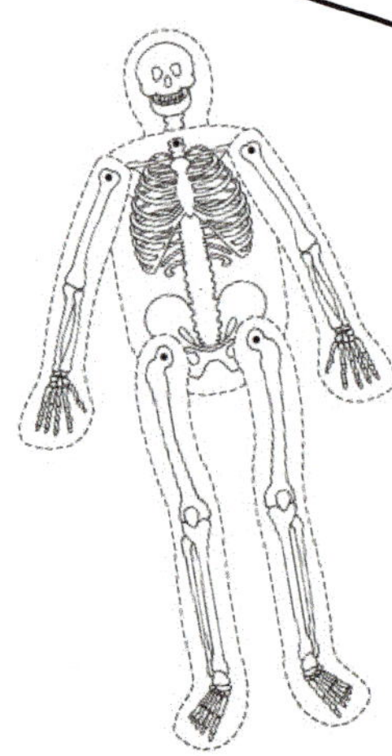

Crafts

- A few children at a time work on the Body/Robot Project (see instructions on page 57)
- Copy skeleton body parts pattern onto cardstock. Children cut out the pieces and join them together with paper fasteners. The skeleton is moveable!
- Provide body-shaped stencils to trace.
- Match the Animals to Their Skeletons Reproducible

Notes & Evaluations

HOW TO: Body/Robot Project

Trace a head and body and glue them together at the neck. (Use a bowl twelve inches in diameter to trace the head and a cafeteria tray approximately 19 x 13 inches for the torso.) Each child chooses four pieces of construction paper. Two are folded lengthwise then cut on the fold for the arms and legs. Discuss with the children where our arms are attached to the body—at the shoulders. The remaining two papers are for the hands and feet. Fold the papers the short way. Trace a hand on the first paper and trace the child's foot on the second paper. Keep the papers folded and show the children how to cut two hands out at one time. Do likewise with the feet. Children glue the arms, legs, hands, and feet to the body. Using markers, children can draw their face and hair. Next, children can decorate their clothes.

Option: Make a silent video with music showing each child holding up their project in front of themselves, lowering it slowly to reveal who's behind it. Watch the movie together. The children enjoy guessing each other!

TIP Show the movie during *Dd* week when families visit the classroom.

	Circle Time	Table Work	Free Choice Play	Crafts
Monday	Beginning: Ending:			
	Story:			
Tuesday	Beginning: Ending:			
	Story:			
Wednesday	Beginning: Ending:			
	Story:			
Thursday	Beginning: Ending:			
	Story:			
Friday	Beginning: Ending:			
	Story:			

Hh WEEK

Fall Harvest

Homes for People

Homes for Animals

Dramatic Play

Continue farm with Harvest Market. Add real pumpkins and gourds.

Learning Objectives

Physical and Motor

- Uses scissors
- Copies and draws simple shapes and letters
- Uses small muscles in hands to color, cut, paste, and paint

Cognitive

- Shows an interest in numbers and names of numbers
- Counts objects out loud

Communication and Language

- Knows print and book rules
- Uses language to control and give directions

Social and Emotional

- Understands others' perspectives
- Role-plays

Approaches to Learning

- Offers ideas and suggestions

Listening Activities and Songs

- Song: "The Farmer, the Goat, and the Missing Letter" (to the tune of "Twinkle, Twinkle Little Star")
- Song: "Spider Song" (to the tune of "Mary Had a Little Lamb")
- Song: "Old MacDonald Had a Farm" (Traditional)

"The Farmer, the Goat, and the Missing Letter"
(to the tune of "Twinkle, Twinkle Little Star")

Teacher sings:
There are letters on the floor.
(Lay about 5 or 6 letters in the center of the circle)

Children sing:
Look, a goat came in the door!
(Teacher, put the goat paper bag puppet on your hand)

T: Now close your eyes really tight.
(Teacher takes one letter away)

C: Hope that goat is out of sight!

T: Open wide and take a look.

C: We can guess the one it took.
(Children each take a turn to guess the missing letter)

Stories

- *Houses and Homes* by Ann Morris
- *How Many Seeds in a Pumpkin?* by Margaret McNamara
- *My Very First Book of Animal Homes* by Eric Carle
- *Last Stop on Market Street* by Matt de la Peña
- *Miss Fiona's Stupendous Pumpkin Pies* by Mark Kimball Moulton
- *Welcome Home, Bear: A Book of Animal Habitats* by Il Sung Na
- *A House for Hermit Crab* by Eric Carle
- *Anasi the Spider* by Gerald McDermott

"Spider Song"
(to the tune of "Mary Had a Little Lamb")

Spiders have eight wiggly legs
Wiggly legs
Wiggley legs
Spiders have eight wiggly legs
Spiders are arachnids!

Spiders spin a sticky web
Sticky web
Sticky web
Spiders spin a sticky web
To catch a bug for lunch!

CIRCLE TIME

Interactive Charts and Props

- Create your own Parts of a Pumpkin chart.
- Class writes a Pumpkin Report.
- Large pumpkin and supplies for carving a shape lantern
- Medium and small pumpkins for the WORKBENCH
- Abacus for counting pumpkin seeds

Parts of a Pumpkin
shell flesh pulp seeds stem

Our pumpkin report	
It weighs this much	15 #
It is this fat	
It is this tall	17 blocks

Circle Time Activities

- Introduce the letter *Hh*.
- Using the large pumpkin, make a **Pumpkin Report.** Record the weight, height (how many blocks tall) and circumference (measure by wrapping a yarn around the pumpkin).
- Give each child a **Pumpkin Picture.** Think about how the class might carve a pumpkin into a shape lantern the following day. Have children draw shapes on their pumpkin picture to plan their ideas. Remind children that the class shape lantern will be a combination of everyone's ideas.

*

TIP Discuss addresses and types of homes for people as well as animal homes.

- Carve a class pumpkin to make a shape lantern. To begin, cut the top opening in the pumpkin and lift the lid. Use the **Parts of a Pumpkin** chart to identify the shell, flesh, pulp, seeds, and stem. Have the children take turns helping to clean out the inside of the pumpkin. Before carving shapes, take this opportunity to demonstrate that a candle needs air (oxygen) to burn. Secure the candle in a candle holder and light the candle. Place a glass jar over the lit candle and watch and count the seconds; the candle slowly goes out as the oxygen is used up. To further the demonstration, place the candle inside the pumpkin shell and light the candle. Place the top on snugly. Begin counting to see how many seconds it takes to use all the oxygen inside the pumpkin. (Light is still visible around the edge of the lid.) As you continue carving, tell the children that is why we need to carve shapes: so the candle can glow. Have the children show their ideas from their pumpkin picture. While carving, discuss and limit the choices, and then vote on the shapes. Also review how pumpkins grow. Save the seeds to count.
- Read the book ***How Many Seeds in a Pumpkin?*** by Margaret McNamara. Teach the class to use an abacus to count the pumpkin seeds.
- Together with the class, write a story describing the shape lantern.

TABLE WORK

- Make a goat paper bag puppet and play **The Farmer, the Goat, and the Missing Letter** Game. Sing the song. The teacher sings the first line, the children sing the next, and so on (everyone gets a turn to take a letter).

- Continue to practice for the **Fall Harvest Show.**

- Teach the children about spiders and their webs. Keep it simple: for example, spiders have eight legs and they spin a web to catch bugs. Why don't spiders get caught in their own webs?

TIP Collect articles from science magazines for children on topics discussed throughout the school year.

- Practice writing the letter of the week. Practice writing the letter *Hh*.

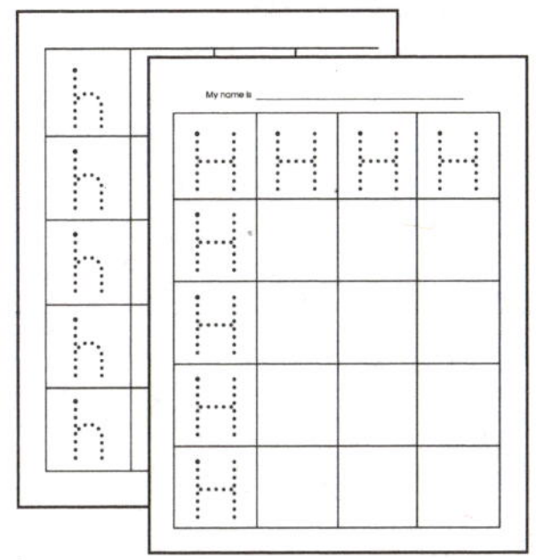

- Phonics Sheet for letter *Hh*.

- Use art foam to create a frame for the photo taken at the Fall Harvest Show.

- **Journal** Write: *shape house*
Children cut out house shapes and assemble and glue them in their journals. Show them how to cut the door so it opens and closes.

FREE CHOICE PLAY

Writing Center

Hh words with alphabet stamps

Board Games

- Hi Ho Cherry-O by Western Publishing Co.
- Count Your Chickens by Peaceable Kingdom

Sensory Table

- Place seeds from the pumpkin carved at CIRCLE TIME first in water to wash, then drain the table and count the seeds.

Workbench

Cut in half the small and medium pumpkins and explore the parts of a pumpkin (use the chart), then lay them flat and use a hammer to pound roofing nails, a screwdriver to screw in wood screws, and a hand drill to put holes in the pumpkin shells.

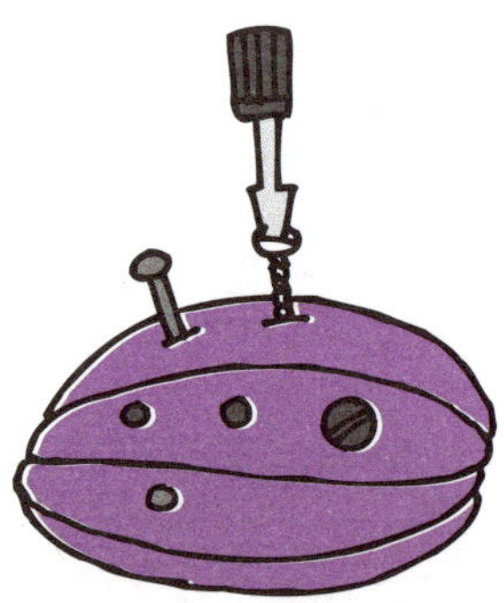

Easel Art

Put the easel away this week.

Crafts

- Marble paint spider webs: Cut a black construction paper circle. Lay it in a box then add a squirt of white tempera paint and a marble. Either close the box and shake it or cut off the box lid and let the children tilt the box slightly and watch as the marble rolls through the paint and makes white spider webs.

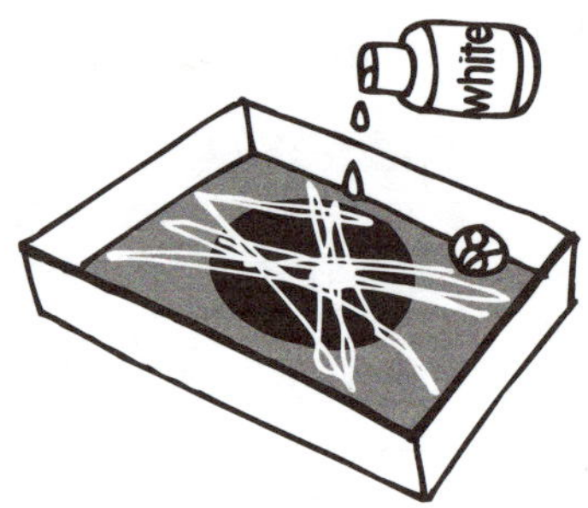

- For another spider web craft, paint a paper plate black. Let it dry overnight. "Draw" a spider's web with glue. Sprinkle with glitter. Or cut ten evenly spaced, one-inch slits around the plate. Tape the loose end of a small ball of white yarn to the back of the plate. Using the yarn, "spin a web" using the slits to hold the yarn in place. To finish, tape the end of the yarn to the back of the plate and stick on a spider sticker.

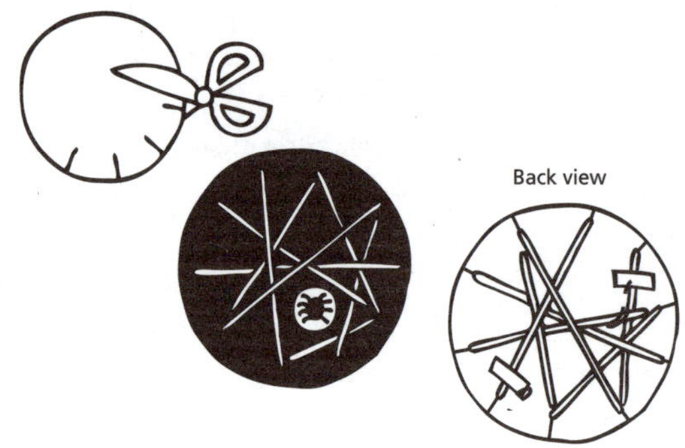

- Children can make a goat paper bag puppet.

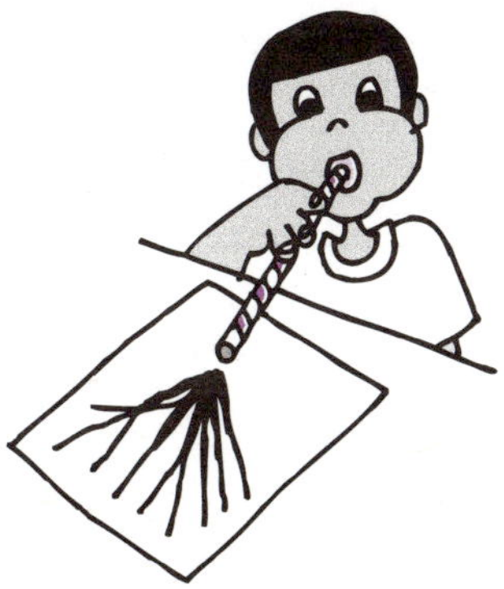

- Blow paint a tree. Add water to black tempera paint and, using an eye dropper, squirt a few drops of the watered paint on glossy paper. Blow the paint with a straw or squeeze a bulb syringe to spread the paint in different directions.

- Create art by gluing dried pumpkin seeds to paper.

- After coloring the fall coloring pages, cut them into four or five pieces to make a fall puzzle (like *Pp* Week).

- The cutout shapes from the shape lantern can be scraped smooth and used as stamps with paint-soaked sponges as the "ink pad."

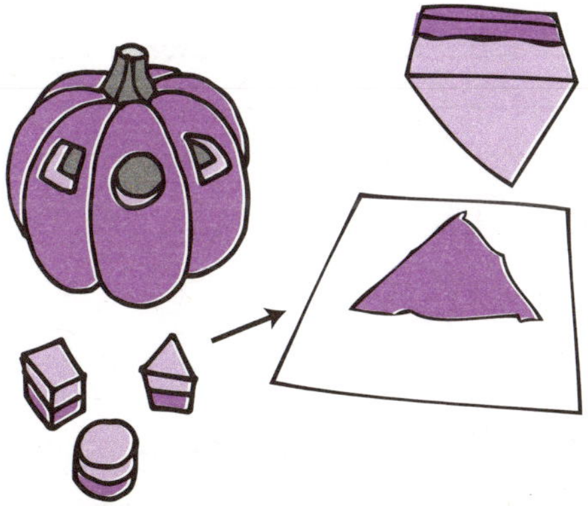

Fall Harvest Show

Using the **Shadow Puppet Stage,** the children hold the puppets while the teacher reads the story **"Great Lion and Tiny Mouse"** (*Ll* Week). (Eight children participate.)

Act out the book ***The Little Old Lady Who Was Not Afraid of Anything*** by Linda Williams (*Xx* Week). (Any remaining child who did not have a part in the Shadow Puppet story participates.)

Sing the children's favorite fall songs. Use props whenever possible.

Notes & Evaluations

	Circle Time	Table Work	Free Choice Play	Crafts
Monday	Beginning: Ending:			
	Story:			
Tuesday	Beginning: Ending:			
	Story:			
Wednesday	Beginning: Ending:			
	Story:			
Thursday	Beginning: Ending:			
	Story:			
Friday	Beginning: Ending:			
	Story:			

Rr WEEK

Car Racing

Ordinal Numbers

Rhymes

Robots

Dramatic Play

Race Car Pit Stop

Add a Darda race track

Learning Objectives

Physical and Motor

- Runs with ease and stops quickly
- Walks on a balance beam or line
- Copies and draws simple shapes and letters

Cognitive

- Recognizes rhyming sounds in words
- Recognizes alliterative sounds in words

Communication and Language

- Pronounces words and letter sounds correctly
- Converses easily with adults

Social and Emotional

- Understands some limits and rules
- Makes friends

Approaches to Learning

- Seeks and accepts help and information

Listening Activities and Songs

- Song: "A-Hunting We Will Go" (Traditional) (Teacher can make up verses to practice rhymes.)
- Song: "Row, Row, Row Your Boat" (Use the verses in the book by Iza Trapani and use the book *Songs in Sign* by S. Harold Collins)
- Song: "This Old Man" (Traditional)

Stories

- *Rumpelstiltskin* retold and illustrated by Paul O. Zelinsky
- *Row, Row, Row Your Boat* as told and illustrated by Iza Trapani
- *Race Car Dreams* by Sharon Chriscoe
- "The Thrifty Tailor" in *Tell It Again 2!* by Shirley C. Raines and Rebecca Isbell
- *"There Are Rocks in my Socks," said the Ox to the Fox* by Patricia Thomas
- *Oh, A-Hunting We Will Go* by John Langstaff
- *The Farmer in the Dell* by John O'Brien
- *This Old Man* by Pam Adams
- *Seven Blind Mice* by Ed Young
- *The Biggest Riddle Book in the World* by Joseph Rosenbloom
- *10 Little Ninjas* by Miranda Paul
- *My Little Blue Robot* by Stephen T. Johnson (This story is used in *Xx* Week and reread to introduce the journal writing activity this week.)
- *1-2-3 Peas* by Keith Baker

CIRCLE TIME

Interactive Charts and Props

- Create your own Car Repair Chart.
- Race Car Game (See FREE CHOICE PLAY section for rules and directions.)
- Seven construction-paper mice to be used with the story ***Seven Blind Mice*** by Ed Young. Make a mouse in each of these colors: red, green, yellow, purple, orange, blue, and white. Also make a set of cards labeled first through seventh.

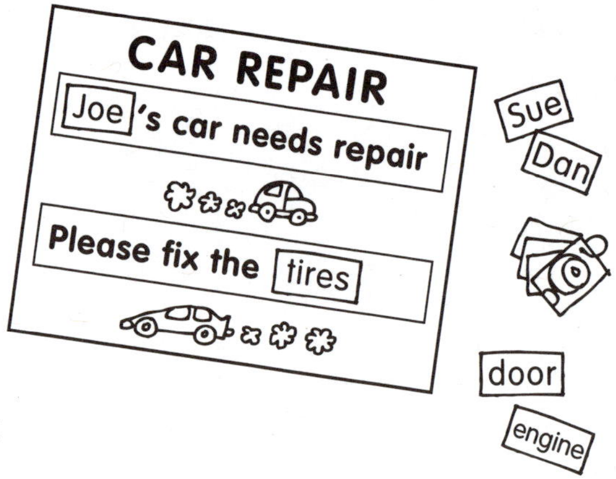

TIP As the story ***Seven Blind Mice*** is read, place each mouse on the floor in no particular order. When the story is finished, lay out the cards labeled first through seventh in order and ask the children to recall which mouse looked at the "strange something" first, second, third, etc. Review the story to check their answers.

Circle Time Activities

- Introduce the letter *Rr*.
- Discuss recycling. We use recycled boxes for the Box Race Car Project. Explain the project: each table of four children will make a race car to share. Race cars have stripes, so each child will paint a stripe on their table's race car at FREE CHOICE PLAY. Cars have headlights and brake lights, so each child can cut one out. Race cars also have numbers on the side, so each child will cut out two numbers for the race car. When the car is complete, the teacher will cut handles in the side so the children can take turns "driving" the car during outside or gym time. (If the box is large enough for two children at a time, cut the appropriate number of handles.)
- Teach and practice rhyming words. Sing **"A-Hunting We Will Go."** (The teacher can make up more verses; have the children also suggest some.)
- Teach the children to play **I Spy a Mouse in the House! Picture Rhymes Game** by Carson-Dellosa
- Use the **Race Car Game** to teach ordinal numbers. Each child can take a turn until the game is finished. Ordinal numbers can also be reinforced when the children line up, take a turn, etc. (See FREE CHOICE PLAY section for rules and directions.)

TABLE WORK

TIP Send home two or three riddles that are a little more difficult for the children to guess with their families. Have them bring back their answers at the end of the week.

- Reread ***My Little Blue Robot*** by Stephen T. Johnson on journal day. Discuss the shape of each piece as it is added to the robot. Explain that the children will be tracing shapes to build a robot in their journals that day.

- Watch the Robot Movie the class made during *Xx* Week. (The movie is shown on the evening the families come for **Family Night**.)

- Discuss: what is a Riddle? Ask the children to guess some simple riddles.

- Sing **"Row, Row, Row Your Boat"** in rounds. Use the book ***Songs in Sign*** by S. Harold Collins and try using American Sign Language signs while singing the song. **TeacherTip: every word does not need to be signed, just the main ones.**

- Tell the story **"The Tortoise and the Hare,"** an Aesop Fable. Discuss storytelling; talk about how people told stories over and over at family gatherings, at bedtime, around a campfire, and so forth. Have the children retell the story "The Tortoise and the Hare." Each child takes a turn; encourage them to use expression and enhance the story if they choose.

- Practice writing the letter of the week. Practice writing the letter *Rr*.

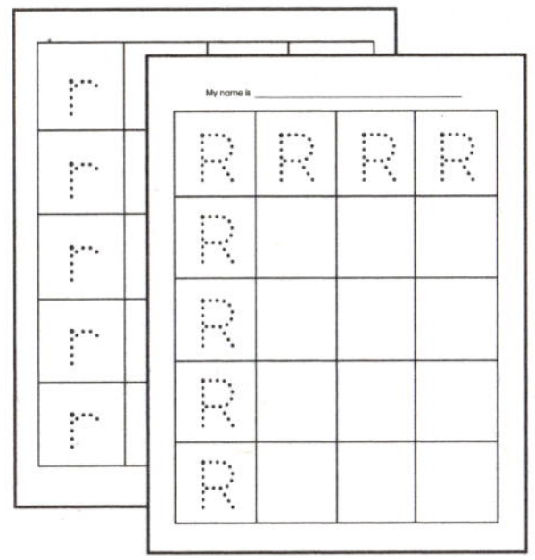

*

- Phonics Sheet for the letter *Rr*

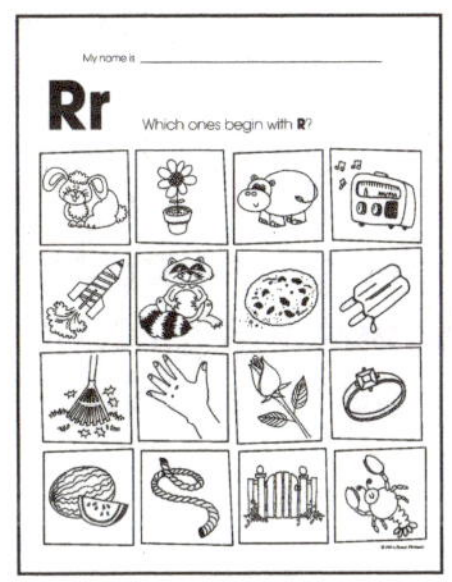

*

- Each table of four children will make a Box Race Car. Two children at the table can cut out a headlight and the other two can cut out a brake light. Each child will also cut out two numbers for her Box Race Car. All four children will write their names on the same half sheet of white construction paper, which is then glued to the back of the Race Car—it is the license plate!

- Rhyming Reproducible

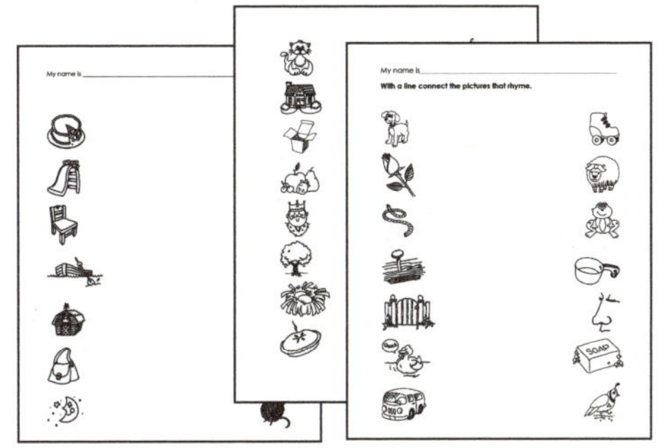

*

- **Journal** Write: *robot*
(Have enough shape patterns for children to share at each table.) Children use shape patterns to trace and construct a robot. Color the robot with crayons.

Rr
WEEK

FREE CHOICE PLAY

Writing Center

Rr alphabet stamps and words

Board Games

- I Spy a Mouse in the House! Picture Rhymes by Carson-Dellosa
- Rhyming BINGO by TREND Enterprises
- Chutes and Ladders by Milton Bradley
- Robot Face Race by Educational Insights

Sensory Table

Fill the table approximately two inches deep with sand. Use oil-changing funnels in a funnel board across the width of the table. Put dump trucks and small blocks in the sand with a few scoops. (The blocks will hold the sand back, which makes a road to drive the trucks.)

OR

Make playdough and put four rolling pins and alphabet letter cookie cutters in the sensory table to roll, roll, roll the dough!

Workbench

Build a Car and Scooter Kit by SnapTite or use any manipulative that can be used to build a car.

TIP Enlarge the **Build a Car and Scooter** instruction sheet and hang it above the WORKBENCH area.

Easel Art

Put the easel away to make room for painting stripes on the race car boxes. When the race cars are painted, the easel can be set up again to use up the rest of the race car paint.

Crafts

- Put out small, cutout construction paper shapes to glue together to make robots.
- Use small cars and stamp pads to "drive a design" with the tires on drawing paper.

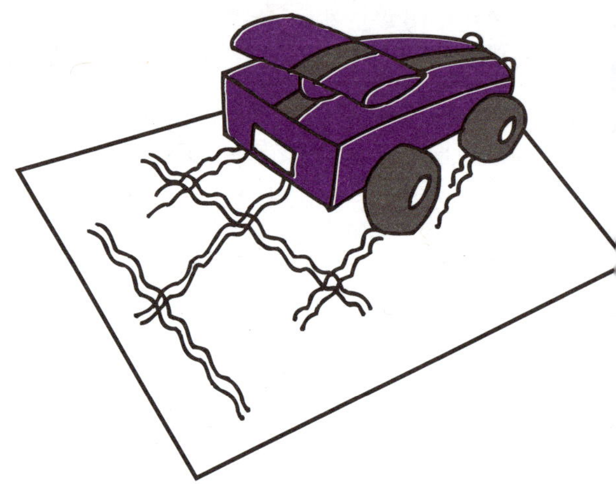

- Use the pictures from the Rhyming Reproducible to make a sheet of rhyming cards to color and cut apart. Children can then take the cards home to practice.

TIP The Rhyming Cards could also be used to play a rhyming memory game.

HOW TO: Play the Race Car Game

You will need the following:

- A game board with six different-colored tracks, each with about nine spaces
- Six small different-colored cars that correspond to six colored tracks
- Two dice or a spinner and a die (one with the numbers 1, 2, 3 and one with the six colors)

Any number of children may play. To begin

- Place the colored cars on the corresponding colored START space.
- The **first player** rolls both dice. Move the colored car the appropriate number of spaces.
- The **second player** rolls both dice and moves the colored car the number of spaces rolled.
- Continue with each player taking a turn.

As each car reaches the FINISH LINE, put the cars in order: first, second, third, etc. There is no winner or loser in this game. Everyone is a winner because they learn about ordinal numbers!

TIP Children want to "be the blue car" or "be the red car" but that's NOT how to play the game! The color dice or spinner determines what color car the player moves on their turn.

Notes & Evaluations

	Circle Time	Table Work	Free Choice Play	Crafts
Monday	Beginning: Ending:			
	Story:			
Tuesday	Beginning: Ending:			
	Story:			
Wednesday	Beginning: Ending:			
	Story:			
Thursday	Beginning: Ending:			
	Story:			
Friday	Beginning: Ending:			
	Story:			

Simple Machines WEEK

Inclined Plane

Screw

Lever

Wheel & Axle

Wedge

Pulley

Dramatic Play

Simple Machines

Set up displays and demonstrations of simple machines throughout the classroom.

Learning Objectives

Physical and Motor

- Makes marks or strokes with drawing tools
- Balances well

Cognitive

- Uses reason to solve problems
- Makes comparisons between objects after observation

Communication and Language

- Asks questions and seeks answers
- Argues, reasons, and uses the word *because*

Social and Emotional

- Plays alone
- Shows increasing patience

Approaches to Learning

- Offers ideas and suggestions

Listening Activities and Songs

- Song: "I've Been Working on the Railroad" (American folksong)
- Audiobook: "The Wheels on the Bus Go Round and Round" Music composed and performed by Bernard Graham Shaw
- Poem: "Jack and Jill" (Traditional)
- Use spoons as musical instruments (two for each child).
- Sounds of motorized machines in the home (washing machine, electric mixer, alarm clock, etc.)

Simple Machines

This unit on simple machines can be used as a themed week on its own, incorporated into an existing week, or spread out over two consecutive weeks—whatever suits the schedule.

TIP A good placement for Simple Machines Week is before *Dd* Week. Each of the simple machines can be displayed in the classroom when the families come to visit on **Family Night.** The children love showing their families what they have learned and how the simple machines make a job easier!

Stories

- *The Simple Story of the 3 Pigs and the Scientific Wolf* by Mary Fetzner
- *Pull, Lift, and Lower: A Book About Pulleys* by Michael Dahl (pulley)
- *Sloping Up and Down: The Inclined Plane* by Gerry Bailey and Felicia Law (inclined plane)
- *The Bee Tree* by Patricia Polacco (screw)
- *Pull the Lever: Who Does What?* by Jane Wolfe (lever)
- *Rumpelstiltskin* retold and illustrated by Paul O. Zelinsky (wheel and axle)
- *The Giant Jam Sandwich* by John Vernon Lord (wedge)
- *How Do You Lift a Lion?* by Robert E. Wells

Reference Books:

- *The Kids' Book of Simple Machines: Cool Projects and Activities That Make Science Fun!* by Kelly Doudna
- *Teaching STEM in the Early Years* by Sally Moomaw
- Starting with Science series: *Simple Machines* by Deborah Hodge

CIRCLE TIME

Interactive Charts and Props

Create a bulletin board display of the six simple machines. Use the stories and reference books to find examples for each. Use the bulletin board as a teaching chart as well.

Circle Time Activities

- Play sounds of motorized machines. First play the sound and just listen. Explain, "These are machines and the sounds they make as they are working." Play them again, stopping after each one to see if the children can guess the machine. Now explain to the children the theme for the week: simple machines, which do not use any electricity, motors, or batteries. Simple machines use people power! Name the six simple machines and show examples of each.

- Explain force, pushing and pulling, friction, work, and power and energy. Sing **"I've Been Working on the Railroad."**

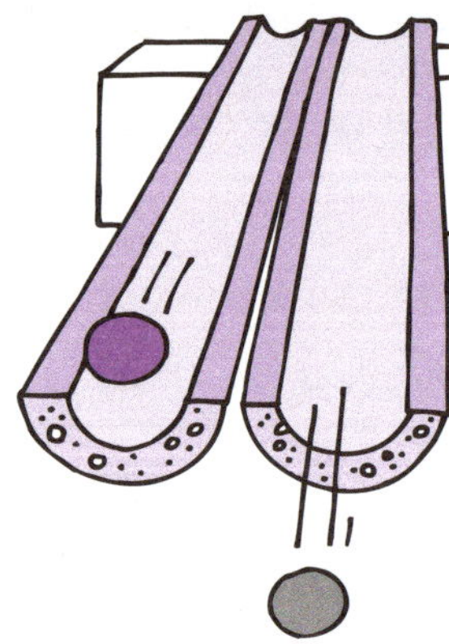

- Explain **inclined planes.** Ask the children to think of examples. Make two inclined planes using a pool noodle sliced in half. Conduct experiments with the two halves, such as racing small balls or marbles and raising the noodles higher and lower using building blocks. Leave the props out so children can try them at FREE CHOICE PLAY. A long board can also be used as an inclined plane. Use two boards, and experiment with sandpaper, felt, waxed paper, etc. on one of the boards. What speeds up or slows down a toy car rolling down the board? Recite the poem **"Jack and Jill."**

- Explain **Levers.** Build a seesaw. Tape a shoebox on each seat and try to balance the seesaw. Then explain the fulcrum and how a lever can be used to make lifting easier. A fun experiment is to use the long board with triangle blocks as the fulcrum. Practice putting items of different weight on each side.

TIP Leave the seesaw with the shoeboxes out for FREE CHOICE PLAY.

- Explain **Screws.** Find a young child's toy screw or bolt and show the children the inclined plane slowly winding its way up and around the screw. Have wood screws at the WORKBENCH with a corrugated cardboard box and screwdrivers. A hand drill could also be used as an example of a screw at the WORKBENCH.

- Explain **Wedges.** Teacher, use a potato and a pumpkin carving knife to carve a few potato stamps. Add the potato stamps to the WRITING CENTER. The children can use the stamps to decorate the pictures they draw for their families. Allow the children to experiment by cutting up potatoes with a pumpkin-carving knife under the direct supervision of an adult, or use plastic cutting tools and playdough.

TIP Letters need to be carved in reverse to print correctly.

- Explain **Wheels and Axles.** Small toy cars are great examples. If there is a wagon available, try moving something heavy in a wagon instead of carrying it. Even better, if there is a wheelchair available use it during FREE CHOICE PLAY for the children to take turns pushing each other. Sing **"The Wheels on the Bus Go Round and Round."**

TIP Take the wheelchair outside, giving each child a turn to ride, and look for inclined planes (wheelchair ramps). Also ask, "Can a person in a wheelchair get to different places in our building by going up or down a ramp?"

- Explain **Pulleys.** Set up a clothesline pulley. Use the pulley to hang the easel art to dry this week. Also set up dollhouse furniture on open shelves. Show how a pulley can move heavy furniture up to the second and third floor of the "shelf dollhouse." For more fun, add some moving vans! (Make a moving trailer by adding wheels and axles to a shoebox and tying it to a toy car.) Sing or say the poem "Jack and Jill."

TABLE WORK

- Use scissors, which are a **double lever**, to cut a snake out of a paper plate. Color and punch a hole in the head to hang.

- Trace school buses on yellow and wheels on black construction paper. Children will cut out and construct the bus using paper fasteners so the wheels turn like a **wheel and axle.** Glue white paper behind the openings and draw faces in the windows.

- Make a paper helicopter. The children are making their own example of a **screw.** This activity is also a great lesson in following directions!

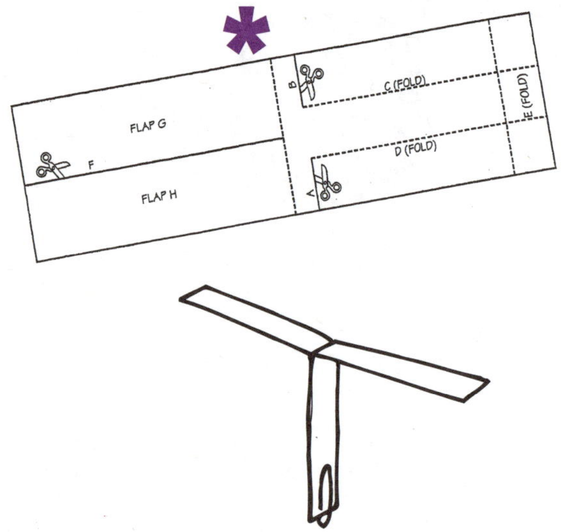

- **Journal** Write: *inclined plane*
  Use a ruler to draw a slanted line or inclined plane. Find transportation stickers and give children stickers to "go down or up" the inclined plane. Encourage them to add scenery in the background.

FREE CHOICE PLAY

Writing Center

Each child draws a picture for his or her family. Use the potato stamps made at CIRCLE TIME to stamp letters on their drawing. Remind the children you used a **wedge** (knife) to make the potato stamps.

TIP Save the pictures for **Family Night.** They can be put in the envelopes with the children's letterw to their families to be completed in *Dd* Week.

Board Games

- Chutes and Ladders by Milton Bradley
- Chickyboom by Blue Orange Games

Sensory Table

Use Marbleworks by Discovery Toys in the sensory table (marble toy with inclined planes). For fun, add water on the last day of the week so the children can pour water down the ramps.

Workbench

Use a screwdriver to screw wood screws into thick corrugated cardboard. Also, a hand drill can be used to drill holes into soft pine wood. **Be sure to wear goggles when working at the WORKBENCH!**

Easel Art

Roll car wheels across a paint pad and print on paper. A small paint roller also can be used. Allow the children to try these **wheel and axle** techniques along with brushes and two to three colors of paint.

Crafts

This week, provide general art and craft supplies on the art shelf. Add some books with pictures of road signs along with shape patterns to trace. Allow the children to use their imaginations!

Notes & Evaluations

	Circle Time	Table Work	Free Choice Play	Crafts
Monday	Beginning: Ending:			
	Story:			
Tuesday	Beginning: Ending:			
	Story:			
Wednesday	Beginning: Ending:			
	Story:			
Thursday	Beginning: Ending:			
	Story:			
Friday	Beginning: Ending:			
	Story:			

Dd WEEK

Dads

Dinosaurs

Dramatic Play

Car Repair

Add a pit stop with race track

Display the six simple machines for Family Night

Learning Objectives

Physical and Motor

- Swings arms while walking
- Uses left or right hand predominantly
- Uses small muscles in hands to color, cut, paste, and paint

Cognitive

- Uses words for time, such as *yesterday* and *today*
- Has increasing memory

Communication and Language

- Uses clear and fluent speech
- Understands the meaning of most preschool words (semantics)

Social and Emotional

- Expresses feelings and emotions with words
- Is sensitive to the feelings of others

Approaches to Learning

- Seeks and accepts help and information

Listening Activities and Songs

- Song: "This Old Man" (Traditional)
- Song: "That's My Family" (to the tune of "This Old Man") (See the schedule for **Family Night** at end of *Dd* Week.)
- Dinosaur Fossils Chant

TIP Find enough names of dinosaurs that swim, stomp, and fly so everyone has a turn. Then adjust the second line of the chart.

For example:
(1st line) Plesiosaurus
(2nd line) They swam and swam and swam and swam

(1st line) Stegosaurus
(2nd line) They stomped and stomped and stomped and stomped.

Stories

- *Coat of Many Colors* by Dolly Parton
- *A Chair for My Mother* by Vera B. Williams
- *Who's in My Family? All About our Families* by Robie H. Harris
- *My Dad Loves Me!* by Marianne Richmond
- *The Kiss that Missed* by David Melling
- *Someone Bigger* by Jonathan Emmett
- *The Little Scarecrow Boy* by Margaret Wise Brown
- *The Grandma Book* by Todd Parr
- *The Grandpa Book* by Todd Parr
- *My Big Dinosaur Book* by Roger Priddy
- *This Old Man* by Pam Adams

CIRCLE TIME

Interactive Charts and Props

- Create your own Family Graph (see the TIP at the bottom of this page).
- Create your own Dinosaur Shadow Matching Chart.
- Suggested props for **"That's My Family"** song (see schedule for Family Night at end of *Dd* Week)
- Music to accompany the movie for **Family Night**

Family Graph	
My family...	
...plays outside together.	XXX
...likes to build things.	XXXX
...likes to work in the yard.	X
...cooks dinner together.	XXXXX
...helps wash the dishes.	XXX
...plays video games.	XXXX
...goes to the zoo.	XX
...likes to go swimming.	X
...likes to play board games.	XXX
...watches movies on TV.	XXXX
	XX

Circle Time Activities

- Introduce the letter *Dd*.
- First, each child takes a turn telling something about their family. Next, explain the **Family Graph** the class will make together. Have the children raise their hands to vote and graph the results (save the graph for **Family Night**).
- Sing the song **"This Old Man."** Then teach the children the song **"That's My Family."** Ask the children which of their family members fit the actions of the song. Fill in the blanks using the correct pronouns. Let them know that family means mom, dad, grandma, grandpa, brother, sister, uncle, aunt, stepmom, stepdad, cousin, and so forth. Ask the children to think of a prop to go with each verse. Tip: use the children's suggestions as much as possible. (See schedule for **Family Night** at the end of *Dd* Week.)

- Teach the children facts about dinosaurs. Allow the children to share what they know about dinosaurs too.
- Continue to practice rhymes.
- Teach the children to play dominoes. Also show them how to build a line of domino blocks and knock them down.
- Read ***The Little Scarecrow Boy*** by Margaret Wise Brown. Discuss with the children about *big* and *little*, *large* and *small*. Explain the comparison of two items, looking closely to see which is *big* and which is *little*. Show examples: dads are big and preschoolers are little in comparison; on the other hand, a preschooler is big compared to a baby.
- If time allows, watch the movie again, accompanied by the music.
- Review the plan and expectations for **Family Night** with the children. Practice the song **"That's My Family"** with the props (see the schedule for Family Night at end of *Dd* Week).

TIP Include some of the things the children say about their families at CIRCLE TIME.

TABLE WORK

- Explain that the teacher will help each child write a letter to his family during FREE CHOICE PLAY. To prepare the children and get them thinking, discuss what their families do together. Refer to the **Family Graph** for some examples. Encourage them to think about what they might say to their families in the letter.

TIP This abstract thinking can be very difficult for children this age, so another approach is to make up a list of questions and the teacher can fill in their answers. The child can write *Family* at the top and sign their own name to the bottom of the letter.

Whatever the family situation, make it personal. If only Grandma is coming to Family Night, then write "Dear Grandma."

- Practice writing the letter of the week. Practice writing the letter *Dd*.

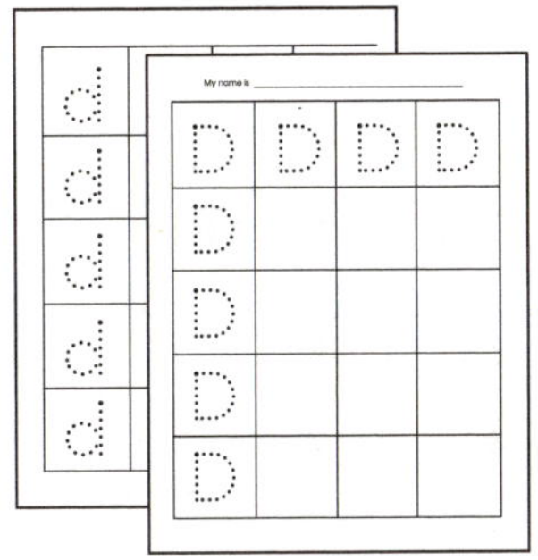

*

- Phonics Sheet for the letter *Dd*

*

- Big and Little Reproducible

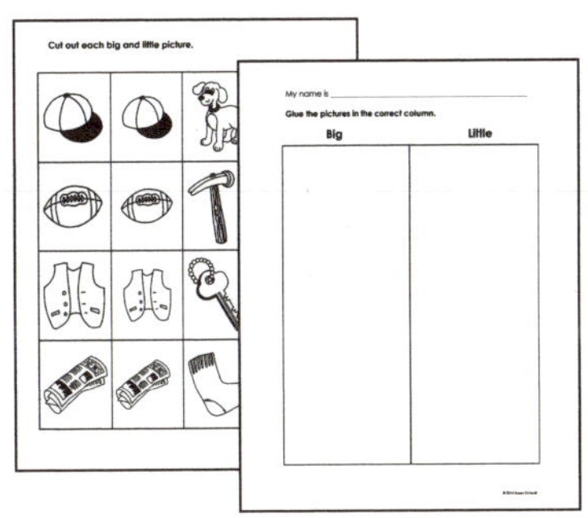

*

- **Journal** Write: *dinosaur shadow*

  Use the Shadow Card Reproducible (page 81) and have children share the dinosaurs. Each child can choose her favorite dinosaur, then cut out the card and glue it into her journal.

FREE CHOICE PLAY

Writing Center

Dd alphabet stamps and words.

Board Games

- Continue using games from the previous week.
- Dominoes
- Any Dinosaur Lotto

Sensory Table

Fill the table about two to three inches deep with modeling sand (sand that stays moist). Add small dinosaurs so the children can create a terrain for the dinosaurs.

TIP Allow children to collect sticks and small rocks when they are outside to create a realistic Dinosaur Land! (No leaves or dirt so the sand can be reused.)

Workbench

Provide hand drills, soft pine wood, and safety goggles. Review safety rules, if needed.

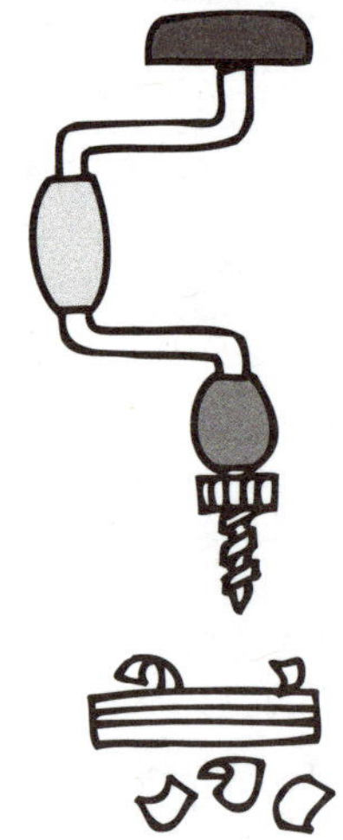

Easel Art

Dot markers and/or dinosaur stencils.

Crafts

- Dinosaur stamps with stamp pads
- Dinosaur rubbing plates
- Dinosaur stencils from the EASEL ART
- Dot-to-dot activity pages

TIP Next week is *Nn* Week and the theme is numbers. The dot-to-dot activity will aid number recognition and counting skills.

- Match the dinosaur to its shadow activity sheet.

- Convert the shadow activity sheet into dinosaur and shadow cards.

- Shaving Cream Color Mixing to make Thanksgiving Cards

HOW TO: Shaving Cream Color Mixing

Supplies needed are shaving cream, baking sheet, food coloring, craft stick, squeegee, and card stock.

- Spray shaving cream onto the baking sheet and smooth it out.
- Drip small drops of food coloring on the shaving cream.
- Use the craft stick to swirl the colors.
- Lay the card stock on the design and press gently.
- Lift the card stock and use the squeegee to wipe off the shaving cream.
- Let it dry, then flatten with a book.

Make a few "prints" before rinsing the baking sheet and starting over.

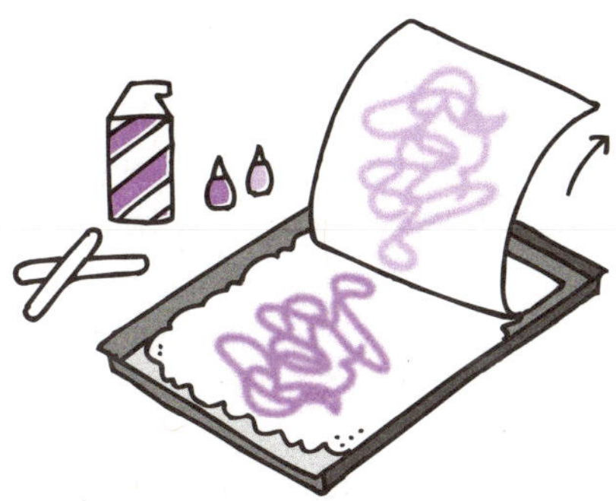

TIP Save the beautiful card stock sheets to make Thanksgiving cards for the children's families next week.

Notes & Evaluations

Notes for Family Night

- Sing the **"Hello Song."** Children can play the spoons for accompaniment.
- Give family members things to look for while their child is touring them around the classroom.

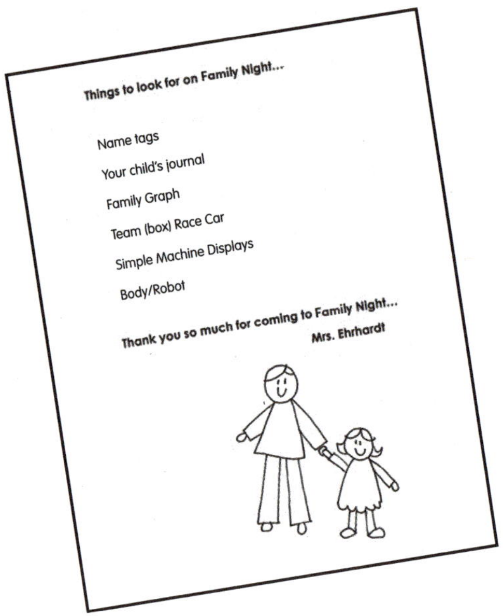

Things to look for on Family Night...

Name tags
Your child's journal
Family Graph
Team (box) Race Car
Simple Machine Displays
Body/Robot

Thank you so much for coming to Family Night...
Mrs. Ehrhardt

Simple Machines Displays

1. Inclined Plane—Use the pool noodles with blocks to create inclined planes. Raise and lower the height. Use ping-pong balls or small cars to race.
2. Lever—Display the seesaw with a moveable triangle block as the fulcrum. You can purchase a new, empty paint can at the hardware store. Use an opener or a screwdriver to pry the lid open.
3. Screw—Have a few of the paper helicopters available so family members can try them out. Also, on a large toy screw you can see the inclined plane wind around the screw. (Follow it with your finger.)
4. Wedge—At the WORKBENCH, have playdough and a pumpkin-carving knife available to cut the dough into pieces.
5. Wheel and Axle—Any vehicle with wheels is a good example. If you have a vehicle with removable wheels, it will show how much easier it moves with wheels and axles.
6. Pulley—Have a simple pulley set up to pull small toys up and down. A fun idea is to use a dollhouse. Move people and furniture from one floor to another.

Children show their family members around the classroom. Play a game, build with blocks, try the race car, etc. (Explore the six simple machines with accompanying activities.)

During this time, the teacher takes a photo of each child in their box race car with their family standing behind them.

Story Time

Choose one of the stories in *Dd* Week to read for Family Night.

- Watch the Robot Movie.
- Sing **"That's My Family"** song with props.
- Pass out the family letters for the children to open and read with their families.
- Thank the families for coming.

"That's My Family" Song
(to the tune of "This Old Man") with prop suggestions:

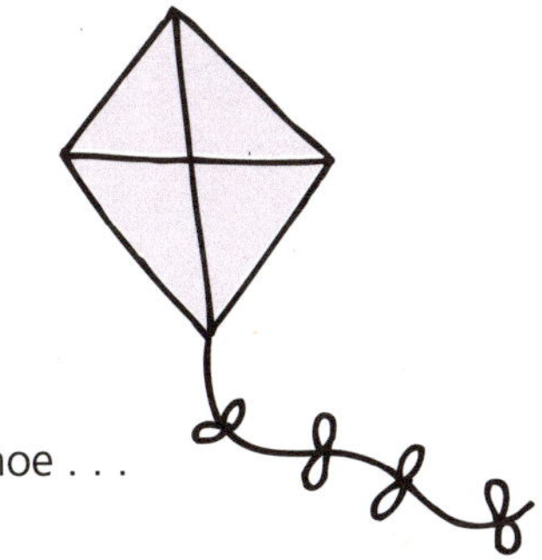

That's my ______, we play one. We play outside just for fun.
With a nick-nack paddy wack, that's my ______. [*He's/She's*] the best friend I ever had.
(prop suggestion: kite—make it with construction paper)

That's my ______, we play two. ______'s teaching me to tie my shoe . . .
(prop suggestion: shoe with a shoestring)

That's my ______, we play three. ______ helps me to climb a tree . . .
(prop: make a tree with poster board)

That's my ______, we play four. ______ tells me, "Don't slam that door" . . .
(prop: bang two blocks together for SLAM!)

That's my ______, we play five. ______ taught me to swim and dive . . .
(prop: dive mask and/or beach towel)

That's my ______ we play six. I help ______ to pick up sticks . . .
(prop: gather some sticks)

That's my ______ we play seven. ______ says, "Bed, that's where you're headin" . . .
(prop: pillow or teddy bear)

That's my ______, we play eight. ______ tells me, "Now don't be late" . . .
(prop: clock or watch)

That's my ______, we play nine. ______ tells me, "You're doing fine" . . .
(prop: sports trophy or medal)

That's my ______, we play ten. We play games again and again . . .
(prop: game board)

That's my ______, we play eleven. I help ______ get dinner in the oven . . .
(prop: paper plate with dinner pictures cut from magazine)

That's my ______, we play twelve. ______'s teaching me to help myself . . .
(prop: pretend bread with plastic knife—to make a sandwich)

End with:
That's my family. I love them and they love me with a nick-nack paddy wack.
That's my family. They're the best, as you can see!

	Circle Time	Table Work	Free Choice Play	Crafts
Monday	Beginning: Ending:			
	Story:			
Tuesday	Beginning: Ending:			
	Story:			
Wednesday	Beginning: Ending:			
	Story:			
Thursday	Beginning: Ending:			
	Story:			
Friday	Beginning: Ending:			
	Story:			

Nn WEEK

Numbers

Nature

Names

Dramatic Play

Camping in Nature. Pitch a small tent and add camping gear, flash-lights, lightweight vests, and so forth.

Learning Objectives

Physical and Motor

- Makes marks or strokes with drawing tools
- Runs consistently without falling
- Uses scissors

Cognitive

- Uses real objects as props during pretend play
- Puts things in order or sequence

Communication and Language

- Uses pronouns in sentences
- Refers to *yesterday* and *tomorrow* correctly

Social and Emotional

- Takes turns
- Shares

Approaches to Learning

- Creates stories, imagining and describing things or situations that do not exist

Listening Activities and Songs

- Song: "Take a Walk in the Forest" (to the tune of "She'll Be Comin' Round the Mountain")
- Small drums, or a large drum with enough drumsticks for groups of children to take turns participating (sing the "Hello Song") (See CIRCLE TIME for another drum activity.)

"Take a Walk in the Forest"
(to the tune of "She'll Be Comin' Round the Mountain"):

Let's take a walk in the forest qui-et-ly.
(sing "quietly" very softly)
Let's take a walk in the forest qui-et-ly.
Let's take a walk in the forest.
Let's take a walk in the forest.
Let's take a walk in the forest qui-et-ly.

Let's listen for the crickets qui-et-ly . . .
(click your tongue)
Let's listen for the squirrels scratching qui-et-ly . . . *(scratch on the floor)*
Let's listen for the frogs croaking qui-et-ly . . . *(ribbit, ribbit)*
Let's listen for the hoot owl qui-et-ly . . . *(hoo, hoo)*

(Ask, "What else do you see in a forest?" Then add more verses.)

Stories

- *The Name Jar* by Yangsook Choi
- *Earth Day Every Day* by Lisa Bullard
- *If Rocks Could Sing: A Discovered Alphabet* by Leslie McGuirk
- *Owl Moon* by Jane Yolen
- *The Legend of the Lady Slipper: An Ojibwe Tale* by Lise Lunge-Larsen and Margi Preus
- *In the Tall, Tall Grass* by Denise Fleming
- *Chicka Chicka 1, 2, 3* by Bill Martin, Jr., Michael Sampson, and Lois Ehlert
- *Stranger in the Woods* by Carl R. Sams and Jean Stoick

Thank You Poem

Thank you winds of the east
For the bright sunshine that begins our day.

Thank you winds of the south
For animals in the forest we can watch at play.

Thank you winds of the west
For the glowing moon and stars which shine nightly in the sky.

Thank you winds of the north
For clear and flowing water as we drift to sleep . . . by and by.
(Say the last line very softly.)

CIRCLE TIME

Interactive Charts and Props

- Show-and-tell bags

TIP Schedule show-and-tell this week if Thanksgiving Week is short due to the holiday.

Remind the children of the Show-and-Tell rules:

1. When you receive a bag, it is your turn the next school day to show-and-tell.
2. Bring only one item.
3. It must fit in the bag.

- Story Stick (a stick decorated with ribbon)
- Tell-A-Story game by Ravensburger

Circle Time Activities

- Introduce the letter *Nn*.
- Ask the children, "What is a neighbor? Tell how you can be a good neighbor."

TIP If the children had difficulty with the first show-and-tell, the teacher can again role-play show-and-tell at CIRCLE TIME.

- Using a drum, tap the syllables of each child's name. Teacher, say, "Su – zy." Tap the drum and say at the same time, "Su (tap) – zy (tap)." Ask, "How many beats?" Suzy says, "Two." If Suzy makes a mistake, repeat the process. Be sure to give each child a turn.
- Teach the children to play the fishing activity in the SENSORY TABLE. (See the SENSORY TABLE on page 88 for the explanation.)
- Ask the children to give examples of the many ways numbers are used. For instance, phone numbers, house numbers, their age, money, license plates on cars, etc.
- Practice counting. Count the children, their brothers and sisters, books, blocks, crayons, etc. Start counting to ten and work up to twenty.
- Count to ten using American Sign Language.
- Practice number recognition. Look around the classroom to find a number one, two, three, and so forth until you reach ten. Again, continue to work up to twenty. Place number cards around the room for the children to find and bring back to the circle and tell what number they found. To end, put the numbers in chronological order.
- Read the story ***Stranger in the Woods***. Sing the song **"Take a Walk in the Forest."** Ask the children, "What else do you see in a forest?" Use the children's ideas to add more verses to the song.

TABLE WORK

- Explain the **Story Stick.** Pick a familiar story or use the game **Tell-A-Story** by Ravensburger. Hold the Story Stick while telling the story. Have the children retell the story. Pass the Story Stick along, each child taking a turn to tell a part of the story. If necessary, tell a second story so everyone gets a turn.

TIP This is an excellent preparation for show-and-tell.

- Teach the children to play the game **Hoot Owl Hoot!** by Peaceable Kingdom.

- Teach the children to play the game **Take a Hike** by University Games, or review it if it was discussed during *Ll* Week. Tell the children this game was invented by a five-year-old named Derek Nelson.

- Practice writing the letter of the week. Practice writing the Letter *Nn*.

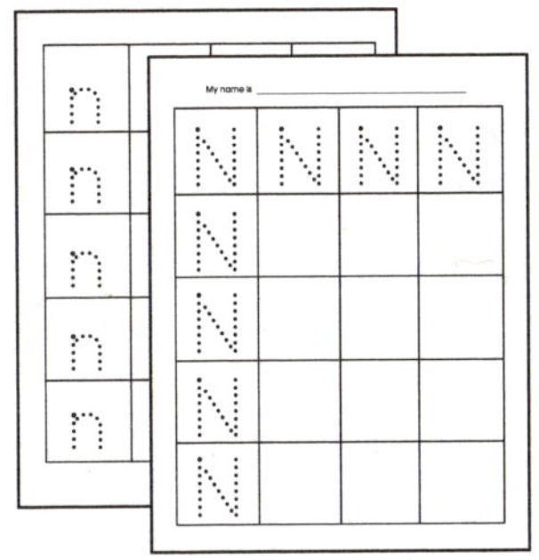

*

- Phonics Sheet for the letter *Nn*

*

- Counting with Stickers Reproducible

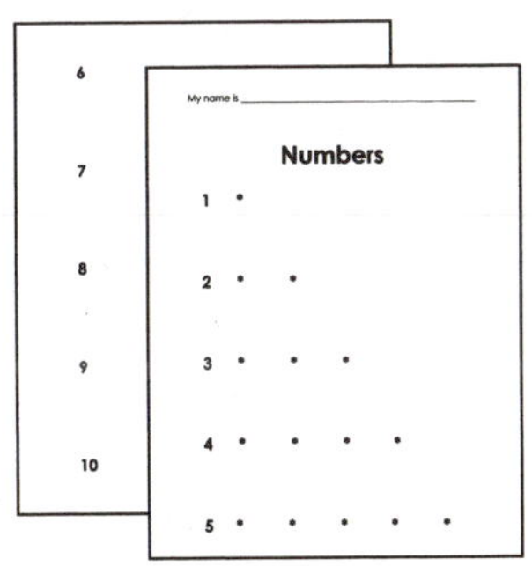

*

- Practice writing numerals.

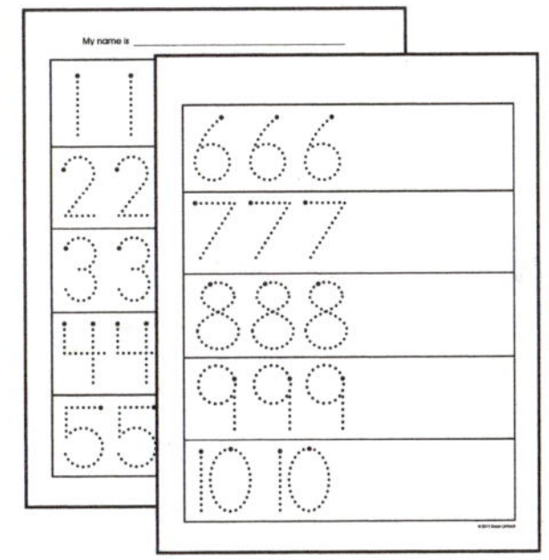

*

- **Journal** Write: *Notice nature*
  Make a drawing of what you might see or hear if you took a walk in the forest.

FREE CHOICE PLAY

Writing Center

Nn picture stamps and word cards.

Board Games

- Hoot Owl Hoot! by Peaceable Kingdom
- Take a Hike created by Derek Nelson, distributed by University Games
- A B Seas by Discovery Toys
- Tell-A-Story by Ravensburger
- Digit by Piatnik

Sensory Table

Fishing for alphabet letters. Use the A B Seas game by Discovery Toys or create your own alphabet-letter fish and place them in the sensory table (with or without water).

Fish for a letter, then place it in an alphabet chart.

TIP Extend the game by making several charts: one with the alphabet letters A to Z, one with the letters mixed up, and finally, one with smaller charts in which players try to get a straight line of letters like Bingo.

Workbench

Create natural colors from foods. Lay a few layers of newspaper on the workbench, then lay a cotton handkerchief or a square of muslin (100 percent cotton fabric). Place a few fresh cranberries (for red), fresh spinach (green), or carrot slices (orange) on the fabric. Lay an old hand towel over the food. Pound with a hammer. The juice from the food will color the fabric. Allow it to set overnight. Rinse the fabric in cold water, squeeze it out, and hang it to dry. Teacher, press the fabric with an iron to set the color.

Easel Art

Tempera paint in fall colors—use red, orange, brown, yellow, and green with paper to paint a tree.

Crafts

- Nature craft: use real things from nature to create art. For example, paint or color a tree trunk then collect and use real twigs for branches.

- Make some coloring pages using the fish stencil from Week 1. Paint with watercolors.
- Make name necklaces with alphabet-letter beads and other beads.
- Use numeral stamps, stamp pads, and fall or nature stickers to make number flash cards to take home for practice.
- Make a dream catcher. Cut out the center of a paper plate and use a hole punch to make eight to ten holes in the rim of the plate. Paint the rim and allow it to dry. Tape one end of a ball of yarn to the back of the plate rim and wrap the yarn ten times around the diameter of the plate to measure a long enough piece of yarn to cut. Optional: decorate with feathers and beads.

TIP Wrap a tiny piece of tape on the cut end of the yarn to make it easier to put through the holes. Weave yarn back and forth through the holes. When all holes are complete, tape the yarn to the back and cut off any excess. Tie a hanger on the dream catcher.

Notes & Evaluations

	Circle Time	Table Work	Free Choice Play	Crafts
Monday	Beginning: Ending:			
	Story:			
Tuesday	Beginning: Ending:			
	Story:			
Wednesday	Beginning: Ending:			
	Story:			
Thursday	Beginning: Ending:			
	Story:			
Friday	Beginning: Ending:			
	Story:			

Thanks-giving WEEK

The First Thanksgiving

We Are Thankful

More Numbers

Dramatic Play

Campground continued

Add picnic table, campfire, cooking utensils, etc.

Learning Objectives

Physical and Motor

- Puts puzzles together
- Balances well
- Uses left or right hand predominantly

Cognitive

- Draws basic shapes and expressive art
- Has a vocabulary of 2,000 to 6,000 words

Communication and Language

- Makes up stories
- Uses correct grammar

Social and Emotional

- Enjoys helping with household tasks
- Shows increasing responsibility

Approaches to Learning

- Works at tasks despite distractions and interruptions

Listening Activities and Songs

- Book with CD: *Grateful: A Song of Giving Thanks* by John Bucchino
- Song: "The Stone Soup Song" (to the tune of "The Farmer in the Dell")
- Use musical instruments from previous week.

"The Stone Soup Song"
(to the tune of "The Farmer in the Dell")

The stone goes in the soup,
The stone goes in the soup,
Now stir and stir and stir some more,
The stone goes in the soup.

The onions go in the soup . . .
The celery goes in the soup . . .
The carrots go in the soup . . .
The potatoes go in the soup . . .
The barley goes in the soup . . .
The milk goes in the soup . . .

(Whatever version of the book is used, put those ingredients in the soup.)

Adapted by Susan Ehrhardt

Stories

- *A Plump and Perky Turkey* by Teresa Bateman
- *A Turkey for Thanksgiving* by Eve Bunting
- *'Twas the Night Before Thanksgiving* by Dav Pilkey
- *Time to Say "Please"!* by Mo Willems
- *Grateful: A Song of Giving Thanks* with CD by John Bucchino
- *Thanksgiving Day Alphabet* by Beverly Barras Vidrine
- *Stone Soup* retold by Heather Forest
- *Emily's Everyday Manners* by Peggy Post and Cindy Post Senning

CIRCLE TIME

Interactive Charts and Props

- Show-and-tell bags (if not done in *Nn* Week)
- Sock puppets used for acting out the book ***'Twas the Night Before Thanksgiving*** by Dav Pilkey.

- Placemat(s) and items needed to review how to set the table
- Card necklaces for **"The Stone Soup Song."** Each child makes a card necklace at the WRITING CENTER this week.

Circle Time Activities

- Do show-and-tell this week if it was not done last week. Remind the children of the rules. Use the show-and-tell schedule and have each group of children give their presentation on the appropriate day.
- Read the book ***Stone Soup*** by Heather Forest. Ask the children, "Would you have tasted the stone soup? Would you like to make stone soup in class? What ingredient does your family keep at home that you could have added to the soup?" Tell the children you will provide the ingredients, but ask the children, "Will you help prepare the soup?"
- Show the children the SENSORY TABLE filled with potatoes. Explain how to scrub them. (The teacher will slice the potatoes right before adding them to the soup because potatoes turn brown quickly). Also, show the children the carrots at the WORKBENCH. Demonstrate how to slice them with a serrated pumpkin-carving knife.
- Sing **"The Stone Soup Song."** Use the necklace card props to create a large "pot of soup" with all the children. When each ingredient is sung, the children wearing that ingredient go into the middle of the circle, which is the soup pot. For more fun, trade necklaces and play again!
- Ask each child to name something she is thankful for. Make a list of all these things. Use this list to make a Thanksgiving Chain of Thanks. (See instructions in the CRAFTS section on page 94.)
- Use the book ***'Twas the Night Before Thanksgiving*** to prepare for the Thanksgiving Show, explain to the children that the book you are going to use is about a class going on a field trip to a turkey farm. Their puppets will be the children in the story. Give each child his own puppet.
- Continue number activities from last week. Use manipulatives and group them in sets of one, two, three, and so on up to ten. Count manipulatives with the children to twenty-five, thirty, fifty, . . . even one hundred if there is time. Lay numeral cards on the floor in the circle and have the children put them in chronological order. Or, pull the cards out of a cloth bag and play "Name the Numeral."
- Tell the story of the first Thanksgiving. Help the children understand the meaning of words such as *tradition*, *harvest*, *pilgrims*, etc.

TABLE WORK

* Review with the children how to set the table. Remind them they can help their family get ready for Thanksgiving dinner. Use placemats that show how to set the table as a guide (see *Tt* Week). Leave props out for the children to practice during FREE CHOICE PLAY.

* Together with the children, make a list of foods that families have for Thanksgiving dinner. Have the children vote for the foods they like. Graph the results.

HOW TO: Make Turkey Stuffing
(turkeys to stuff in the sock puppets)

Purchase a piece of Thanksgiving-themed fabric printed with turkeys about two to three inches in diameter. Make sure there are enough turkeys—one for each child. Cut a circle around the turkey and another circle the same size, using the turkey fabric or a piece of felt. Sew the circles together, leaving a small opening to stuff the turkey with batting. Sew the little opening closed. **Once the turkeys are made, keep them with the other props.**

* Write the Numerals

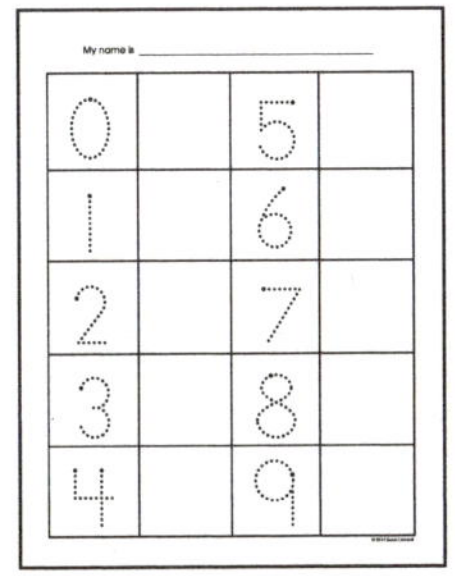

* Circle the Correct Number

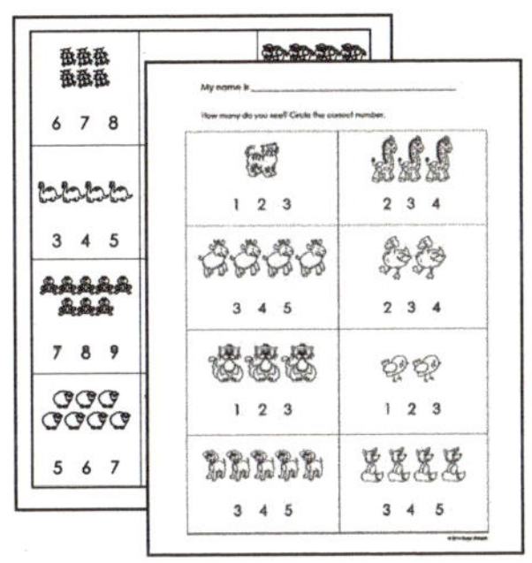

* Make an art foam frame for the photo taken on Family Night. Use a kit from a local craft store or create your own.

* **Journal** Write: *Thanksgiving Turkey*
Show the children an example of a handprint turkey. Trace each child's hand in her journal. Color the turkey with crayons.

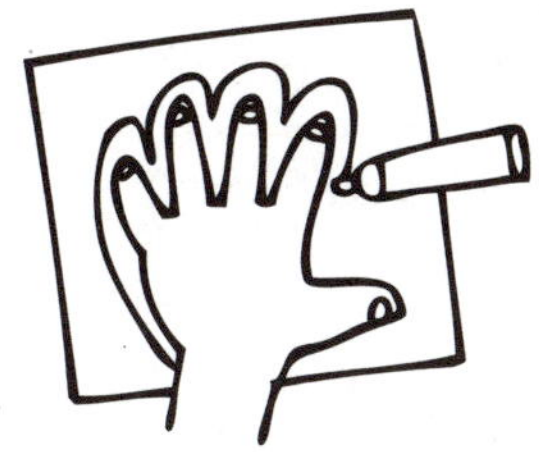

TIP Mount the frame on an adhesive magnet.

FREE CHOICE PLAY

Writing Center

Use the book ***Stone Soup*** and teacher-made cards with both the word and picture of each ingredient that went into the soup. Have the children copy two of the ingredients in their journals and one other ingredient on their own index card. Make their cards into necklaces to sing the **"The Stone Soup Song."**

Board Games

Use the same games from previous week.

- Gobblet Junior by Blue Orange Games

Sensory Table

Scrub potatoes, carrots, celery and any other vegetables that need to be scrubbed to make stone soup this week.

Workbench

Allow children to use pumpkin knives to slice carrots after they are scrubbed.
Or the teacher can slice all the ingredients.

Use the workbench surface to set out plain placemats to practice setting the table. Display a "How to Set the Table Placemat" as a guide.

Easel Art

Have easel paper cut into large circles. Children paint the entire paper with bright colors (this circle is the turkey's tail feathers). Allow the painting to dry. Trace turkey heads, wattles, and beaks. Children cut them out and glue them to the bright-colored tail feathers. Draw eyes with a black marker.

TIP This project will get messy. Cover the easel with newspaper.

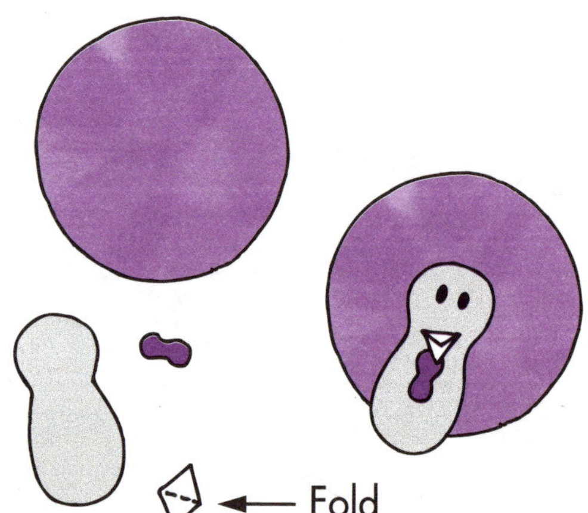

Crafts

- Make thank-you cards from the beautiful colored card stock the children made with shaving cream during *Dd* Week. Fold the paper in half like a greeting card and have the children write "Thank You" on the inside of their cards. Don't forget to sign it "Love" and the child's name.

- Make a **Thanksgiving Chain of Thanks** using the list of things the children said they were thankful for at CIRCLE TIME. Children cut the strips apart and staple them together, making a chain.

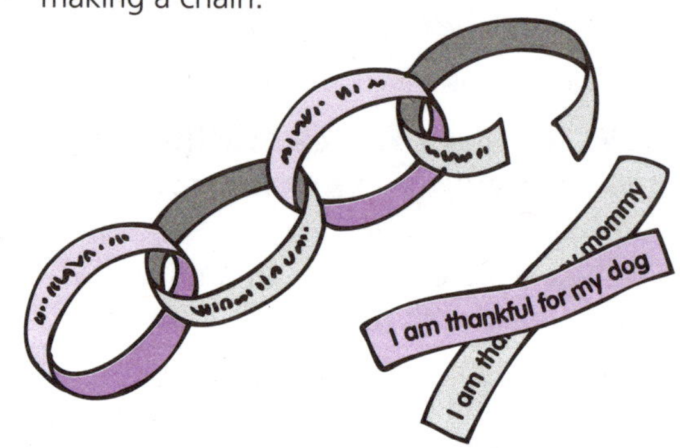

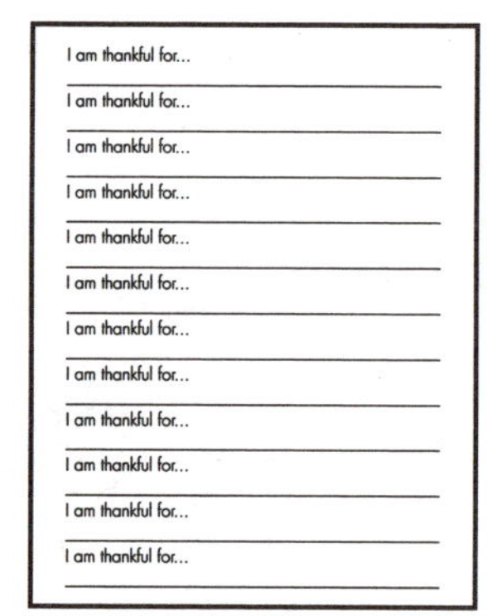

*

- Make a paper plate turkey. Paint a large paper plate and a small paper plate brown. Let them dry. Use the same beak and wattle from the EASEL ART project to glue onto the small plate. Draw the eyes with a black marker. Have colorful strips of construction paper cut ahead of time to use as feathers. Add legs and feet to finish.

TIP **Thanksgiving Chain of Thanks** strips could be used as feathers for the turkey.

- Make handprint turkeys like the ones in the children's journals.

- Make Thanksgiving puzzles. Find easy Thanksgiving pictures. First, color the picture. Next, glue the picture to a piece of colored construction paper. Finally, print a word that describes the picture at the bottom and draw lines so the children can cut it into strips, one for each letter in the word. For example, the turkey is cut into six strips because *turkey* has six letters.

Take the opportunity in Thanksgiving Week to make a thank-you card for the parents. Thank them for their help and support. And thank them for trusting you with their children!

Thanksgiving Show
Children act out the story as you read the book ***'Twas the Night Before Thanksgiving***. Props for the show are the sock puppets and "stuffed turkeys." Another prop could be a poster board school bus. Put on the show for parents or younger preschool classes or just for fun.

*

Notes & Evaluations

	Circle Time	Table Work	Free Choice Play	Crafts
Monday	Beginning: Ending:			
	Story:			
Tuesday	Beginning: Ending:			
	Story:			
Wednesday	Beginning: Ending:			
	Story:			
Thursday	Beginning: Ending:			
	Story:			
Friday	Beginning: Ending:			
	Story:			

Ss WEEK

Seasons

Symmetry

Sorting

Sequencing

Drawing Stars

Dramatic Play

Campground

Add some birdhouses and some stuffed winter animals along with mittens and scarves.

Learning Objectives

Physical and Motor

- Makes marks or strokes with drawing tools
- Builds and stacks with several small blocks
- Uses left or right hand predominantly

Cognitive

- Sorts or describes objects by one or more attributes
- Puts things in order or sequence

Communication and Language

- Uses language to express feelings, wants, and needs
- Has an expanding vocabulary, up to 6,000 words

Social and Emotional

- Seeks attention and approval
- Is self-directed

Approaches to Learning

- Approaches new situations with increasing flexibility

Listening Activities and Songs

- Song: "What Happens Each Season?" (to the tune of "It's Raining, It's Pouring")

"What Happens Each Season?"

(to the tune of the the first line of "It's Raining, It's Pouring")

It's spring; it's spring. We plant the seeds in spring.
It's summer; it's summer. We water the garden in summer.
It's autumn; it's autumn. We harvest the crops in autumn.
It's winter; it's winter. We eat the food in winter.

It's spring; it's spring. Trees sprout leaves in spring.
It's summer; it's summer. Trees give shade in summer.
It's autumn; it's autumn. We rake leaves in autumn.
It's winter; it's winter. Trees are bare in winter.

Stories

- *Seasons* by Blexbolex
- *Draw Me a Star* by Eric Carle
- *Laura's Star* by Klaus Baumgart
- *Six Dots: A Story of Young Louis Braille* by Jen Bryant
- *We're Going on a Bear Hunt* by Michael Rosen
- *Four Seasons Make a Year* by Anne Rockwell
- *We Both Read about Seasons* by Sindy McKay
- *Night Tree* by Eve Bunting
- *Special People, Special Ways* by Arlene Maguire
- *Strega Nona* by Tomie dePaola
- *Otto and the New Girl* by Nan Walker
- *Sort It Out!* by Barbara Mariconda
- *The Jacket I Wear in the Snow* by Shirley Neitzel

CIRCLE TIME

Interactive Charts and Props

- Create your own How to Draw a Star Chart (use ***Draw Me a Star*** by Eric Carle).
- Either purchase at a school supply store or create a poster for each of the four seasons. (Save these for the Winter Show at the end of the *Cc* week.)

Circle Time Activities

- Introduce the letter *Ss*.
- Talk about the seasons. Sing the song, **"What Happens Each Season?"** Then ask the children, "What do you wear in the spring?" Repeat with summer, fall, and winter. Make a list. (Save the list for a later activity.) Be sure to give each child a turn.
- Talk about the season of winter. Lead the discussion toward what animals do in the winter. Can we help them? Explain to the children how to make a bird feeder. Keep it simple and choose a method the children can do without assistance. One idea is to string "circle" cereal and cranberries onto yarn or pipe cleaners.
- Ask the children, "In what season is your birthday?" Graph the results.
- Teach symmetry using building blocks. Very simply, each side looks exactly the same. Explain and demonstrate EASEL ART activity.
- Ask the children what is symmetrical? Lead the discussion to people—our bodies are the same on both sides! Talk about two arms, two legs, two hands, and two feet. And our face is the same: two eyes, two ears, half of our nose and mouth (use this CIRCLE TIME activity before "Drawing of Me" at TABLE WORK).
- Teach sequencing. Have the children work in groups of two or three with 6-Scene Sequencing Cards by Frank Schaffer. Have the children put them in order then take turns "telling the story" of what is happening on the cards. To extend the learning, the teacher can take photos of the children doing an activity in sequence. Some suggestions are putting on outerwear to go out to play in the snow, setting the table, or drawing a simple picture. The photos can become sets of class sequencing cards!
- Discuss sorting. Sort buttons (or any small manipulative) by shape, color, number of holes, etc. Use hula hoops to group the items into sets. Also, the list of which clothing is worn each season can be sorted. Do this by cutting apart the list of clothing (made previously) and sorting. Use the hula hoops again to show that some articles of clothing are worn in more than one season.

TIP Take the sorting a step further by intersecting the hula hoops to show a Venn diagram. Ask the children, "Do some of the manipulatives fit into both sets?"

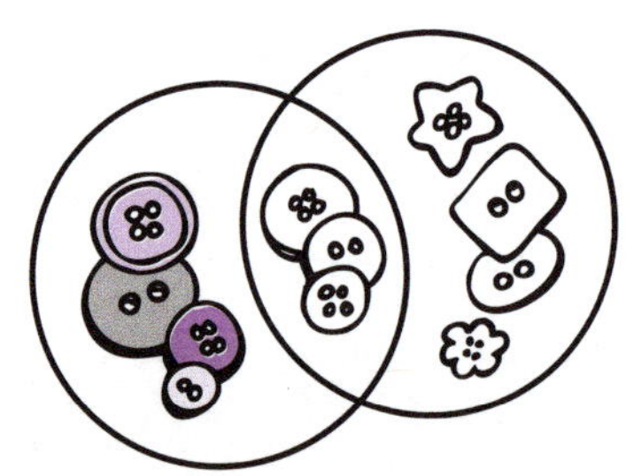

TABLE WORK

- Teach the children how to play the board game **Wild Woods** by Discovery Toys.

- Teach the game **Chinese checkers.** To begin, sort the marbles by color. Notice the design of the game board is in the shape of a star. Also mention that when we clean up our classroom, we sort game pieces, blocks, art supplies, etc.

- Review the letters of the alphabet the children have learned so far: *O*, *T*, *L*, *P*, *X*, *H*, *R*, *D*, *N*, *S*. Practice the sounds and think of some words beginning with each letter. Ask, "Does anyone's name begin with one of the letters?"

- Practice writing the letter of the week. Practice writing the letter *Ss*.

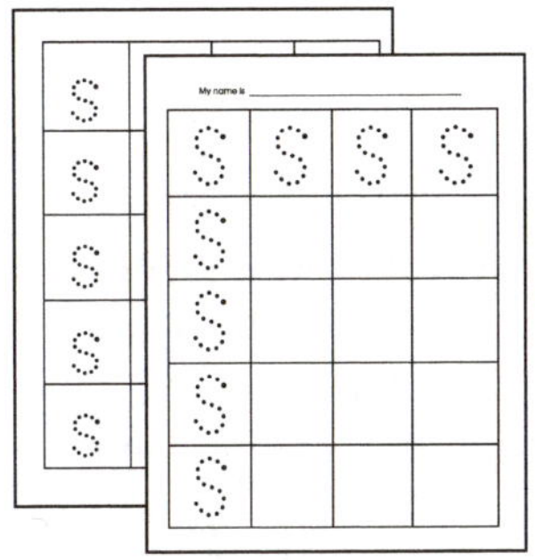

*

- Phonics Sheet for the letter *Ss*

*

- **Drawing of Me:** Review what you discussed about symmetry at CIRCLE TIME. People are symmetrical. Have the children draw a picture of themselves. Remind them about feet, hands, ears, and so forth.

- **Journal** Write: *See the star*
  Using the book ***Draw me a Star*** by Eric Carle, make a dot-to-dot diagram for the children to follow to draw a star. Have the children glue the diagram in their journals after drawing, then coloring the star. To introduce the lessons, read the book at TEACHING CIRCLE before sitting down to TABLE WORK.

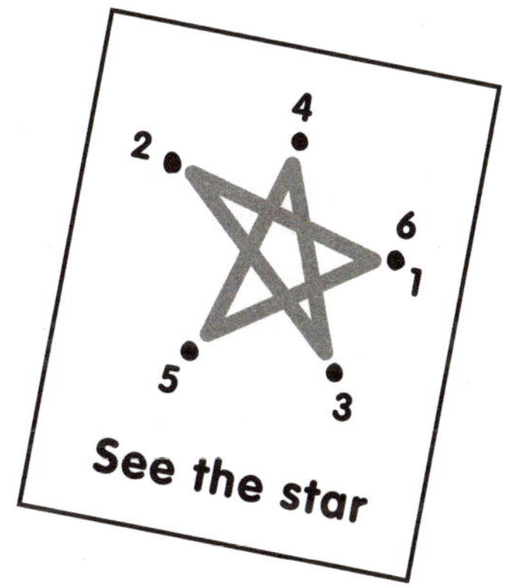

FREE CHOICE PLAY

Writing Center

Alphabet Stamps

Board Games

- Wild Woods by Discovery Toys
- Chinese checkers

Sensory Table

Thread blunt embroidery needles with cotton string and tie a circle cereal at the end. Inside the table, tape the different patterns the children learned during *Pp* Week: ABABAB, AABBAABB, AABAABAAB, ABBABBABBA.

Place containers of circle cereal and dried fruit to string in the sensory table. When a child is finished, the teacher should tie it into a circle and cut off the needle.

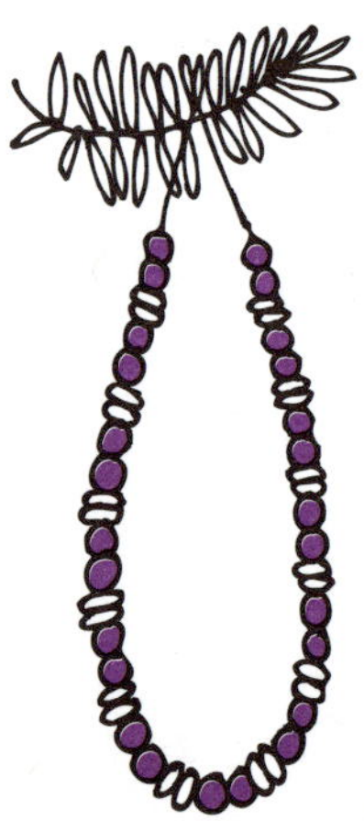

TIP Dried fruit like craisins or raisins are easier to pierce.

TIP Teacher, make a sample animal feeder and tell the children their animal feeder must be as long as yours before they can move on to another activity.

Workbench

Make pierced-star sun catchers. Lay a piece of indoor/outdoor carpet on the workbench. Teacher, trace stars on yellow construction paper. Children cut out a star and place it on the carpet. Punch holes in the star using a corn cob holder (finer holes can be punched with a pushpin). Punch a larger hole in one point of the star and tie a ribbon to hang.

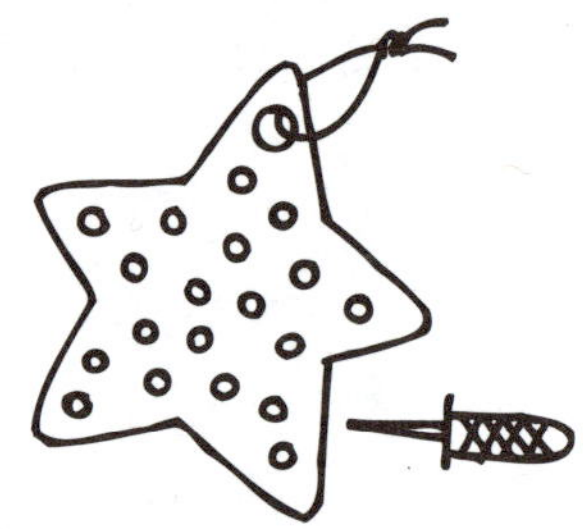

Easel Art

Before hanging the paper at the easel, fold a piece of easel paper in half. Paint a simple design on one side of the paper. Take the paper off the easel and lay it on a table. Refold the paper and rub your hand firmly over the paper to print a symmetrical picture.

Crafts

- Make glitter stars without a mess! Have enough stars traced so each child can make one. Mix glitter with clear hair gel. First, cut out the star. Then use a paintbrush to spread the "glitter gel" on the star. Allow to dry. Punch a hole and tie a ribbon if you want to hang it.
- Fold paper in half and use shape stickers to create symmetrical designs. Remind the children that what is on one side must be on the other side for balance.
- Build a Snowman in Sequence Booklet (see instructions on page 101).

Notes & Evaluations

- **Star:** Glue five wooden craft sticks together to form a star. When the glue dries, allow the children to paint and even glitter their star!

TIP Tiny buttons can be used to decorate the face. But to keep the snowman really warm, a small piece of fleece fabric or ribbon can be made into a scarf. Be sure to clip one end to look like fringe.

How To: Build a Snowman in Sequence

Teacher: fold a piece of light blue construction paper in half to make a booklet. Make a label for the front of the booklet that says, "I Can Build a Snowman." Then, trace nine circles on white construction paper: four large circles, three medium circles, and two small circles.

Children: place the label "I Can Build a Snowman" on the first page (front) of the booklet. Next, cut out the nine circles and sort them into small, medium, and large around his neck. In sequence, the first page has one large white circle, the second page has one large and one medium snowball, and finally, the third page a large, medium, and small snowball stacked to make a snowman. The last page is for decorating the snowman. Restack the large, medium, and small snowballs and tell the children to use markers to draw stick arms and a face on their snowman. They can also draw a scarf around his neck.

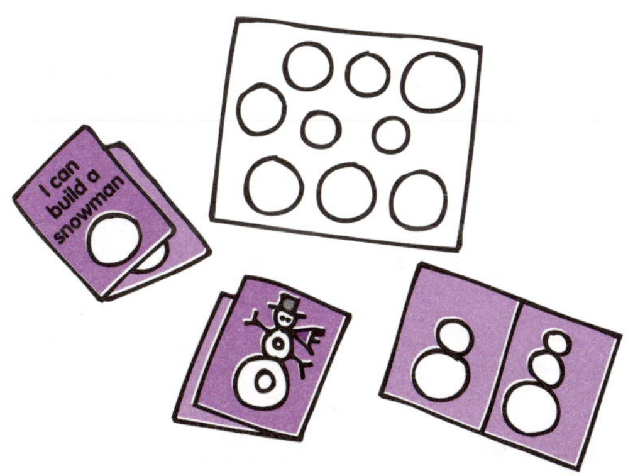

	Circle Time	Table Work	Free Choice Play	Crafts
Monday	Beginning: Ending:			
	Story:			
Tuesday	Beginning: Ending:			
	Story:			
Wednesday	Beginning: Ending:			
	Story:			
Thursday	Beginning: Ending:			
	Story:			
Friday	Beginning: Ending:			
	Story:			

Dramatic Play

Kitchen with table and chairs, dishes, play food, babies and high chairs, aprons for dress-up.

Learning Objectives

Physical and Motor

- Uses scissors
- Jumps into the air with both feet
- Uses small muscles in hands to color, cut, paste, and paint

Cognitive

- Knows half or more letter sounds
- Knows half or more letter names

Communication and Language

- Sings songs, fingerplays, and rhymes with increasing accuracy
- Uses sentences with seven words or more

Social and Emotional

- Likes to be silly and make others laugh
- Expresses feelings and emotions with words

Approaches to Learning

- Purposefully explores new things or ideas

Listening Activities and Songs

- Song: "If You're Happy and You Know It" by L. Smith. Extend the song for *Jj* Week by adding the following verses:
  you can jump
  you can jiggle
  shout for joy hoo-ray!
  (*Use this song for the* ***Winter Show****, which is in* Cc *Week*)
- John Jacob Jingleheimer Schmidt (Traditional)
- "*Frére Jacques* (Are You Sleeping?)" (Traditional)

Stories

- *Journey* by Aaron Becker
- *Have You Filled a Bucket Today? A Guide to Daily Happiness for Kids* by Carol McCloud
- *The Most Magnificent Thing* by Ashley Spires
- *The Berenstain Bears and Too Much Junk Food* by Stan and Jan Berenstain
- *The Juice Box Bully: Empowering Kids to Stand Up for Others* by Bob Sornson and Maria Dismondy
- *I Am Jane Goodall* (Ordinary People Change the World series) by Brad Meltzer
- *Where the Wild Things Are* by Maurice Sendak
- *Get the Giggles: A First Joke Book* by Bronwen Davies
- *Silly Jokes for Silly Kids* by Silly Willy
- *Knock-Knock Jokes for Kids* by Rob Elliott

Jj WEEK

Jokes

Junk

Jump and Jiggle

Making Gifts

CIRCLE TIME

Interactive Charts and Props

- Create your own Classroom Words with Photos interactive chart (Copy five of the words in the children's journals this week—see CIRCLE TIME ACTIVITIES.)
- Either purchase from a school supply store or create a sign for each month of the year (these will be used at the Winter Show along with the posters of the four seasons from last week). The **Winter Show** is in *Cc* Week.

Classroom Words

paper	glue	book
easel	marker	game
pencil	crayon	eraser
table	paint	block
scissors	tape	puzzle
chair	envelope	door

Label these items in the classroom.

Circle Time Activities

- Introduce the letter *Jj*.
- Together with the children, make the **Interactive Chart with Classroom Words** by finding each item in the classroom and taking a photo. Make two word cards for each item photographed. Use one to label the item in the classroom and the other to match the photo taken for the chart.
- Explain the WRITING CENTER activity for this week—instead of stamping and copying words at the WRITING CENTER, the children should carry their journals around the classroom and find five words to copy. Tell the children to use the labels that were placed by the items when the photos were taken to make the **Interactive Chart.**

- Explain the EASEL ART activity: making wrapping paper. Demonstrate sponge painting.
- After reading the book ***The Most Magnificent Thing*** by Ashley Spires, talk about creating a class sculpture with all the supplies at the WORKBENCH. Tell the children that it will be displayed at the Winter Show.
- Sing the songs **"John Jacob Jingleheimer Schmidt"** and **"Frére Jacques"** anytime this week.
- Ask the children, "Who feels happy today?" Another word for *happy* is *joy*. Joy starts with the letter *Jj*. Sing **"If you're Happy and You Know It"** by L. Smith. Extend the song and sing the added verses. Ask the children, "What makes you happy?" Give each child a turn and make a list.
- At STORY TIME read ***Have You Filled a Bucket Today?*** Refer to the list of what made the children happy. Maybe a few more things can be added.
- Explain that the CRAFTS this week are gifts that can be made for family and friends. Show each craft: "joy" door hanger, make a stamp and print stationery, decorate art foam frames for photos taken at Family Night, paper strip hangers, and color-by-number pictures. Simple, inexpensive craft kits can be purchased to extend the variety of gifts to make.

TABLE WORK

- Remind the children of the four seasons they learned last week. Have them repeat after you the months of the year. Notice that three of the months start with the letter *Jj*. Now work together to sort the months into the season in which they belong. (This sorting exercise can also be part of the **Winter Show**.)

- Discuss the meaning of junk food. Have the children name some of their favorite junk foods. Ask, "Can you ever eat junk food?" Name some healthy alternatives.

- Read from the joke books listed in STORIES. Have the children choose their favorites. Each child should pick a joke to tell for the **Winter Show**. Practice as needed until the children learn their jokes.

- Again this week, have the children review the letters of the alphabet studied so far: *O*, *T*, *L*, *P*, *X*, *H*, *R*, *D*, *N*, *S*, and *J* (upper and lower case, of course!). Lay alphabet letter cards or puzzle pieces in the circle and have children take turns identifying them. (This week the children will copy the letters at TABLE WORK.)

- Teach the children to make a simple gift tag using old greeting cards. Try tracing a star on construction paper, then gluing on a small picture from an old greeting card to decorate the shape. Be sure children sign their names on the gift tag. Save the tag so it can be taped to their family's gift that is wrapped this week during FREE CHOICE PLAY.

- Practice writing the letter the letter of the week. Practice writing the letter *Jj*.

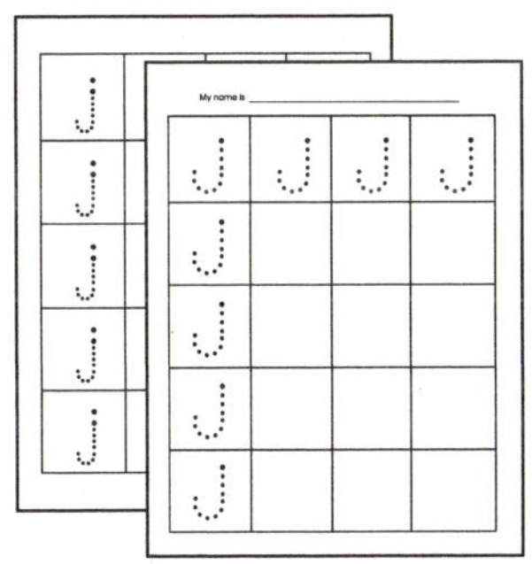

*

- Phonics Sheet for the letter *Jj*.

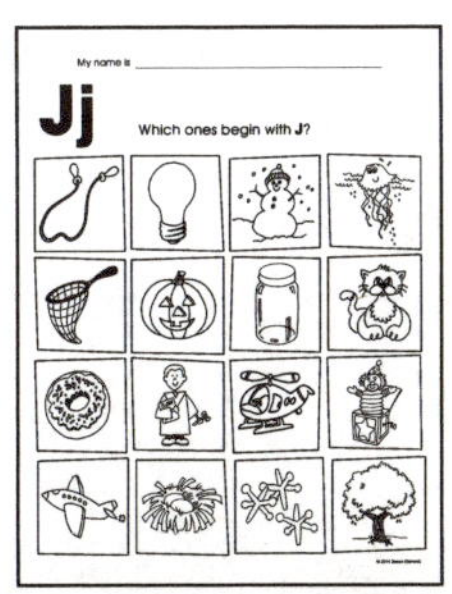

*

- Practice copying the alphabet letters studied so far.

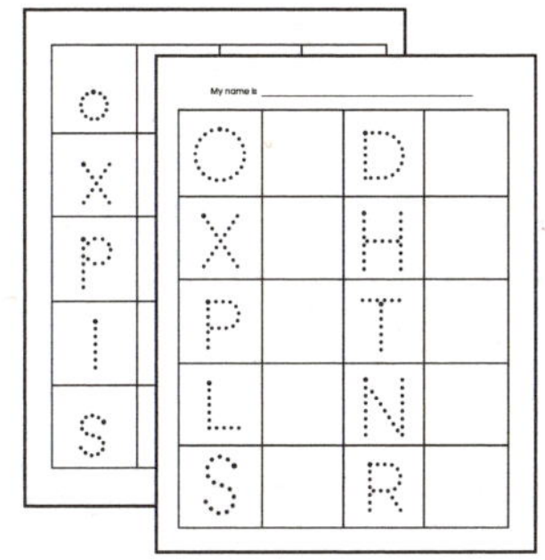

*

- **Journal** Write: *juice box*
  Draw a juice box (an upright rectangle). Don't forget the straw! Color the juice box with a crayon. Tell the children to use the color of their favorite flavor of juice. The teacher can help the children write the flavors in their journals.

*

FREE CHOICE PLAY

During FREE CHOICE PLAY, children can wrap the gifts they make for family and friends. Use the sponge, painted wrapping paper made at EASEL ART. Then take their packages to a table to decorate with ribbons and their gift tag. **Be sure each gift tag made at TABLE WORK is securely taped to its package!**

Writing Center

This week the children will carry their journals around the classroom and copy five classroom words from the index word cards which label items around the classroom.

Board Games

- ABC Match and Learn by Scholastic
- Picture Link by Binary Arts

Sensory Table

Use kitchen utensils, measuring cups, and spoons to pour water into bowls.

Workbench

Supply lots of "junk" to create a class sculpture. Collect items like old thread spools, pipe cleaners, paper cups and dessert plates, paper scraps, old pieces of toys, puzzle pieces, colored pasta, beads, and so forth.

Easel Art

Sponge paint easel paper to make wrapping paper for the children's gifts. Extra wrapping paper can be made to take home as well.

Crafts

- After learning to make a gift tag at TABLE WORK, leave the supplies out so the children can make more gift tags.

- **"Joy" door hanger:** five half-size and one regular-size wooden craft sticks are needed. Cut red or green nine-by-twelve inch construction paper in half. Also, ahead of time, trace letter *O*s with yellow construction paper. Remind the children how to cut the middle out of the letter *O*. Children glue the craft sticks and the letter *O* in place, spelling the word *JOY*. Use a hole punch to make two holes and tie a piece of ribbon to hang the door hanger.
- **Make a gift:** Have several small, stamp-sized blocks of wood with sanded edges so that there are no rough corners. Children will make a stamp by drawing a simple design on art foam that is the same size as their block of wood. Cut out the design carefully. Help children glue the art foam to the wood using waterproof glue. Allow to dry completely. Have children stamp paper and envelopes to make stationary as a gift for someone special.

- Decorate art foam frames for the photos taken on Family Night. Mount each photo on adhesive magnet paper and glue the photo in the frame.

- Use a coloring page to make a color-by-number picture. The activity can be done without assistance if you make a color word chart. Number the chart from 1–8 with a corresponding color for each number. Number the picture and make copies so the children can color by number. This can be done with a few pictures if the children like the activity!

- Make paper-strip ornaments by cutting paper strips different lengths and stapling them together at the top and bottom. Cut all strips about one-and-a-half inches wide. Make a heart by cutting two 12-inch strips and two nine-inch strips. Make a teardrop by cutting two twelve-inch strips, two ten-and-a-half-inch strips, and one nine-inch strip. See illustration above to assemble into ornaments. Hang with a ribbon.

- Make pretty punched pine trees. Cut two pine trees at one time using decorative-edged scissors. Open them like a book and glue a few pieces of brightly colored paper to one tree. Also add a tree trunk to the bottom of that same side. Punch approximately eight holes in the other tree. Carefully place a few drops of glue in between the holes and put the tree back together. Hang with a ribbon.

Notes & Evaluations

Winter Show

Have the junk sculpture on display.

The children name the four seasons. (Four children can hold the four season posters.)

Sing **"What Happens Each Season."** Twelve children pick up the month signs and sort them into each season while singing "What are the months in spring, in spring?" The three months—March, April, and May—say their months and stand by the spring poster. Repeat for each month.

Each child tells a joke.

Sing **"If You're Happy and You Know It"** with the added verses.

	Circle Time	Table Work	Free Choice Play	Crafts
Monday	Beginning: Ending:			
	Story:			
Tuesday	Beginning: Ending:			
	Story:			
Wednesday	Beginning: Ending:			
	Story:			
Thursday	Beginning: Ending:			
	Story:			
Friday	Beginning: Ending:			
	Story:			

Dramatic Play

Continue the kitchen. Remove the play food and let the children bake and decorate cookies.

Learning Objectives

Physical and Motor

- Uses large muscles to throw, climb, skip, hop, jump, catch, turn somersaults, and bounce
- Makes marks or strokes with drawing tools

Cognitive

- Expresses interest in creative movement
- Can stay with the same activity for five to ten minutes (increasing concentration)

Communication and Language

- Uses clear and fluent speech
- Follows two-to-three-step directions

Social and Emotional

- Engages in pretend play
- Shows independence

Approaches to Learning

- Reflects on past experiences and applies information to new situations

Listening Activities and Songs

- Practice the favorite songs from *Ss* and *Jj* Weeks (be prepared for the **Winter Show**).
- Set up the headphones near enough to the EASEL so the children can listen to music while they paint. (See EASEL ART activity on page 112.)

Stories

- *Peter's Chair* by Ezra Jack Keats
- *Chrysanthemum* by Kevin Henkes
- *You're Wonderful* by Debbie Clement
- *Hooray for You! A Celebration of You-ness* by Marianne Richmond
- *Incredible You! 10 Ways to Let Your Greatness Shine Through* by Dr. Wayne W. Dyer with Kristina Tracy
- *Chicka Chicka Boom Boom* by Bill Martin Jr. and John Archambault
- *Charlie the Caterpillar* by Dom DeLuise
- *Too Many Carrots* by Katy Hudson
- *Corduroy* by Don Freeman
- *Who Stole the Cookies from the Cookie Jar?* By Margaret Wang

Cc WEEK

Wonderful Children

Cards

Cookies

CIRCLE TIME

Interactive Charts and Props

- Make the photos of classroom words from *Jj* Week into enough bingo cards for each child to have one. Make up a verbal clue for each word so the children can guess the words as the game is played.

- Be sure to have all the props needed for the **Winter Show.** (See Notes for the **Winter Show** on page 114 for suggestions.)

Circle Time Activities

- Introduce the letter *Cc*.

- Be sure the children know the songs you plan to use for the sing-along at the **Winter Show.**

- Practice the **Winter Show** this week. Have the children use props and set up one of the days before the show. That day, take a photo of each child and a group photo as a keepsake. (The group photo can be glued into the journal for *Jj* Week.)

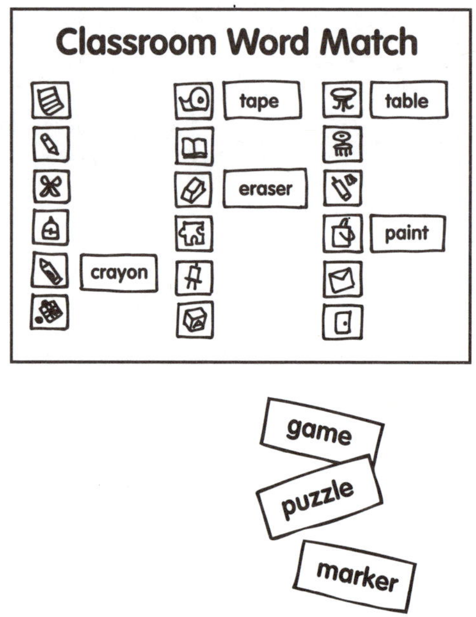

- Review the **Classroom Word Match interactive chart.** Give each child a turn to pick a word and match it to a photo on the chart. If the children need to move, have them also find the item in the classroom.

- Play classroom bingo with the cards prepared ahead of time using the photos taken. Be sure all cards have photos in a different sequence so everyone doesn't "bingo" at the same time! Make up clues so the children can guess the words. For example, say, "When you cut something out, you use a ____." [The answer is *SCISSORS*.]

- Review tangrams from *Tt* Week. Show the children the four tangrams for *Cc* Week. They are *cat*, *candle*, *chicken*, and *camel*. Cut up a tangram square into the seven magic shapes. Pass out the pieces to the children. Then they can take turns adding pieces until the four puzzles are complete. Have them name the shape as each piece is added. Show the children how they can assemble their own puzzles and glue them to paper. They can also trace around the pieces and take them home in an envelope to show their families how they can build the puzzle. Tell them the tangram puzzles will be in the CRAFT AREA.

TABLE WORK

- Practice writing the letter of the week. Practice writing the letter *Cc*.

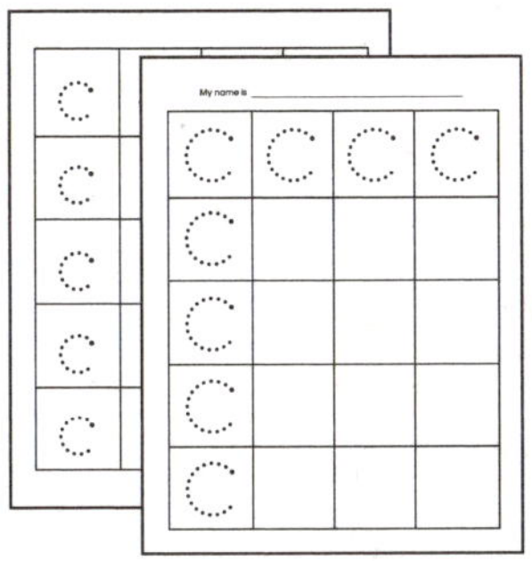

- Phonics Sheet for the letter *Cc*

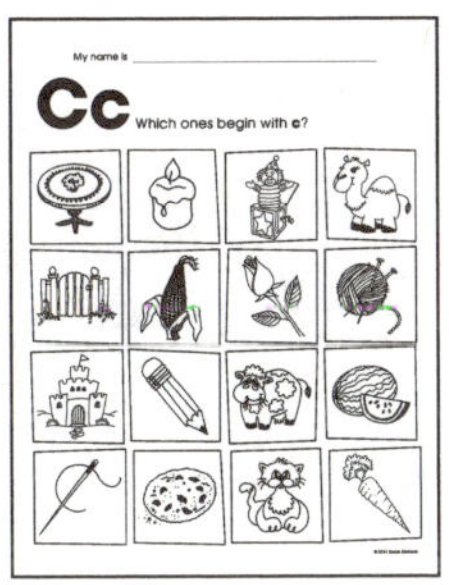

- Have children make a pop-up card for their families. To make the card, fold two pieces of construction paper in half. Decorate the front of the card. In the center of the other folded paper, cut two slits about an inch apart on the folded edge—two pencil marks can be made about an inch apart to guide them. Open the card push out the strip. Show the children where to write "Love," and sign their name. Put glue on the back of the inside of the card. Be careful not to get any glue on the tab that will pop up. Children can create or cut out a small picture for the pop up. Carefully glue it in place.

TIP An easy way for children to do this is by opening their scissor wide and make one complete cut, then open wide again and make another cut on the lines you've drawn.

- **Journal** Write: *Concentric circles*
Explain that concentric circles share the same center. Draw an example for the children. It looks like a bullseye! Have the children draw colorful concentric circles in their journals or make a block print of concentric circles using a Styrofoam tray. To make the block print, draw the circles with a blunt pencil. Brush easel paint on the Styrofoam tray, covering the drawing completely. Lay a piece of manila paper over the paint and roll with a brayer (teacher can press and rub with a gloved hand). Carefully peel the paper off the tray and hang to dry. Later glue the print in the journal.

TIP Have children practice drawing concentric circles on scrap paper before pressing the circles into the Styrofoam tray.

FREE CHOICE PLAY

Writing Center

Alphabet Stamps

Board Games

- Play the board games from *Ss* and *Jj* Weeks.
- Candyland by Hasbro
- Counting Cookies by Learning Resources

Sensory Table

Roll out and cut playdough cookies with cookie cutters. Cookie sheets, spatulas, and even a pretend oven (small shelf right next to the sensory table) with potholders would be fun!

Workbench

Make a catapult. To begin, saw a piece of a board to get a wood block. Sand the block smooth—no splinters! Use a hot glue gun or carpenter's glue to adhere a spring clothespin and tongue depressor to the block. Then glue a plastic bottle cap near the end of the tongue depressor, leaving a little space for a child's finger to release the lever. If there are two or more players, each player can make different-colored crumpled paper balls. See how far you can catapult the paper balls or aim for the shoe boxes to score!

TIP To be safe, the teacher will need to use the hot glue gun away from the children.

Easel Art

Paint while listening to music. Set up the headphones near the easel and just turn on the music! Ask the children, "Did the music help you to decide what to paint?" "What colors did you choose?"

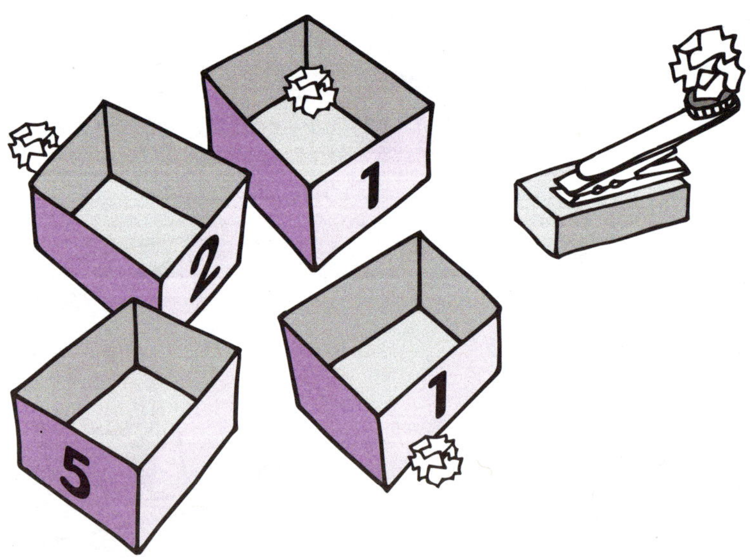

Crafts

- Make cookies by using construction paper and cookie cutters to trace cookies. Then cut them out. Put glue in the paint for icing, then sprinkle with glitter or real candy sprinkles. Just like in a bakery, make a dozen cookies and take them home in a small bag. Children also can have fun trading cookies. You could even have an old-fashioned cookie walk!

- Following the explanation at CIRCLE TIME, make tangrams. Provide pretraced tangram squares and visual directions for assembling the cat, candle, chicken, and camel. The children should cut the tangram square into the seven magic shapes. Then they can assemble the puzzle and glue it to paper, or trace around the assembled shapes to outline the puzzle, which lets them take the pieces home in an envelope to show their families.

- After making pop-up cards at TABLE WORK, keep the supplies out to make more cards for family members, friends, and neighbors.

- Block printing is a messy activity, so have it available only during FREE CHOICE PLAY on the day it is done as a journal writing activity.

- Cut coffee filters into snowflakes. The snowflakes can be used to decorate for the Winter Show.

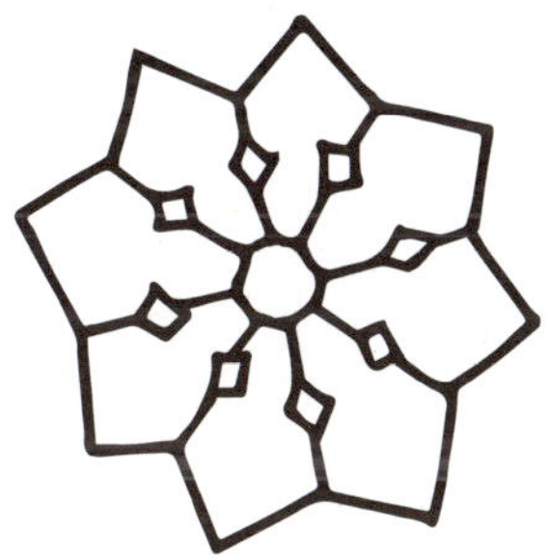

Notes & Evaluations

Cc
WEEK

Cc WEEK

NOTES FOR THE WINTER SHOW

Before the Winter Show:

- Decorate the space with the snowflakes cut from coffee filters (*Cc* Week).

- Have the junk sculpture on display (*Jj* Week).

The Show, the Props, and the Characters

1. Four children name the four seasons and hold up a poster of that season.
    - Spring: A tree with green buds made with fingerprints or dabbed with a Q-tip
    - Summer: A tree with tissue paper flowers
    - Autumn: A tree with red, yellow, and orange leaves
    - Winter: A bare tree with branches

TIP Have the children create the posters.

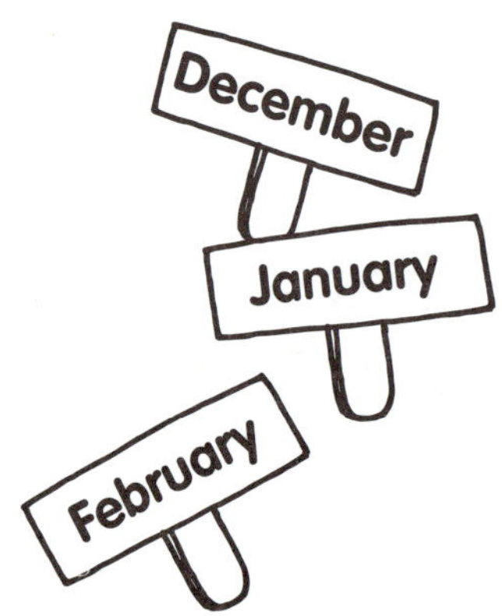

2. All the children sing "What Happens Each Season" (tune of "It's Raining, It's Pouring")
3. Twelve children pick up the month signs and sort themselves in front of the correct season. Each child with a month sign says, "I'm January," "I'm February," and so forth until all twelve have had their turn. All bow, then sit down.

4. Next, explain that during *Jj* Week the children had fun learning and telling jokes. Each child tells a joke.

5. For a finale, the class sings "If You're Happy and You Know It"
   [Clap your hands . . .
   Tap your toe . . .
   Nod your head . . .
   You can jump . . .
   You can jiggle . . .
   Shout for joy, Hoo-ray!]

6. All bow.

Notes & Evaluations

	Circle Time	Table Work	Free Choice Play	Crafts
Monday	**Beginning:** **Ending:**			
	Story:			
Tuesday	**Beginning:** **Ending:**			
	Story:			
Wednesday	**Beginning:** **Ending:**			
	Story:			
Thursday	**Beginning:** **Ending:**			
	Story:			
Friday	**Beginning:** **Ending:**			
	Story:			

Ff WEEK

Food

Friends

Feelings

American Flag

Dramatic Play

Grocery Store

Use the five food groups to make five areas and spread them throughout the classroom so the children can push a grocery cart to shop.

Learning Objectives

Physical and Motor

- Swings arms while walking
- Balances or hops on one foot
- Copies and draws simple shapes and letters

Cognitive

- Knows some names of coins and bills (money)
- Uses measurement terms

Communication and Language

- Makes up stories
- Retells a story in sequence

Social and Emotional

- Plays with other children
- Understands others' perspectives

Approaches to Learning

- Invents new purposes for objects

Listening Activities and Songs

- Song: "*Frères Jacques*" (Traditional)
- Song: "You're a Grand Old Flag" by George M. Cohan
- Song: "A-Shopping We Will Go" (to the tune of "A-Hunting We Will Go")

"A-Shopping We Will Go"
(to the tune of "A-Hunting We Will Go")

A-shopping we will go,
A-shopping we will go.
Let's buy some ___________
And put it in the cart.
A-shopping we will go.

Adapted by Susan Ehrhardt

Stories

- *The Flag We Love* by Pam Muñoz Ryan
- *F is for Flag* by Wendy Cheyette Lewison
- *The Pledge of Allegiance* published by Scholastic
- *Good Enough to Eat* by Lizzy Rockwell
- *The Case of the Hungry Stranger* by Crosby Bonsall
- *We Are Best Friends* by Aliki
- *Not Norman: A Goldfish Story* by Kelly Bennett
- *Fish Is Fish* by Leo Lionni
- *A Fly Went By* by Mike McClintock
- *Miss Fannie's Hat* by Jan Karon
- *Before We Eat: From Farm to Table* by Pat Brisson and Mary Azarian
- *How Did That Get in My Lunchbox? The Story of Food* by Chris Batterworth

CIRCLE TIME

Interactive Charts and Props

- Show-and-tell bags

- Create a word card with a picture for each food item in the grocery store.

TIP To create interest, add a few real food items to the grocery store—but be sure they will last the two weeks.

- MyPlate from the US Department of Agriculture (ChooseMyPlate.gov)
- American flag (to count stars and stripes)
- Feeling cards (either purchase a set or make a set of feeling faces from the book ***Ed Emberley's Fingerprint Drawing Book).***

Circle Time Activities

- Have show-and-tell this week. Remind the children of the rules. Use the show-and-tell schedule and have each group of children give their presentation on the appropriate day.
- Introduce the letter *Ff*.
- To set up the grocery store, gather all the food and place it in the center of the circle. Teach the five food groups. Together sort the food brought to the circle into the five food groups. Have the children help put the food items away in the proper places in the classroom grocery store.

- Explain the grocery store rules: Using the **food cards**, write a grocery list before shopping and only buy what is on the list. Push the cart to the check-out counter. All grocery items are $1. The cashier has the money box with $5 bills and $1 bills. The cashier places a food sticker on the grocery list. The shopper must put the items back on the shelf. Keep the grocery lists this week to make sure every child has written at least one for the week. Choose the best one to glue in their journals. (Purses and wallets can also be part of the DRAMATIC PLAY.)
- Children love to play with money, and the grocery store is a good opportunity to talk about other money values, for example, saving for things they want, how much things cost, and taking good care of the things we buy!
- Bring in a favorite can of vegetables. Look at the labels. What information is found on a food label? Talk about portion sizes of the food. Also review how many servings per day of each of the five food groups are needed to be healthy. Discuss eating a healthy diet.
- Show the children the American flag. Read the story ***F is for Flag*** by Wendy Cheyette Lewison or ***The Flag We Love*** by Pam Muñoz Ryan. Count the stars and stripes. Explain that every country has a flag. Show some examples of flags of other countries. Say the Pledge of Allegiance. At TABLE WORK, color an American flag (see TABLE WORK on page 119).
- Listen to and sing **"You're a Grand Old Flag."**
- Discuss Fire Safety. The children will practice stop, drop, and roll. The teacher should role-play a 911 phone call. When someone calls 911, an operator answers, "911, what is your emergency?" Have each child take a turn talking with the "911 operator."

TABLE WORK

- Sing **"Frères Jacques"** in French and English.

- Discuss feelings using **Feeling Faces**, which are simple to draw using ***Ed Emberley's Fingerprint Drawing Book.*** A set of feeling cards can also be purchased from a school supply store. Talk about each feeling and have the children tell what would make them feel that way.

- On journal day, read the book ***We Are Best Friends*** by Aliki. Talk about the word *friend* with the class and how they can be a good friend. Explain that the children will draw two names at a time, and those two children will stand together for a photo before they sit down for TABLE WORK.

- Meet my friends Hernando and Harriet. Explain the **Creative Writing Project** to the children. That same day, send home the letter that explains the project. Pick names and display a list of who takes the puppet the first week, second week, etc. (see CREATIVE WRITING PROJECT on page 122 for an explanation and a copy of the letter).

- Practice writing the letter of the week. Practice writing the letter *Ff*.

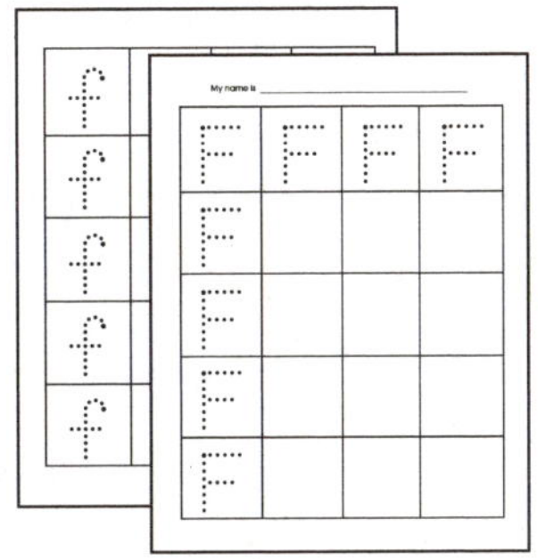

- Phonics Sheet for the letter *Ff*

- Color a prepared coloring page of the American flag. Direct the children to color the blue first, then give them fifty star stickers. Be careful to color the stripes in a pattern beginning with red.

- Color the MyPlate plate, which can be obtained from ChooseMyPlate.gov.

- **Journal** Write: *My friend* ___________. At CIRCLE TIME, the children drew a friend's name and had their photo taken together. Instruct children to find their name cards and give them to their friends to copy in their journals. When printing the photos, make two copies of each. The photo of the two friends can be glued in their journals at a later date.

FREE CHOICE PLAY

Writing Center

Alphabet Stamps

Board Games

- Shopping Spree (from Spain) by Educa Borras, SA
- My Feelings Game by Sensational Learners
- MyPlate Pursuit Board Game by Learning ZoneXpress
- Shopping List Memory Game by Orchard Toys

Sensory Table

Place a balance scale in the table with different-sized deli containers. Fill two dishpans with different bulk food items to weigh, for example, pasta shells and grapes (real or pretend). Have the fruits and vegetable food group nearby with baskets for weighing the produce in the sensory table weigh station. If there is enough space, a food scale can also be in or near the sensory table.

OR Make a funnel board that fits across the table. Provide different sizes and types of funnels so the children can experiment. Use sand in the table.

Workbench

This center becomes the **meat department** of the grocery store. Meat, chicken, fish, and beans are on a shelf nearby. Styrofoam trays, tape, scissors, and waxed paper (taken out of the box with the sharp edge) are on the workbench for wrapping the meat.

TIP Plastic wrap is too difficult for young children to handle.

Easel Art

Put the easel away. Fingerpaint at a table.

Crafts

- Provide food ads. Children can clip coupons.
- Cut pictures of healthy food from old magazines. Either put them in a paper bag to make a "healthy sack lunch" or glue them to a paper plate for a "healthy meal."
- Use ***Ed Emberley's Fingerprint Drawing Book*** to draw feeling faces. Make sure the stamp pad has washable ink for the fingerprints. Keep wipes nearby for easy cleanup. There are also lots of other things to draw with fingerprints in the book!

- Make a craft-stick American flag. Paint seven sticks red and six sticks white. Have blue squares traced for the children to cut. Use a pinky finger or an eraser tip dipped in white paint for the stars. Assemble and glue all the pieces together on poster or mat board.

TIP If the children are interested, help them count fifty stars.

- Make embossed foil pictures. Gather very simple coloring book pages that the children could trace. Lay about four layers of newspaper on a flat surface. Next lay a piece of aluminum foil on the newspaper, then the coloring page on top. Trace the picture with a blunt pencil. Lift off the picture and color the foil with a permanent marker. To finish, the foil can be folded around a piece of cardboard and taped.

- Color, then cut out the pieces of the Sandwich Reproducible. Make a sandwich by gluing what you like on your sandwich. Or save all the pieces to make sandwiches again and again.

- Make a pretty folded fan. Use a six-by-twelve-inch piece of pretty paper. Wallpaper works well, or use construction paper. Accordion-fold the paper widthwise with one-inch folds. Staple in the center to hold the folds in place. Glue a craft stick to each side of the staple. With a small line of glue, connect the fan together to form a semi-circle (point out the semicircle to the children). Close the fan by bringing the sticks together and securing them with a rubber band. Allow the fan to dry. To open the fan, spread the paper open into a full circle and secure the sticks with the rubber band.

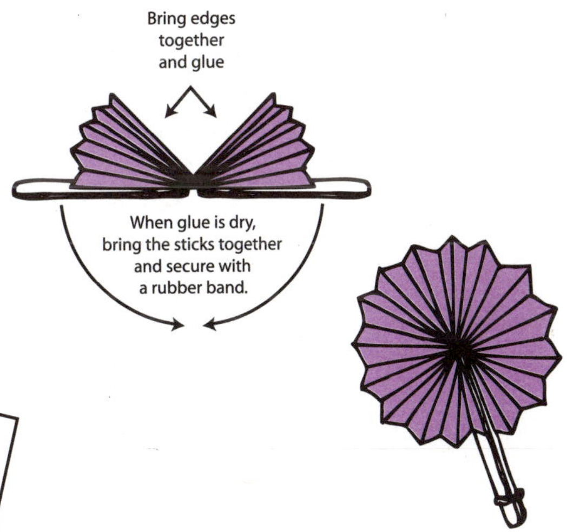

TIP Tell the children they can make sandwich pieces and play "Sandwich Shop" with friends and family.

Notes & Evaluations

CREATIVE WRITING PROJECT

The teacher introduces the puppet as a friend in *Ff* Week.

Each group will need the following:

- Stuffed animal puppet
- Plastic bin with a handle
- Book about the animal
- Journal (like the one used at TABLE WORK)

Suggestions include a hamster, guinea pig, hedgehog, and a porcupine—a stuffed animal would be sufficient.

Here are books that can be used with each animal:

- Hamster: *Hamsters on the Run* by Miah Pluta
- Hedgehog: *Hedgie's Surprise* by Jan Brett
- Porcupine: *A Porcupine Named Fluffy* by Helen Lester
- Guinea Pig: *I Love Guinea Pigs* by Dick King-Smith

TIP Draw names and make a list so the children know who has the puppet and who gets the puppet next.

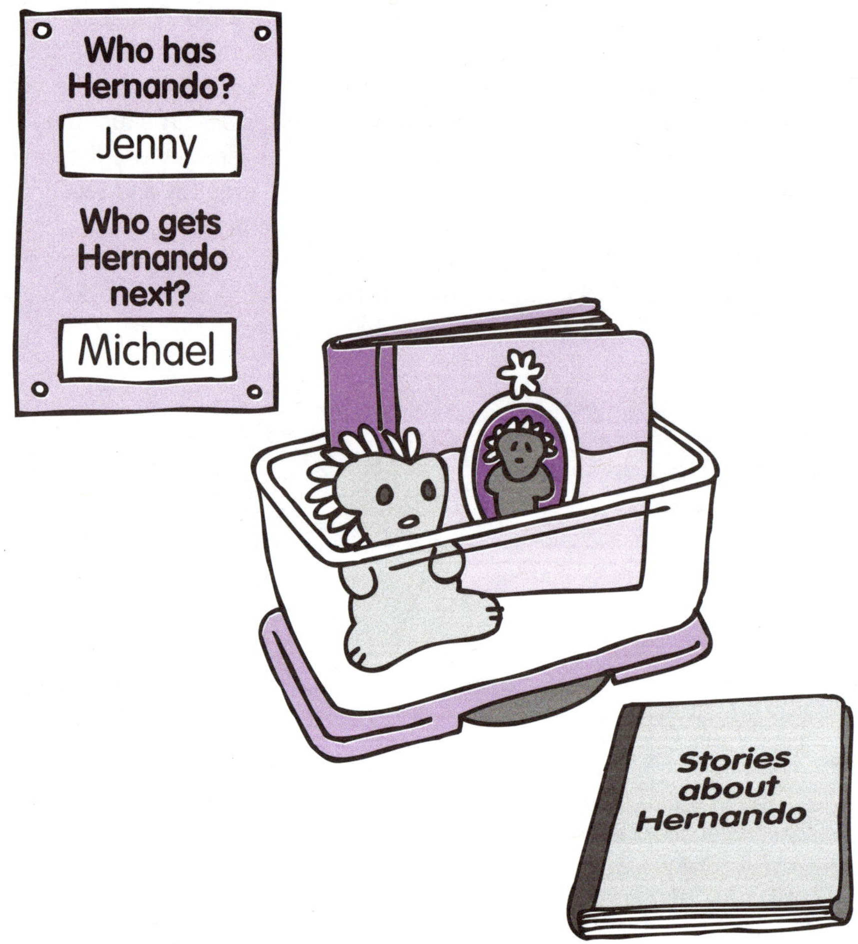

Send a letter about the Creative Writing Project to the families:

Creative Writing Project Letter

[date]

I would like to introduce a creative writing project during this second half of the school year. The purpose is for the children to use their imaginations and develop their storytelling skills. Make it fun! And don't be alarmed . . . the pet is a puppet.

Meet Hernando!

Hernando is a Spanish name which means "bold voyager," "daring," and "adventuring." It is a perfect name for our new class pet. He is a guinea pig. However, he doesn't live at school. Each child in the class will have a turn to care for him.

Please take Hernando home with you for one week, ***from Thursday to the following Wednesday.*** Play with him and have fun, but be sure to take care of him. Keep him away from your pets and watch him carefully when little brothers and sisters want a turn with him.

Even though you take special care of him, something very peculiar happens every night while you are sleeping! Hernando escapes and has pretend adventures in your house!

With your child, write a story about one of his adventures. A one-page story is plenty. Make it exciting. Hernando is a curious guinea pig, and he usually gets into mischief. Use your imagination and tell us what happens when he visits at your house.

Be sure to bring back Hernando, his cage, the book, and the journal on Wednesday.

Thanks for letting Hernando visit your family,

[your signature]

Creative Writing Project Letter

[date]

I would like to introduce a creative writing project during this second half of the school year. The purpose is for the children to use their imaginations and develop their storytelling skills. Make it fun! And don't be alarmed . . . the pet is a puppet.

Meet Harriet!

Harriet is a French name which means "ruler of the home." It is a perfect name for our new class pet. She is a hedgehog. However, she doesn't live at school. Each child in the class will have a turn to care for her.

Please take Harriet home with you for one week, **from Thursday to the following Wednesday.** Play with her and have fun, but be sure to take care of her. Keep her away from your pets and watch her carefully when little brothers and sisters want a turn with her.

Even though you take special care of her, something very peculiar happens every night while you are sleeping! Harriet escapes and has pretend adventures in your house!

With your child, write a story about one of her adventures. A one-page story is plenty. Make it exciting. Harriet is a curious hedgehog, and she usually gets into mischief. Use your imagination and tell us what happens when she visits at your house.

Be sure to bring back Harriet, her cage, the book, and the journal on Wednesday.

Thanks for letting Harriet visit your family,

[your signature]

	Circle Time	Table Work	Free Choice Play	Crafts
Monday	Beginning: Ending:			
	Story:			
Tuesday	Beginning: Ending:			
	Story:			
Wednesday	Beginning: Ending:			
	Story:			
Thursday	Beginning: Ending:			
	Story:			
Friday	Beginning: Ending:			
	Story:			

Gg WEEK

Graphing

Gingerbread Boys and Girls

Position Words

Community Helpers

Dramatic Play

Grocery Store

Learning Objectives

Physical and Motor

- Dresses with little assistance
- Makes marks or strokes with drawing tools
- Uses small muscles in hands to color, cut, paste, and paint

Cognitive

- Estimates numbers in a group
- Engages in fantasy play, making up plots

Communication and Language

- Likes to learn new words
- Listens for details

Social and Emotional

- Shows strong emotions
- Plays simple games with rules

Approaches to Learning

- Seeks and accepts help and information

Listening Activities and Songs

- *The Three Billy Goats Gruff* by Paul Galdone
- Song: "The Green Grass Grew All Around" (Traditional)
- "Good-bye Poem" (Use this poem the second half of the year instead of the "Good-bye Song")

"Good-bye Poem"

Good-bye, my friends.
See you later, alligator.
Toodle-loo, honeydew.
After a while, crocodile.
Ta-ta, mama llama.
Give a hug, little bug.
Take care, panda bear.
See you soon, macaroon.
No cryin', little lion.
Out the door, with a ROAR!

Adapted by Susan Ehrhardt

Stories

- *The Gingerbread Boy* by Paul Galdone
- *Gingerbread Baby* by Jan Brett
- *Gingerbread Friends* by Jan Brett
- *Babushka Baba Yaga* by Patricia Polacco
- *Miss Tizzy* by Libba Moore Gray
- *Germs Make Me Sick!* by Melvin Berger
- *Helpers in My Community* by Bobbie Kalman
- *Up, Down, and Around* by Katherine Ayres
- *A Kiss Goodbye* by Audrey Penn
- *The Three Billy Goats Gruff* by Paul Galdone
- *Martin's Big Words: The Life of Dr. Martin Luther King, Jr.* by Doreen Rappaport (Read this book the week of the celebration of Dr. Martin Luther King, Jr. Day.)

CIRCLE TIME

Interactive Charts and Props

- Create your own Blank Graph Chart.

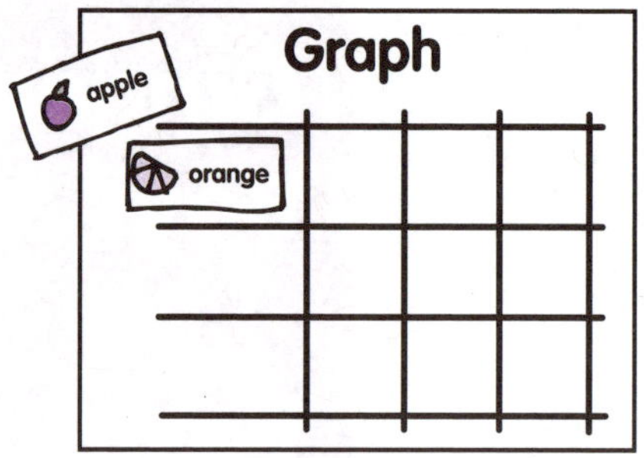

- Create your own position-word cards: (have one for each child):

in	**below**	**on**	**in front**
out	**over**	**off**	**in back**
before	**under**	**beside**	**bottom**
after	**around**	**near**	**behind**
above	**through**	**far**	**between**

- Purchase a bulletin board display of community helpers (occupations). Put a magnet on the back and display them on the whiteboard. On a smaller scale, the cards from a community helpers lotto could be used.

- Make a bridge to pantomime ***The Three Billy Goats Gruff*** story. (Turn a small wooden table upside down so the three billy goats can "trip, trap, trip, trap" across the bridge.) Also, a picture or word card can be made for the small, medium, and big billy goat. The troll can wear a funny wig and an old tattered shirt. Be sure to set up a few chairs for an audience!

Circle Time Activities

- Introduce the letter *Gg*.

- Teach the children about graphs. To practice, graph some groceries. For example, gather all the apples, pears, oranges, strawberries, and cherries from the fruit and vegetable group in the grocery store, then lay them out on the **Blank Graph Chart.** To give all the children a turn, divide the class into the five food groups. Repeat the above graphing activity.

- More graphing practice could be graphing the children by the color of their shirts, hair, eyes, etc. Another fun thing is to graph what numbers come up when a die is rolled. First, place cards on the floor, numbered 1–6. Let each child roll the die once. Whatever number is rolled, the child should stand in a row by that number card. It's a child-size graph!

- Sing the song **"The Green Grass Grew All Around."**

- After reading the story ***The Gingerbread Boy*** by Paul Galdone at STORY TIME, use gingerbread people to teach position words. Set up a gingerbread-boy-sized obstacle course using blocks and shoe boxes. Take turns placing the Gingerbread Boy in the appropriate place in the obstacle course. Leave the obstacle course set up during FREE CHOICE PLAY. The children will probably rebuild it the next day!

- Discuss community helpers (occupations) using the display. Ask the children, "Who are the community helpers in your neighborhood?" Ask, "Would you like to do any of those jobs when you become an adult?"

- Listen to the book ***The Three Billy Goats Gruff*** by Paul Galdone. Pick four children to help act out the story as it is read (use the props listed). Tell the children they can take turns acting out the story during FREE CHOICE PLAY. Be sure the area for the pantomime is away from activities that need to be quiet.

TABLE WORK

- Discuss how not to share germs. Read or use the book ***Germs Make Me Sick*** by Melvin Berger as a reference. Show the children how to cover a cough and sneeze. Ask them, "What should you do with a tissue that you've used?" Explain and show the craft that goes with the lesson. Review with the children how to wash their hands. Remind them that eating a healthy diet will also keep them from getting sick.

- Read the story written by the first child who took home Hernando or Harriet (creative writing project introduced during *Ff* Week on page 122). Pass the puppet to the next child on the list.

TIP This is done every week until all the children have had a turn to share their story with the class.

- Practice writing the letter of the week. Practice writing the letter *Gg*.

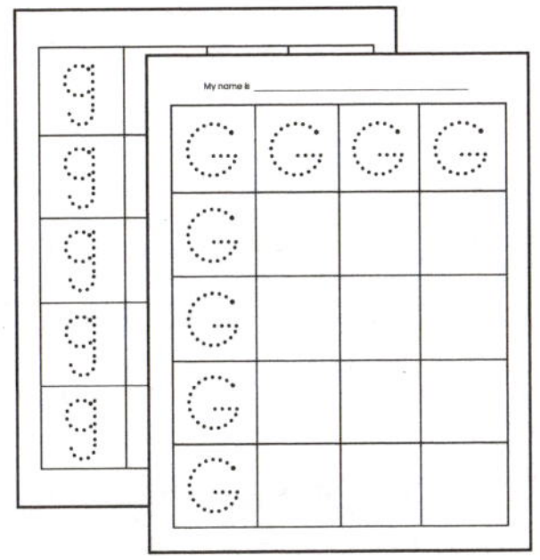

- Phonics Sheet for the letter *Gg*

- Graph Reproducible

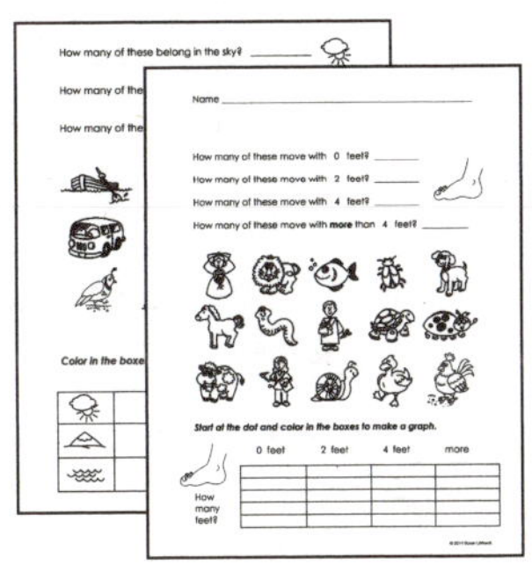

- **Journal** Write *Gingerbread boy* **or** *Gingerbread girl*
Children trace a boy or girl gingerbread person using a cookie cutter or pattern. Then they can decorate their gingerbread person with crayons.

FREE CHOICE PLAY

Writing Center

Alphabet Stamps OR Glue a complete (five-item) grocery list in children's journals

Board Games

- Keep the games from last week
- A community helpers lotto game
- To Grandma's House We Go by Milton Bradley

Sensory Table

Continue weighing bulk food from last week.

Or Use uncolored playdough, rolling pins, and gingerbread people cookie cutters. Then color a batch of playdough with a few different bright colors for decorating the cookies.

Workbench

Continue using the workbench to wrap meat for the grocery store.

Easel Art

Put the easel away this week to make enough space for ***The Three Billy Goats Gruff*** pantomime area.

Crafts

- Continue to have coupons available for the children to cut out and play with in the grocery store.
- If the children are using the sandwich-building activity from last week, leave it out for one more week.
- Also make the ***Ed Emberley's Fingerprint Drawing Book*** available this week. Don't forget to leave out the stamp pads and wipes for cleanup.
- Trace occupation stencils with markers. Be sure to have thin markers for the tiny spaces!
- Allow the children to borrow some of the cookie cutters from the SENSORY TABLE to trace gingerbread people to color and cut. Or make some cardboard patterns for the children to use.
- Make a "How Not to Share Germs" poster. Have a head and hand traced on multicultural skin-toned construction paper. Everyone needs to learn to stay healthy! The instructions for the project were given at CIRCLE TIME. A little fun fact: the eyes on the poster are drawn closed because when a person sneezes they always close their eyes!
- Have large gingerbread people traced on tan construction paper. Buy a variety of colors of glitter glue. First decorate the gingerbread people with the glitter glue, then let them dry. When the glue is thoroughly dry, cut out the gingerbread person. Be sure to put away the glitter glue in time to allow the projects to dry by the end of the week.

- Have children make a background picture of a "pretty little tree with green grass growing all around" by drawing grass lines all along the bottom of the page with markers or crayons. Next draw a simple tree trunk. Then make it a "pretty tree," by making the foliage of the tree using small squares of tissue paper in various shades of green. Teach the children to roll the tissue paper with their fingertips or around the tip of a pencil eraser and glue in place. Make a pattern of a giraffe, gorilla, goat, or any *Gg* animal to trace onto the background. The children can draw a little bird to put in the tree like the song **"The Green Grass Grew All Around."**

TIP There are fingerprint birds in ***Ed Emberley's Fingerprint Drawing Book.***

Gingerbread Cookie Activity

Decorate a large gingerbread cookie for children to take home for their families to enjoy. Each child receives her own cookie. Provide colored icing and a variety of candies children can use to decorate their cookies. Children can invite their grandparents to help. Take a photo of the gingerbread cookie when they finish as a keepsake.

TIP Substitute Crispy Marshmallow Treats for gingerbread. Press the Marshmallow Treats into a gingerbread mold or cookie cutter. The children love them and there is no baking required!

Notes & Evaluations

	Circle Time	Table Work	Free Choice Play	Crafts
Monday	Beginning: Ending:			
	Story:			
Tuesday	Beginning: Ending:			
	Story:			
Wednesday	Beginning: Ending:			
	Story:			
Thursday	Beginning: Ending:			
	Story:			
Friday	Beginning: Ending:			
	Story:			

Yy WEEK

Fitness through Yoga

Counting

Sharing

Yuck and Yum

Dramatic Play

Fitness Center with Yoga Studio

Include mats, balance beam, exercise ball, jump ropes, and beanbag weights.

Learning Objectives

Physical and Motor

- Manages zippers, snaps, and buttons
- Learns to tie shoes
- Runs with ease and stops quickly

Cognitive

- Counts twenty or more objects with accuracy
- Understands the words *whole* and *half* and uses them in sentences

Communication and Language

- Uses correct grammar
- Enjoys books

Social and Emotional

- Understands some limits and rules
- Engages in group play

Approaches to Learning

- Offers ideas and suggestions

Listening Activities and Songs

- Song: "Yankee Doodle" (Traditional)
- Book on tape: *The Doorbell Rang* by Pat Hutchins
- Classical instrumental music for yoga relaxation

RECIPE: Yuck

2 parts cornstarch
1 part water
Food coloring (optional)

Stir all ingredients to mix thoroughly. Store in an airtight container. It will last about a week.

TIP Experiment by adding more water until it is equal parts cornstarch and water. At this consistency, it can be used as sidewalk paint that rinses off with water.

Stories

- *My Daddy Is a Pretzel: Yoga for Parents and Kids* by Baron Baptiste
- *Tie Your Shoes with Slipknot Sam* by Paul Bennell
- *I Can Tie My Own Shoelaces* by Oakley Graham and Barry Green
- *Who Stole the Cookies from the Cookie Jar?* by Margaret Wang
- *The Doorbell Rang* by Pat Hutchins
- *Yertle the Turtle and Other Stories* by Dr. Seuss
- *My Little Yellow Taxi* by Stephen T. Johnson
- *The Crayons' Book of Numbers* by Drew Daywalt
- *Bal Yoga for Kids* by Glenda Kacev and Sylvia Roth
- *Yoga Games for Children* by Danielle Bersma and Marjoke Visscher
- *Extra Yarn* by Mac Barnett

CIRCLE TIME

Interactive Charts and Props

- Use the book ***Yoga Games for Children*** by Danielle Bersma and Marjoke Visscher as a reference.
- *The Kids' Yoga Deck: 50 Poses and Games* by Annie Buckley (set of cards)
- Props for acting out the story ***The Doorbell Rang*** by Pat Hutchins: two trays, twenty-four cookies, twelve small plates, two aprons (for mom and grandma), bell
- Use the book ***Who Took the Cookies from the Cookie Jar?*** by Bonnie Lass and Philemon Sturges, a cookie jar, first and last name cards, and enough cookies for every child (one day have real cookies!).
- A pair of real shoes to practice tying shoes
- Cut one-by-twenty-inch strips of fleece—one for each child—to practice tying a knot (see FLEECE PROJECTS at the end of this chapter).

Circle Time Activities

- Introduce the letter *Yy*.
- Teach the children to tie a knot using a one-by-twenty-inch piece of cut fleece (see FLEECE PROJECTS at the end of this chapter).
- Play "All Tied Up!" Divide the class into groups of six or more. The more children in the group, the more complex the knot. Have each group gather in a close circle facing one another. Everyone grasp the hand of a friend; each hand should be holding a different person. Now slowly, carefully untangle the knot without letting go. Do this activity indoors or out. It's great for problem solving, communication, and stretching!
- Demonstrate how to tie shoestrings, then encourage the children to practice tying the shoes you have brought for use in the classroom. Also, demonstrate the CRAFT activity that lets them make a poster board shoe and shoestring for more practice.
- Make the **Yuck** for the SENSORY TABLE with the children. Let them help measure the ingredients and then stir, stir, stir!
- Fill the cookie jar with cookies and play "Who Took the Cookie from the Cookie Jar?" Use name cards with the children's first and last names. Say, "Tommy Johnson took the cookie from the cookie jar." Tell the children this week they will begin practicing writing their first and last names for TABLE WORK.

TIP

FIELD TRIP IDEA!
In the spring, either plan a field trip to the public library or invite the children's librarian to visit the class. Ahead of time, send a library application home to complete so each child can get their very own library card. The library card application requires the child to sign their name—first and last!

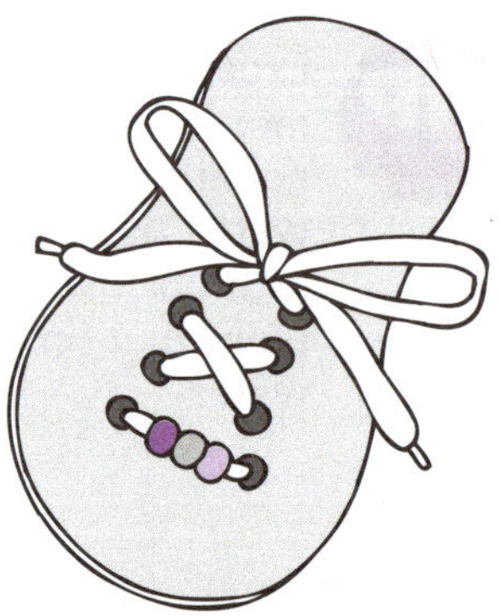

TABLE WORK

- Show the children a geo-board and how to follow a pattern and make a design with rubber bands. Divide the children into pairs and have them pick a pattern and make a picture with their friend.

- Act out the story ***The Doorbell Rang*** by Pat Hutchins. Use the props listed on the previous page and leave them out so more children can pantomime the story at FREE CHOICE PLAY.

- Read the second Hernando or Harriet story. Pass the puppet on to the next child.

- Sing **"Yankee Doodle."** Once the children know the song, practice galloping and singing at the same time.

- Use the yoga cards at CIRCLE TIME to follow along and learn the positions. Each day, use a different card, then leave them in the DRAMATIC PLAY area during FREE CHOICE PLAY.

- Practice writing the letter of the week. Practice writing the letter *Yy*.

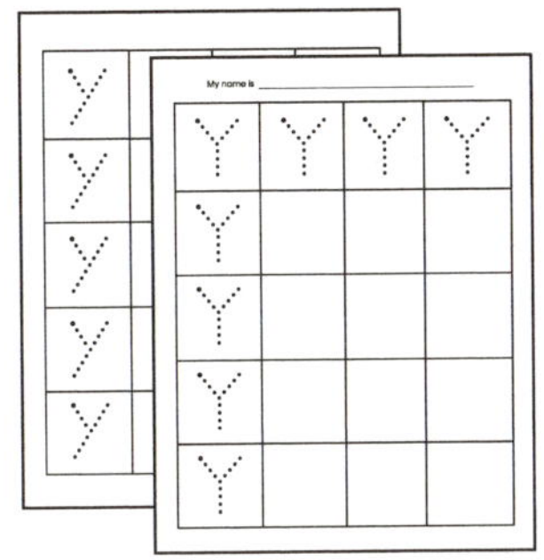

*

- Phonics Sheet for the letter *Yy*

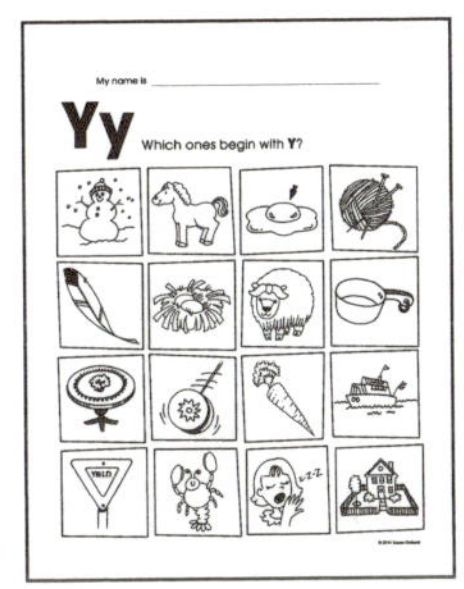

*

- Practice writing first and last names. Simply draw ten lines equally spaced on the paper. Print each child's name on the top line so it is practiced correctly.

TIP Make extras for later in Snow Week and *Ee* Week.

- Untangle the Yarn Reproducible

*

- **Journal** Write: *I love you*
  Have each child trace his hand on skin-tone-colored construction paper. Cut out the handprint. Place glue on the palm of the hand and glue in the journal. Dot glue on the third and fourth fingers and bend them down to make the American Sign Language sign for "I love you."

FREE CHOICE PLAY

Writing Center

Alphabet Stamps

Board Games

- Trouble by Milton Bradley
- Yahtzee by Hasbro
- 1, 2, 3 Treasures in the Sea: Counting Up to 30+ by Carson-Dellosa

Sensory Table

The **Yuck** made at CIRCLE TIME can be contained in a dishpan, or enough can be made to cover the bottom of the table. Add small scoops, spoons, plastic knives, or spatulas. Use jelly roll, pizza, or muffin pans to contain the Yuck. Have the children suggest other utensils to use after seeing how the Yuck behaves.

Workbench

Place one or two pieces of one-inch thick plywood on the workbench. Draw a large circle on each board. Tell children to pound nails around the circle leaving them to stick up at least ½ inch. The children can use a finger to measure about a ¾-inch space between nails. Have some small balls of yarn in a basket. When the ring of nails is complete, tie one end of a ball of yarn to a nail and go from nail to nail, winding once to create a design. The children may need some help tying the yarn when the ball runs out—it's difficult to keep the yarn taut and tie at the same time. These design boards are a class project, and many children should add yarn to the design before it is finished. Display each board carefully because they are heavy.

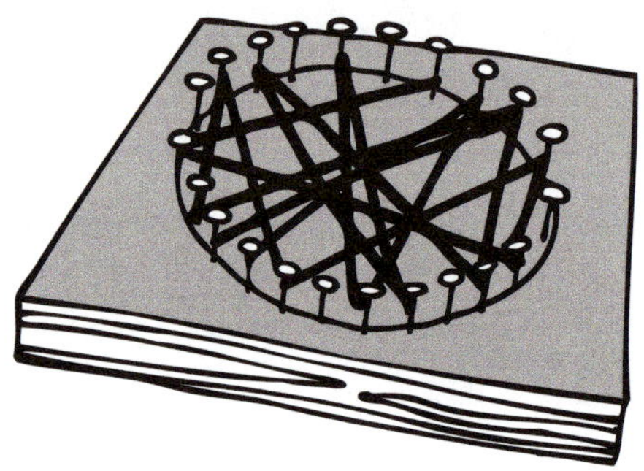

Easel Art

Have paint at the easel and paper so the children can paint whatever they choose.

Crafts

- Use the leftover one-by-twenty-inch fleece strips to practice tying knots. I allow them to tie a fleece strip on anything—for example, table and chair legs, cabinet handles, doorknobs, hooks, etc. The last day of class that week, at cleanup time, allow them to cut off all the strips. Remind them to go slowly and carefully because they are using scissors!

- Sew plastic canvas shapes with yarn. Thread blunt needles with yellow yarn. Add small beads for creative decorating.
- Decorate construction-paper cookies with glitter glue. Provide a variety of circle patterns for the children to trace. Teach them to look in the scrap box for pieces of construction paper to use to make the cookies. Remember, glitter glue should be applied sparingly or it will take a long time to dry!

- Use different-colored yarn pieces to draw with yarn. Simply "draw" with glue, then lay the yarn on the line of glue. Try a design that goes around and around. Part of the picture could be done with yarn and then completed with markers. For example, make the shell of a turtle with yarn, then add the legs, head, and tail with a marker.

- Make a "take–home shoe and shoestring" to practice tying shoes at home. Make the shoe by having the children stand on a piece of poster board and then tracing around their shoes. Cut out the shoe and punch holes to lace a shoestring. A hole punch with a long reach will be needed to line up the holes correctly. Very cheap shoestrings or cording can be purchased at a craft or hobby store.

- This is a good week to put out a spirograph, by Kahootz. The drawings made with a spirograph will look like the yarn art activity at the WORKBENCH.

Notes & Evaluations

WORKING WITH FLEECE

Project Descriptions and How-To Instructions

There are three projects to complete with fleece. Buy a variety of print designs so the children can choose one they like.

Project 1: Fleece Pillow
Get the children excited about the project so they will want to learn to tie a knot this week. After practicing, the children really will be able to make a fleece pillow.

TIP Ask for extra adult help this week so when the children are tying knots, there is one adult for every two children.

Project 2: Fleece Quilt
The children use the four-inch square scrap cutouts to make a fleece quilt during *Qq* Week.

Project 3: Knot Tying
The one-inch strips to practice tying a knot are used this week, *Yy* Week.

HOW TO: Make a Fleece Pillow

The teacher should prepare this project ahead of time.

Three pillows can be made from 1¼ yards of fleece fabric. Fleece is 60 inches wide, so cut the pillow squares 20 inches by 20 inches (see the FABRIC LAYOUT on the next page).

1. Lay two 20-by-20-inch squares on top of each other—wrong sides together.
2. Cut out the four corners—four-by-four-inch squares, which yields eight squares. Save these for the fleece quilt (project 2 in *Qq* Week).
3. Baste the two pillow pieces together diagonally with a single contrasting thread. This holds the pillow together while you cut the knotting strings. It also holds the pillow together while the children tie the knots.
4. Cut the tying strings by cutting four inches into the pillow (as deep as the corner cutouts) and approximately one inch wide (guide is indicated in purple on the FABRIC LAYOUT on the next page).

Put the pillow shells aside.

TIP Save the four-inch squares for *Qq* Week. Use the 1-inch-by-20-inch strips to learn to tie a knot this week—*Yy* Week.

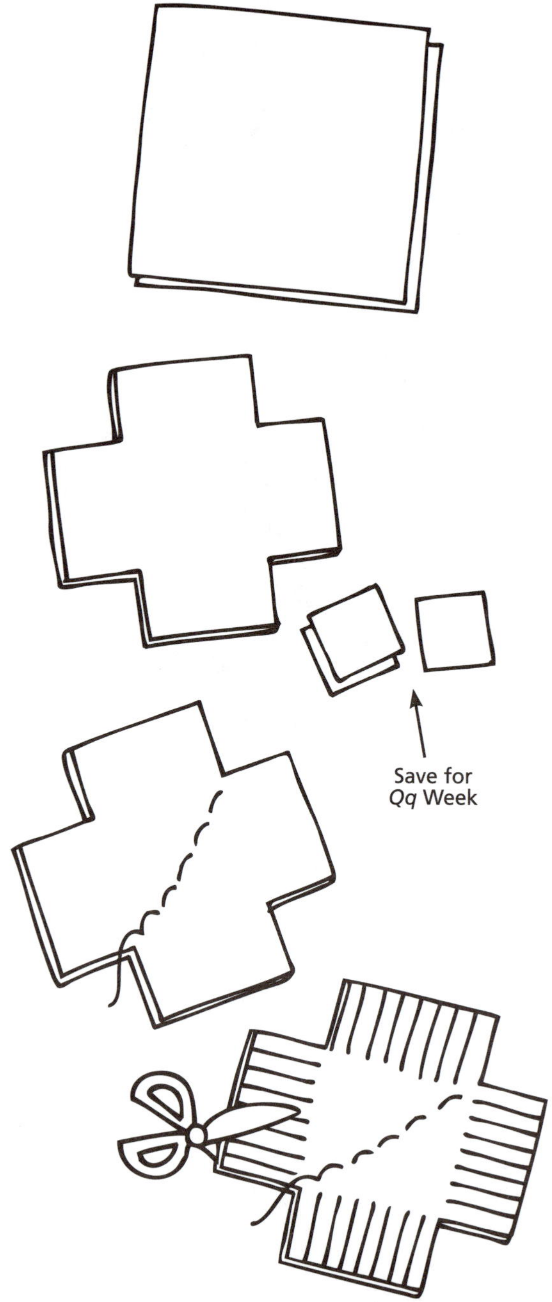

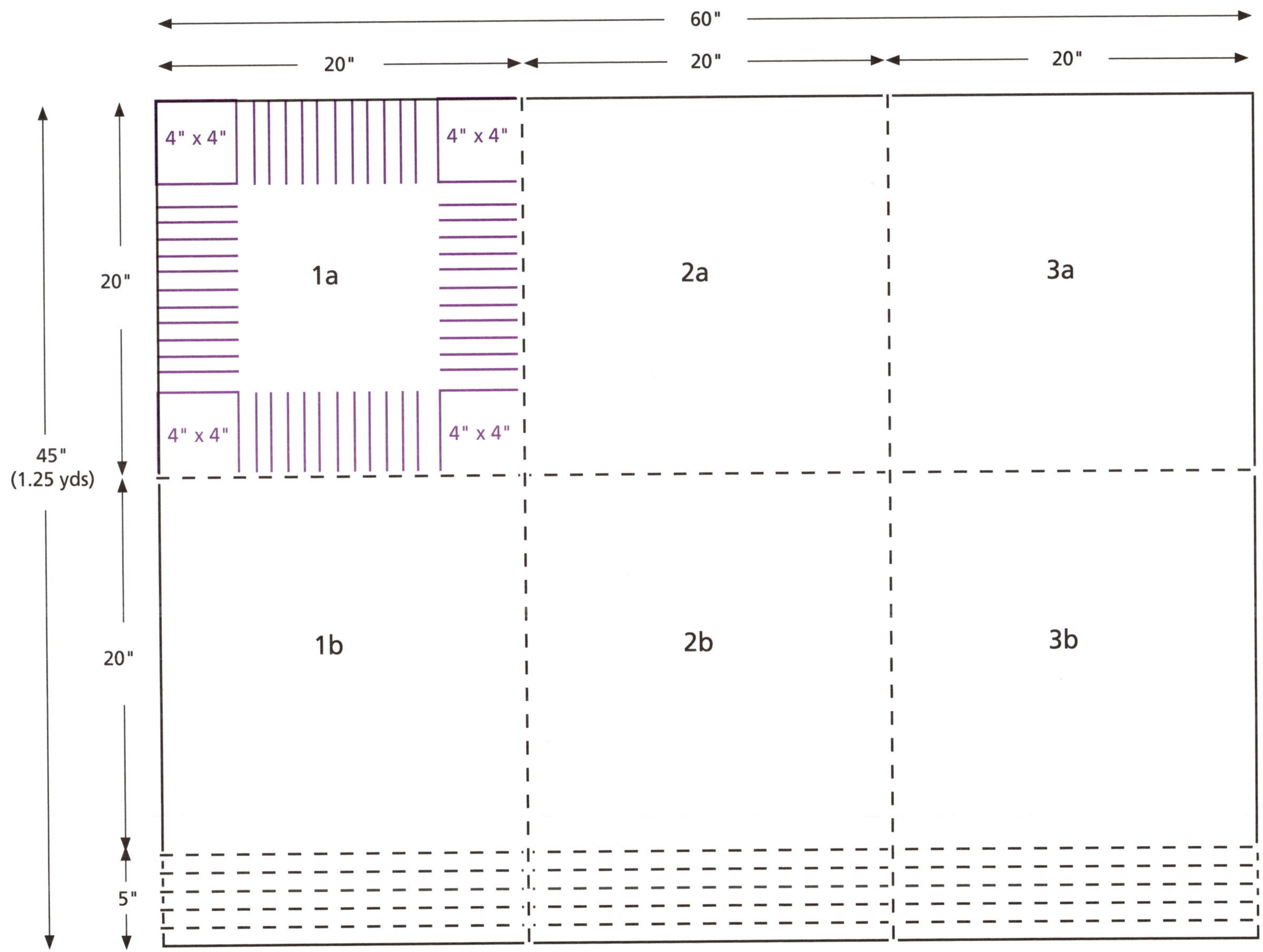

Fabric cut according to this layout will yield

- three pillows
- fifteen strips for practice tying
- twenty-four squares for fleece quilt

	Circle Time	Table Work	Free Choice Play	Crafts
Monday	Beginning: Ending:			
	Story:			
Tuesday	Beginning: Ending:			
	Story:			
Wednesday	Beginning: Ending:			
	Story:			
Thursday	Beginning: Ending:			
	Story:			
Friday	Beginning: Ending:			
	Story:			

Snow Week

Snow

Snow People

Writing Numerals

Rhymes

Dramatic Play

Continue fitness center and play with snow indoors—winter, winter everywhere!

Learning Objectives

Physical and Motor

- Builds and stacks with several small blocks
- Runs consistently without falling
- Uses scissors

Cognitive

- Notices patterns
- Understands concepts such as age, number, and distance

Communication and Language

- Speaks when spoken to
- Uses language socially (pragmatics)

Social and Emotional

- Plays with peers, sharing ideas and toys
- Follows and makes simple rules

Approaches to Learning

- Invents new purposes for objects

Listening Activities and Songs

- Song: "S-N-O-W-Y" (to the tune of "B-I-N-G-O")

"S-N-O-W-Y"
(to the tune of "B-I-N-G-O")

There was a day when it was cold
and snowy was the weather.
S-N-O-W-Y, S-N-O-W-Y, S-N-O-W-Y
And snowy was the weather.

(Other verses can be made up for other five-letter words: *frost*, *scarf*, etc.)

This unit on snow can either be used as a themed week on its own or incorporated into an existing week or spread through the winter months—whatever suits the schedule. Most importantly, take time to practice writing numerals and review rhymes.

Stories

- *The Mitten* by Jan Brett
- *The Snowy Day* by Ezra Jack Keats
- *The Biggest Snowman Ever* by Steven Kroll
- *Snowballs* by Lois Ehlert
- *Sneezy the Snowman* by Maureen Wright
- *The First Day of Winter* by Denise Fleming
- *Animals in Winter* by Henrietta Bancroft and Richard G. Van Gelder
- *The Three Snow Bears* by Jan Brett
- *Trouble with Trolls* by Jan Brett
- *Stranger in the Woods* by Carl R. Sams II and Jean Stoick
- *The Missing Mitten Mystery* by Steven Kellogg

TIP A good placement for Snow Week or parts of Snow Week might be when the children have experienced the first big snowfall of the year if you live in a snowy climate.

CIRCLE TIME

Interactive Charts and Props

- Create your own Build a Snowman interactive chart

> We can build a snowman,
> One step at a time.
> Roll three snowballs and stack them,
> One step at a time.
> Now let's decorate together,
> One person at a time.

TIP Have buttons, sticks, hats, shapes, fleece scarves, mittens, etc. to decorate the snowman.

- Use the rhyming cards (found in *Rr* Week in the CRAFTS section) to play Match the Mittens Memory Game. Trace and cut enough mittens to glue each rhyming card on a mitten. Make as many pairs of rhyming mittens as children in the class. Take turns until each child has a pair of matching mittens!

TIP For fun, place the cards in pairs of real mittens.

- Create your own large numeral cards labeled from 1–10.
- Indoor snow for the SENSORY TABLE (Insta-Snow Powder by www.SteveSpanglerScience.com)
- A lot of cotton balls!

Circle Time Activities

- Have the children help make snow in the SENSORY TABLE. Pass out the Numeral Cards (1–10) to ten children to hold in no particular order. Make the snow according to the directions on the container. Have the remainder of the children add one cup of water at a time as the teacher mixes. Tell the children they can play in the **Snow** at FREE CHOICE PLAY. Count as each cup of water is added and have children identify the **numeral.** For example, "That's two cups of water. Show me the two." Take a few minutes to continue asking the children about numeral recognition, giving every child at least one turn.

- Discuss what the children know about snow. In what season does it snow? Ask them if they've ever built a snowman. "What happens to the windows in your house when it is very cold outside? Did your car ever look like it had fuzz on it? What about the grass in your yard? That's called **Frost**!" Make Frost with the children. To make Frost you will need a large tin can, crushed ice, salt, and a wooden spoon. Fill the can with crushed ice and sprinkle with at least one cup of salt. Start stirring, giving each child a turn. Watch the outside of the can . . . it's Frost! Allow the children to touch the Frost then describe how it feels.

- Explain the **Pop-Up Snowman Counting Book** Craft. Review the pop-up technique that was learned during *Cc* Week. Show the children step-by-step how to add more pages to make a snowman pop-up book instead of just a card. (Note: the book is folded the long way so it can hold many pop-ups on each page.) Tell the children the Pop-up Snowman Counting Book will be with the CRAFTS so they can make their own during FREE CHOICE PLAY.

- Play with a class-sized parachute or king-size sheet and cotton balls. Sing "S-N-O-W-Y" while shaking the parachute. Make up verses for the words *frost*, *scarf*, or any five-letter word.

- Use the **Build a Snowman interactive chart** giving each child a turn.

- Demonstrate how to make a **Potato Masher Snow Person.** Use a round potato masher to stamp three circles onto brightly colored construction paper. Tell the children

TABLE WORK

the paint must dry before they can decorate. Make a plan together and gather the supplies needed to make the "sample" snow person. Show what it means to coordinate colors and patterns. Make available a variety of colored pipe cleaners for arms, wallpaper samples for hats and scarves, orange foam triangles for noses, and a variety of real buttons (see CRAFTS section).

For added interest and fun, have a snow person parade! Hang the completed snow people in a row. Have each child give their snow person a name. Below each picture display a name card.

- Review rhymes. Match the **Mittens Memory Game,** giving each child a turn to find two rhyming mittens.

TIP This activity is a good evaluation tool to see if each child understands rhymes.

- Read the Hernando or Harriet story. Pass the puppet on to the next child.
- Explain how to play **Pengoloo** by Blue Orange.
- Explain how to play **Thin Ice** by Pressman.

- Practice writing numerals 1–5.

- Count the Snowmen Reproducible

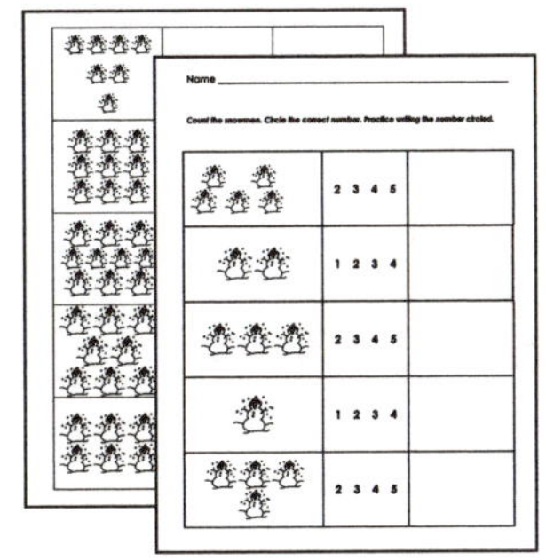

- Practice writing numerals 6–10.

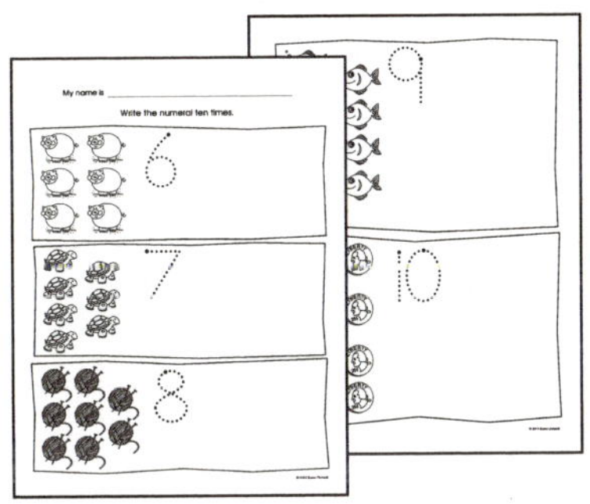

- Practice the children's last names.

FREE CHOICE PLAY

Writing Center

Display numerals 1–10. Tell the children to write the numerals in their journals.

Board Games

- Thin Ice by Pressman
- Picture Rhymes by Carson-Dellosa
- Rhyming BINGO by TREND Enterprises
- Pengoloo by Blue Orange

Sensory Table

Snow made at CIRCLE TIME (Insta-Snow Powder by www.SteveSpanglerScience.com)

TIP Put out pairs of stretchy gloves so the children can wear the gloves while playing with the pretend snow.

OR Provide a lot of cotton balls with ten bowls (numbered 1–10), tweezers, dice. Roll the dice and fill the bowls using the tweezers—don't touch the cotton balls!

Workbench

To make a craft-stick snowman, paint seven craft sticks white and two more craft sticks another dark color. Let the craft sticks dry overnight. The next day, build the snowman by placing the white sticks side by side and spreading two lines of glue across the white sticks where the two colored sticks will be placed for the brim of the hat. To keep them in place, be careful not to touch the sticks with the glue bottle. Provide moveable eyes, orange foam triangle noses, and cut pieces of pipe cleaners for the mouth to put a face on the snowman. To hang, adhere a ribbon to the back of the two top corners using masking tape.

TIP Build the snowman on a piece of waxed paper so it can be moved easily to a safe place to dry.

Easel Art

Children use white paint to draw a snowy picture on 12-by-18-inch blue construction paper. When the painting is complete, place it on a tray and bring it to a nearby table. While the paint is still wet, use a salt shaker to sprinkle salt on the painting. Allow the painting to dry flat on the tray. When the paint is dry, the salt will sparkle like ice crystals!

Crafts

- To make a Potato Masher Snow Person, saturate a large flat sponge with white tempera paint. Use a round potato masher to stamp three circles onto brightly colored construction paper. Allow the paint to dry and decorate it the next day. Tell the children to make a plan of how they will decorate their snowman or snow lady. Then gather their supplies. Provide a variety of colored pipe cleaners for arms, wallpaper samples for hats and scarves, orange foam triangles for noses, and a variety of real buttons.

Hang the snow people in a long line to make a snow person parade! Below each picture, display a name card.

Notes & Evaluations

- Make numerals with cotton balls. Stretch out one cotton ball to make the numeral *1*; use two cotton balls to make the numeral *2*, etc. Tell the children to be sure to arrange the cotton balls before they glue them on paper.

- Make a Snowman Pop-up Counting Book. To make the book, fold the pieces of construction paper in half, lengthwise. Write "Count the Snowmen," and decorate the front of the book. Along the folded edge of the other papers, cut two slits about an inch apart for every pop-up that will be displayed on that page—two pencil lines for each pop-up can be made about an inch apart to guide them, then pop out and mark each pop-up tab so it is easy to see where to glue each little snowman. (Remember the tip for cutting the slits: Tell the children to open their scissors wide and make a complete cut, then open wide again and make another cut on all the lines drawn.) Open the card and push out each pop-up tab. Glue the back of the inside of each page, being careful not to get any glue on the pop-up tabs. Carefully glue each little snowman in place.

- Make a string of snow people paper dolls. Show the children how to accordion-fold paper. Fold the paper in half and bring each raw edge to the fold, which will make four snow people in a row.

TIP Ahead of time, fold the paper and make the correct size snowman pattern.

Demonstrate how to trace the pattern on the folded paper. Point out to the children where the edges touch the folds on each side and explain how to avoid cutting the folds. Cut it out and stretch out the snowmen paper dolls to show what happens. The snow people will connect at the lower body and at the arms. Decorate with crayons or markers. For fun, tape or staple a few strings of snow people together!

- Make available different-sized circular items to trace. Children can use them to draw snow people. Glue on cotton balls to make the snow people soft and fluffy. Decorate!

	Circle Time	Table Work	Free Choice Play	Crafts
Monday	Beginning: Ending:			
	Story:			
Tuesday	Beginning: Ending:			
	Story:			
Wednesday	Beginning: Ending:			
	Story:			
Thursday	Beginning: Ending:			
	Story:			
Friday	Beginning: Ending:			
	Story:			

Qq WEEK

Quilts

Shapes

Friendship

Ask Questions

Dramatic Play

Friendship Card Factory

Children make a card for each child in the class

Learning Objectives

Physical and Motor

- Copies and draws simple shapes and letters
- Swings arms when walking
- Uses left or right hand predominantly

Cognitive

- Names simple shapes
- Knows some names of coins and bills (money)

Communication and Language

- Uses language to control and give directions
- Uses pronouns in sentences

Social and Emotional

- Makes simple choices (between two objects or two ideas)
- Has an increasing attention span

Approaches to Learning

- Purposefully explores new things or ideas

Listening Activities and Songs

- Song: "The Muffin Man" (Traditional)
- *Qq* Poem

"The Muffin Man"

Do you know the muffin man, the muffin man, the muffin man?
Do you know the muffin man who lives in Drury Lane?

Oh, yes, we know the muffin man, the muffin man, the muffin man.
Oh, yes, we know the muffin man who lives in Drury Lane.

TIP This week, change the words to practice the names of the children's streets.

Do you know my good friend Sue, my good friend Sue, my good friend Sue?
Do you know my good friend Sue who lives on Shady Lane?

TIP The story ***Sweet Clara and the Freedom Quilt*** could be saved for *Kk* Week when cartography (map making) is discussed.

Stories

- *The Quilt* by Ann Jonas
- *The Quiet Book* by Deborah Underwood
- *The Patchwork Quilt* by Valerie Flournoy
- *The Josephina Story Quilt* by Eleanor Coerr
- *The Keeping Quilt* by Patricia Polacco
- *The Three Questions* by Jon J. Muth
- *The Quiltmaker's Gift* by Jeff Brumbeau
- *Sweet Clara and the Freedom Quilt* by Deborah Hopkinson

Qq **Poem**

Queen Q was writing questions in her brand new book.

King Quail was singing, "quack, quack, quack," and everyone turned to look.

Queen Q whispered, qu . . ., qu . . ., qu . . ., quiet!

CIRCLE TIME

Interactive Charts and Props

- Create your own What Keeps Me Warm on a Cold Winter Day? interactive chart.

- A real quilt or photos of quilts
- Create your own Question Words Chart.

?? Question Words ??	
Who	is in your family?
What	is your name?
When	is your birthday?
Where	do you live?
Why	do you like school?
How	old are you?

- A decorated question box

Circle Time Activities

- Introduce the letter *Qq*.
- Tell the children about the project for the week: to make a friendship card for each classmate. Explain that each day during CIRCLE TIME, you will give the children a new idea for a card they can make (see CRAFTS on page 148 for a number of handmade card ideas). Pass out a class first-name list.

Have the children find their name and check to be sure it is correct. Next, give each child a pocket folder. Tell them, "This is your folder to keep your friendship cards in." When they sit down for TABLE WORK, have them put their name on their folder and cross their own name off the name list, because they do not need to make a card for themselves. Show the children the cards already stamped with TO: and FROM: and show them where their name and their friend's name belong.

- Sing **"Do You Know the Muffin Man?"** Then change the words to practice the street names of the children.
- Practice the ***Qq* Poem.**
- Tell the children about quilts. Read one of the quilt stories listed under STORIES to further explain. Explain the WORKBENCH activity and the QUILT CRAFT activity. Show the children a real quilt, or at least photos of some quilts. Review shapes and then look for different shapes in the quilts—notice how they all fit together. It's like a puzzle!
- Use the interactive chart **What Keeps Me Warm on a Cold Winter Day?** Think of lots of answers to give everyone a turn.
- Explain the word *question*. Talk about the question words: *who*, *what*, *when*, *where*, *how*, and *why*. Look at the **Question Words Chart.** Ask each child a question. Then, to practice, let each child ask the teacher or a classmate a question.

TABLE WORK

- Using the decorated **Question Box**, play a "guess what's in the box game." Tell the children to each take a turn asking you a question that will help them guess what you have placed in the box. Let a few children make a guess until someone guesses correctly. For fun, don't tell who guessed correctly and let them vote on which answer they think is correct. Show what's in the Question Box! Show the children how to play the **Guess Who?** game by Winning Moves Games.

- Gather one hundred pennies, four quarters, and a dollar bill. Count twenty-five pennies; do it four times to make four piles of pennies. Ask the children to remember when you talked about pizza and fractions during *Pp* Week. Draw a circle, a line through the middle to show half, and another line to show one-quarter. Now compare the circle to the money that you just counted. That's why it's called a quarter!

- Read the Hernando or Harriet story. Pass the puppet on to the next child.

Write friendship cards at the start of TABLE WORK each day this week (see CIRCLE TIME).

- Practice writing the letter of the week. Practice writing the letter *Qq*.

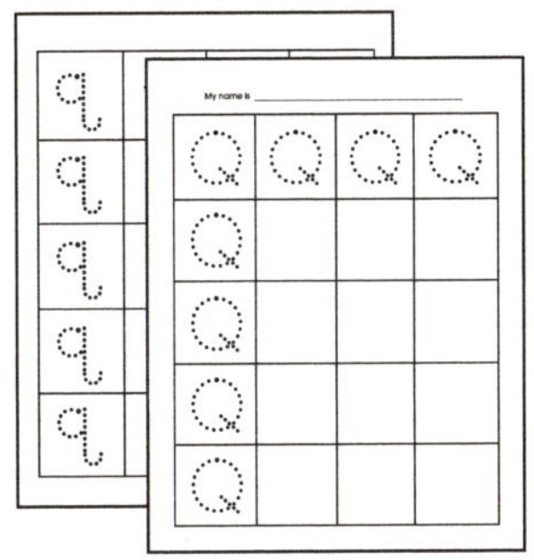

*

- Phonics Sheet for the letter *Qq*

*

- Practice Drawing Shapes

*

- **Journal** Write *A quarter is 25¢*. Use a quarter and a crayon to make a "rubbing" of the front and back of the coin.

NOTE: During FREE CHOICE PLAY

Complete the "Mom Questionnaire" with children individually during FREE CHOICE PLAY. (If children don't have a mom, encourage them to fill out the questionnaire about another special family member.)

*

FREE CHOICE PLAY

Writing Center

Skip the Alphabet Stamps this week and use the writing table as an activity center for making cards. (The children will be doing lots of writing this week!)

Board Games

- Any shapes lotto
- Guess Who? by Winning Moves Games
- Qwirkle by MindWare

TIP Qwirkle is a great game, but to make it more child-friendly, use only four colors and four shapes and simplify the scoring.

Sensory Table

Have a Quack Race. Gather identical small rubber ducks, heavy clear glass bowls, and large spoons or ladles. Make a mark on each bowl at exactly the same depth. Put a rubber duck in each bowl. Say, "Get set . . . go!" Start filling the bowl, one spoonful at a time, until the rubber duck and the water level gets up to the mark on the bowl. If they don't figure it out, show them that if they are careful, less water spills when filling the bowl!

Workbench

Make a class fleece quilt. This project uses the small fleece squares (see "Working with Fleece" in *Yy* Week). Use a large roll of paper, at least thirty-six inches wide. Lay the heavy roll behind the workbench and bring up the paper to rest on the surface. Make the first row by gluing a row of squares evenly across the bottom edge of the paper so the quilt starts out level.

TIP Glue the first row of squares in a pattern to give the children the idea.

After a week of gluing rows of fleece squares, simply trim off the paper edges and hang up the quilt.

TIP Try hanging the soft fleece quilt in the hallway with a sign that says "PLEASE TOUCH!"

Easel Art

Put the easel away to make room for a card-making activity.

Crafts

- **Quilt Craft Activity:** Cut a supply of squares from old wallpaper books or decorative paper, sized to fit the "__________ 's Quilt" Reproducible. Children should draw a face and hair, then do all coloring first. Lastly, glue a pre-cut square to each of the nine squares to create a colorful quilt.

TIP Use the fleece squares from the WORKBENCH activity. Cut in fourths to make a soft quilt.

- **Handmade Card Suggestions** (Make four heart patterns: small, medium, large, and very large.)

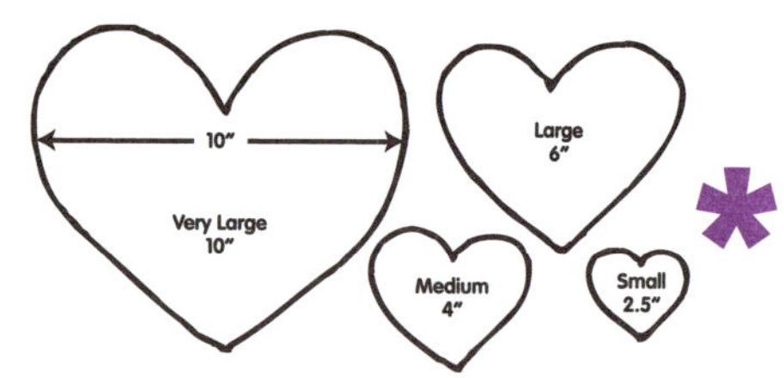

1. Pattern Cards: Using two colors, trace one of each of the four different-sized hearts, onto

full and half sheets of construction paper. Stamp TO and FROM on the "very large" heart. Children choose two different colors and cut out all the hearts which is eight. Put the hearts in four piles: small, medium, large, and very large. Glue one on top of the other from "very large to small" in an ABAB pattern, alternating the two colors. (Be sure the TO and FROM shows on the back of the "very large" heart.) This makes two cards at a time!

2. **Hanging Card:** Cut a "large" heart pattern in half, then punch five holes evenly spaced around the edge of the pattern. Use a half sheet of construction paper and fold in half. Trace the "half large" heart pattern on the fold. Mark a dot in each of the five holes punched. Stamp TO and FROM inside the folded heart. The child cuts the half heart and punches the five holes while the paper is still folded. When the heart is opened, there are ten holes and the TO and FROM is on one side. Thread a piece of yarn or ribbon through the holes, starting at one hole at the top of the heart—don't pull all the way through, leave a few inches—and ending at the hole on the other side of the heart at the top. Tie the two ends of yarn or ribbon loosely, leaving enough space to hang the heart on a hook or doorknob.

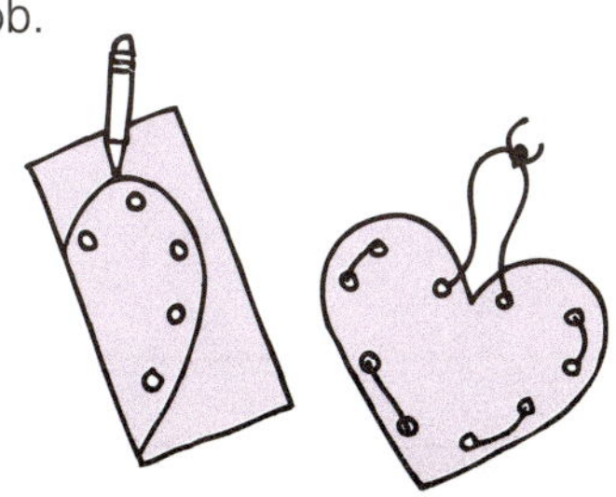

3. **Hi There! Card:** Fold a half sheet of construction paper in half. Trace the "medium" heart pattern with the side edge against the fold. Children cut out the heart, being careful not to cut the fold edge. Open and punch two eye holes on the front of the card. Refold the card and carefully make a dot with a marker in the opening of each eye hole. Open the card and glue a moveable eye on each dot. Children can draw more of the face with the marker if they wish. Write "Hi there!" on the inside of the card. The TO and FROM stamp should be on the back of the card.

4. **Heart Friend:** Trace one "large heart" and four "small hearts" on a sheet of construction paper. Stamp TO and FROM on the back of the "large heart." Cut out all five hearts.

Punch two holes on each side of the "large heart." Using two ten-inch pieces of yarn, thread one piece of yarn in and out of the two holes on each side of the "large heart." Tape a "small heart" to each end to be the hands and feet of the Heart Friend. Glue on moveable eyes. Draw eyelashes and a big smile.

5. **Stamp a Friendship Message:** Trace the "very large" heart pattern on manila or construction paper and stamp TO and FROM on the back. Set up a table with a stamp pad and alphabet stamps to spell a message. For example, "I LOVE YOU" or "BE MY FRIEND." Make a display for the children to copy.

TIP This card-making activity could be set up at the WRITING CENTER.

6. **Encourage the children to use their imaginations:** Fold half sheets of construction paper in half to make a card. Stamp TO and FROM on the inside of the card. Gather ribbon, yarn, paper doilies, buttons, sequins, wallpaper and construction paper scraps, paper quilt squares, crayons and markers, etc. Children can be creative and decorate the front of the card.

7. **On the last day of the week, try Marble Painting Cards:** (See CRAFTS in *Hh* Week on how to marble paint.) Trace the "very large" heart pattern on manila paper, stamp the TO and FROM on one side, and marble paint the other side to decorate. This activity is a quick way to finish the last few cards when children begin to lose interest. Moreover, marble painting is a great solution if a child is absent and needs to catch up.

	Circle Time	Table Work	Free Choice Play	Crafts
Monday	Beginning: Ending:			
	Story:			
Tuesday	Beginning: Ending:			
	Story:			
Wednesday	Beginning: Ending:			
	Story:			
Thursday	Beginning: Ending:			
	Story:			
Friday	Beginning: Ending:			
	Story:			

Vv WEEK

How to Mail a Letter

Addresses

Patterns

Dramatic Play

Friendship Card Factory continued from last week. Add a Post Office with a mail slot for each child and teacher.

Learning Objectives

Physical and Motor

- Balances well
- Makes marks or strokes with drawing tools
- Uses small muscles in hands to color, cut, paste, and paint

Cognitive

- Recognizes own name in print
- Sorts or describes objects by one or more attributes

Communication and Language

- Knows book and print rules
- Pronounces words and letter sounds correctly

Social and Emotional

- Shows increasing patience
- Sows increasing responsibility

Approaches to Learning

- Approaches new situations with increasing flexibility

Listening Activities and Songs

- Song: "The More We Get Together" (Traditional)
- Song: "A-Tisket, A-Tasket" (Traditional)
- Use an audio recorder to record voices—first other teachers and staff, then the children's voices (explanation at CIRCLE TIME).

"A-Tisket, A-Tasket"

Change the words to:
A-tisket, a-tasket,
on my arm a basket.
I wrote a letter to my friend and on the way I lost it . . . I lost it . . .

Teacher answers,
"I found it . . . I found it . . . "

The first time, ask:
"Who lives on Shady Lane?"

The next time, say:
"This person lives on Shady Lane. What's your house number?"

Finally, say:
"This is Tommy's letter. Tommy, what is your address?"

Stories

- *Dear Annie* by Judith Caseley
- *Delivering Your Mail: A Book about Mail Carriers* by Ann Owen
- *It Came in the Mail* by Ben Clanton
- *Growing Vegetable Soup* by Lois Ehlert
- *The Velveteen Rabbit* by Margery Williams
- *Verdi* by Janell Cannon
- *Sally Goes to the Vet* by Stephen Huneck
- *My Mouth Is a Volcano!* by Julia Cook

CIRCLE TIME

Interactive Charts and Props

- Seven Steps to Mail a Letter Cards

- Create your own What's on the Envelope Poster (address, return address, stamp).

- Have an envelope for each child with their house number and street.

Circle Time Activities

- Introduce the letter *Vv*.

- Discuss the **What's on an Envelope Poster.** Be sure to talk about what city and state you live in. And don't forget the zip code. It really is a secret code for the Post Office!

- Explain the easel art for the week (see EASEL ART on page 154).

- Give the children the envelopes you have prepared with their house number and street name. Show them that each one is different because they all live at a different address (unless there are siblings in the class). Teach the children the song **"A-Tisket, A-Tasket"** using the original words. Collect the letters, put them in a basket, and explain to the children you are going to change the words of the song and play a game. You can walk around the outside of the circle the first time and drop one of the envelopes in the middle of the circle. You sit down, pick up the envelope and sing: "I found it . . . I found it . . ." Use the **first-time words** to help the children learn their street name. The child whose letter is found can carry the basket and walk around the circle. Repeat the game until all letters have been lost.

  (Words to the full song can be found in the LISTENING ACTIVITIES AND SONGS section.)

  (Sing and play this game three consecutive days at CIRCLE TIME, learning more of the children's addresses each day.)

- Look at and discuss the **Seven Steps to Mail a Letter Cards.**

- Ahead of time, record the voices of adults in your program giving a little message to your class—but don't let them give away who it is. Play the messages and see if the children can guess who is speaking to them by listening to the sound of their voice. Now make a recording of all the children speaking. Have them each tell three things: "Hi, my name is _______. I live on _______ street. I like to play _______." (Set up a listening center so the children can listen to their friend's voices at FREE CHOICE PLAY.)

- Use the Pattern Cards from *Pp* Week and the Color Bears from Week 2 to review patterns.

TABLE WORK

- To introduce the board game **ABC Match and Learn** by Scholastic, place each of the cards from the game in an envelope. Pass out an envelope to each child—there may be a few extras because there are twenty-six cards—one for each letter of the alphabet. Begin with the extras. Open each envelope and tell what letter of the alphabet the card represents. Each child takes a turn to open her envelope and tell what's on her card and what letter it begins with. Briefly explain how to play the board game.

- Read the Hernando or Harriet story. Pass the puppet on to the next child.

- Practice writing the letter of the week. Practice writing the letter *Vv*.

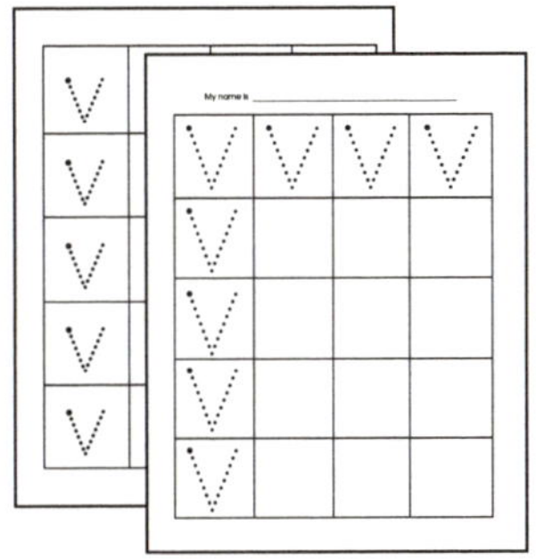

- Phonics Sheet for the letter *Vv*

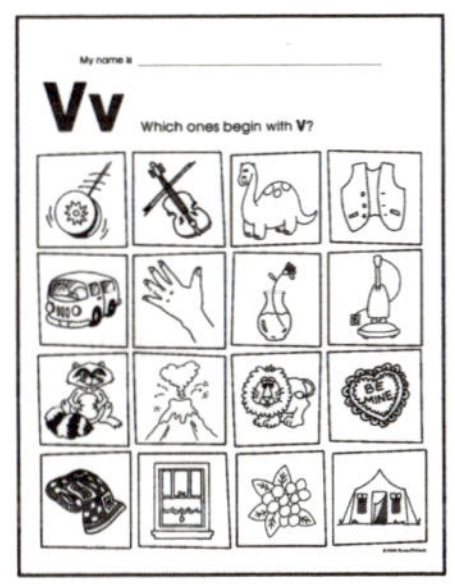

- Color a Heart Pattern Reproducible (Display pattern cards used in *Pp* Week: ABABAB, AABBAABB, AABAAB, ABBABBA.)

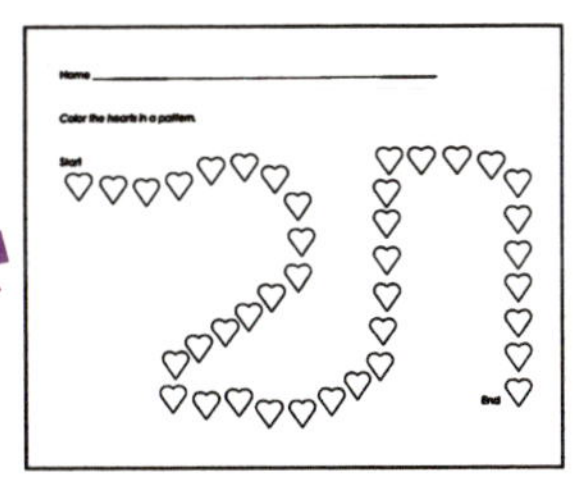

- **Journal** Write: *My address*
  Glue each child's envelope with his address in the journal. (Use the envelope from Interactive Charts and Props on p. 152) Help each child find the line with his house number and street on his envelope. Copy his house number and street name in his journal.

FREE CHOICE PLAY

Writing Center

Alphabet Stamps

Board Games

- ABC Match and Learn Game by Scholastic
- Keep board games out from *Qq* Week

Sensory Table

Four pairs of chopsticks, large bowl of heart erasers, four small bowls, timer, and dice. Show the children how to hold the chopsticks, and let them practice moving hearts from one bowl to the other. Use the timer and dice to make up simple games.

TIP Children can use tweezers if chopsticks are too difficult, but give them enough time and encouragement to learn a new skill.

Workbench

Explain to the children how a vice can help at the workbench. Place a piece of soft pine in the vice and let the children take turns using the handsaw. Remember the safety rules: Always wear goggles and keep two hands on the saw. Remember, a sign-up sheet can be placed near the workbench so the children don't waste time waiting for a turn with the saw.

Easel Art

When the **Shapes Around the House** project was done during *Oo* Week, the frame of the house cut-out was saved for this project. Ahead of time glue the house frame on easel paper. Also write each child's street name on a brightly colored strip of construction paper, leaving space for house numbers. Provide enough of each number from 0–9 traced for all the children's house numbers. At the easel, children paint inside the frame of the house. Let the painting dry overnight. The next day, display the street name strips for the child to choose their street, then glue on the correct house numbers. Glue the address strip to the house painting. Hang the houses for a beautiful display!

Crafts

- Leave out card-making supplies from last week to continue making friendship cards for friends and family.
- Put out a basket of shape stencils to trace. Use the stencils to make patterns the children can decorate.

CLASS CRAFT:
Make a photo card for a favorite staff person at the school. We make a card for our custodian. The card says "We love you, Mr. (or Ms.) ____________." Trace the letters needed for the message. Have each child color one letter—add hearts to color if there are more children than letters. When everyone has finished, pose the children and take a photo.

Notes & Evaluations

	Circle Time	Table Work	Free Choice Play	Crafts
Monday	Beginning: Ending:			
	Story:			
Tuesday	Beginning: Ending:			
	Story:			
Wednesday	Beginning: Ending:			
	Story:			
Thursday	Beginning: Ending:			
	Story:			
Friday	Beginning: Ending:			
	Story:			

Ww WEEK

Water

Wind

Worms

Days of Week

Weight

Weaving

Dramatic Play

Laundry

Washer, dryer, clothesline with clothespins, doll clothes, ironing board, and iron.

Learning Objectives

Physical and Motor

- Uses left or right hand predominantly
- Copies and draws simple shapes and letters

Cognitive

- Has increasing memory
- Knows half or more letter names

Communication and Language

- Argues, reasons, and uses *because*
- Listens for details

Social and Emotional

- Makes friends
- Plays alone

Approaches to Learning

- Works at tasks despite distractions and interruptions

Listening Activities and Songs

- Any "days of the week" jingle
- Song: "The Mulberry Bush" (Traditional)
- Song: "He's Got the Whole World in His Hands" (Traditional)

Stories

- *Abuela's Weave* by Omar S. Castañeda
- *Weaving the Rainbow* by George Ella Lyon
- *Wonderful Worms* by Linda Glaser
- *Wiggling Worms at Work* by Wendy Pfeffer
- *The Wind Blew* by Pat Hutchins
- *The Red Balloon* by A. Lamorisse
- *Tillie and the Wall* by Leo Lionni
- *Whistle For Willie* by Ezra Jack Keats
- *Mirette on the High Wire* by Emily Arnold McCully
- "The Boy Who Cried Wolf" in *Tell It Again! 2* by Rebecca Isbell and Shirley C. Raines
- *Water Dance* by Thomas Locker

CIRCLE TIME

Interactive Charts and Props

- Create your own Days of the Week cards and a blank calendar chart.
- Two small weaving frames

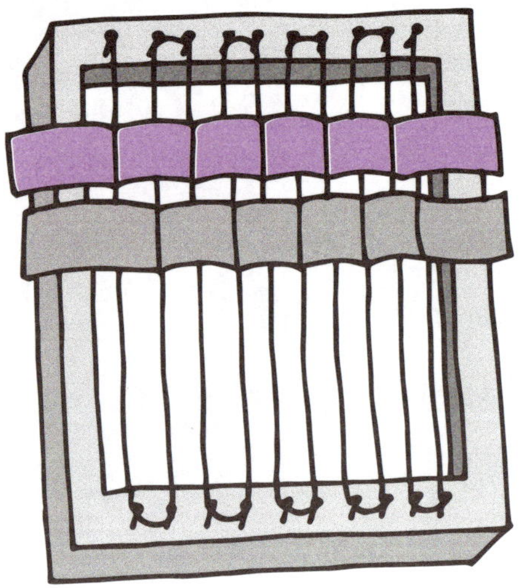

- Globe of the world
- Wagon (any size—to collect word cards)

Circle Time Activities

- Introduce the letter *Ww*.
- Explain that this week, each child will weave a placemat. It can be taken home when completed. Demonstrate how to weave on a large frame (anything could be used—a ladder, a fence, or a frame made from a large cardboard box). Give each child a turn to weave on the large frame. The class can say, "Over, under, over, under . . ." as each child weaves.

TIP Ask for extra adult help this week if possible, so when each child is weaving there is at least one adult to assist two children.

- Allow the children to observe while you mix the paint to be used at EASEL ART this week. Explain that water in the ocean is many colors of blue. Use different amounts of blue, blue + white, blue + green, and blue + green + white to create the various colors to paint the water.
- Sing **"Days of the Week"** jingle. Show the children the **Blank Calendar Chart** and the **Days of the Week cards.** Look at the calendar for the current month that is displayed on the bulletin board in the classroom. Now set up a calendar for the upcoming month. Show how you know where to begin and fill in the numbers. Practice saying the days of the week by going around and around the circle, with each child saying a day. When you do this four or five times around the circle, each time the children will answer a different day. (If the total number of children is a multiple of seven, then you can join the activity.)

TIP This is a great activity while the class is gathered and you have a few minutes to spare—just circle up and practice the days of the week.

- Sing **"The Mulberry Bush."** Each verse sings about a day of the week. It may also give children a few new ideas for ways to play in the laundry DRAMATIC PLAY area.
- Show the children water in different forms—solid, liquid, and gas. Then explore the properties of water:
  - **Water evaporates**. Set up two glass bowls with equal amounts of water. Cover one tightly with plastic wrap. Record the results every day.
  - **Water can be absorbed**. Try a terry cloth towel and a paper towel and see which one absorbs more water.
  - **Water magnifies**. Fill a large glass jar with water and drop in a few items that will sink. Place those same items outside the jar. Even though they are the same size, do the items in the jar look bigger?
  - **And water can even affect sound**. Set up three glasses filled with different amounts of water. Tap the glasses and listen to the different sounds (see SENSORY TABLE on page 160).

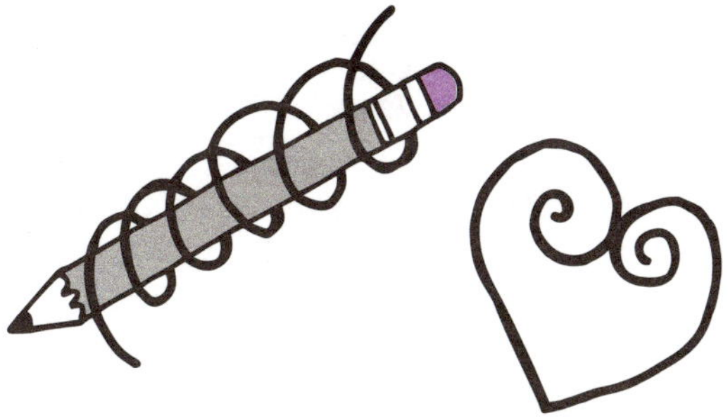

- Use a pliable length of plastic-coated wire to create wire sculptures. Demonstrate how to mold the wire into shapes, wrap the wire around a pencil to form a corkscrew, form shapes using cookie cutters, etc. Tell the children the wire sculpting will be at the WORKBENCH.

- Using a food scale and a balance scale, weigh different items found in the classroom (different sizes of blocks work well). Tell the children to try holding a different item in each hand, then close their eyes and see if they can feel which is heavier. For fun, bring out four brown paper "mystery bags," each one heavier than the other. Ask the children to lift the bags and place them in order from heavy to light. Finally, weigh each bag to see if they guessed correctly. Use items of various sizes—try a bigger item that is lightweight and a small item that is heavy—to show that size does not always indicate weight.

- Sing **"He's Got the Whole World in His Hands."** Talk to the children about taking care of our world. Look at a **globe** and discuss.

- Ask the children if they can guess this riddle:

  I am small and hard to find.
  I am weak but I am kind.
  I am quiet; I make no sound.
  I am a helper, the best around.
  When I move, I must wiggle.
  If you touch me, you may giggle.
  Look for me in the garden.
  (*Answer:* an earthworm)

  To learn about earthworms, read one of the books about worms. After a rain, go outside and dig for earthworms so the children can see them up close. Be sure to put them back in the ground so they can do their work!

- Review the alphabet letters learned so far. First, practice letter recognition. (If you are learning ASL, practice signing each letter.) Next explain that letters are used to make words. Show the children that many words can be made from the letters they've learned so far. (See the reproducible used for TABLE WORK for a list of letters and words.) Print each word on a card and place them in a path on the floor. Bring in a **wagon** and make a sign for it that says "Word Wagon." Go for a walk with the wagon and pick up words!

- Read ***The Wind Blew*** by Pat Hutchins. Have children tap a beach ball to keep it up in the air. When the ball touches the floor, the child must sit down. Last child standing is the winner!

- Teach the children the water tricks set up in the SENSORY TABLE (see SENSORY TABLE, Day 4).

- Read the Hernando or Harriet story. Pass the puppet on to the next child.

- Practice writing the letter of the week. Practice writing the letter *Ww*.

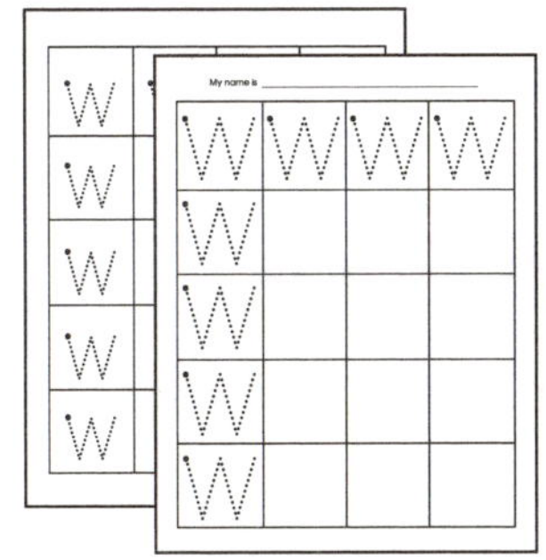

- Phonics Sheet for the letter *Ww*

- Letters and Words Reproducible

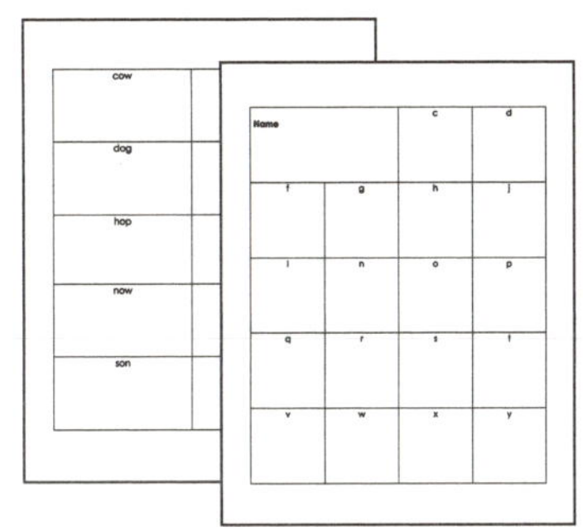

- **Journal** Write *My backpack weighs* ______. Have the children look inside their backpack and draw what is inside that makes it weigh so much (children could also weigh five blocks, a number of books, and so forth).

Ww WEEK

FREE CHOICE PLAY

Writing Center

Alphabet Stamps

Board Games

• Wild Woods by Discovery Toys

• Scrabble Junior by Hasbro

Sensory Table

Use the sensory table for a variety of water activities and experiments each day of the week:

Day 1. Freeze four or five very large ice blocks (food storage containers are a good size—varied sizes could be used). Float the ice blocks in a small amount of water. Set up a timer and see how long it takes for the solid water to turn to liquid water. Ask, "Do larger blocks take longer to melt? How much longer?"

Day 2. Place a few small washcloths and sponges in the water. Teach the children to wring out the washcloths and sponges so they don't drip.

TIP This activity strengthens children's hands and is great practice for when they want to help wipe tables with you!

Day 3. Experiment with how water can affect sound. Place a wire rack in the table that will hold a few glasses above the water level. The children can fill the glasses with different amounts of water and tap the glasses with a rubber tapper and listen to the sounds. Does more water make the pitch higher or lower?

Day 4. Save at least four water bottles with the lids. Make three holes in a row on the bottom of each bottle with a hot nail. After demonstrating the water tricks at CIRCLE TIME, leave the water bottles in the sensory table.

Trick one: turn the water on and off. When the bottle is filled with water, screwing the top off and on will start and stop the water sprinkling from the holes.

Trick two: tie a knot with water. While the water is sprinkling from the holes, pull together and pinch the three streams of water with your fingertips—the three become one stream of water!

Workbench

Remind the children of the rule to always **wear goggles at the workbench.** Place goggles, a pair of wire cutters, a variety of widths of dowel rods, and different-shaped cookie cutters at the workbench. Ahead of time, cut wire in twelve-inch lengths and loosely coil it. (A long length of wire is not easily managed and can be unsafe for young children.)

TIP Save the children's wire art by sticking them in a piece of Styrofoam. Cover the Styrofoam with silver paper and display with the art gallery at the end of the school year. Alexander Calder is an artist that the children will study later in Artist Week; he made mobiles and wire sculptures.

Easel Art

Trace whales on a full sheet of gray construction paper. First, before painting at the easel, the children cut out the whale. Second, using the various hues of blue that were mixed at CIRCLE TIME, paint water on the bottom half of the easel paper. Next, glue the whale so it is floating on the surface of the water. Finally, paint water spouting from the whale's blowhole.

*

Crafts

- Each child will take a turn weaving a placemat. Ahead of time, cut into strips different colors of 1-by-12-inch construction paper. An adult needs to string a small weaving frame with yarn to prepare the loom before each child weaves a placemat. The children begin weaving the paper strips **over then under** the yarn. The second paper strip starts **under then over.** Sometimes the last strip is difficult to weave, so you may need to do it for them. Take the placemat off the loom very, very carefully. Later the placemats will need to be laminated to hold the woven strips securely. This project is time consuming, but it will be one of their favorites!

TIP Adult supervision is helpful for this project, so ask for extra adult help this week if possible. When each child is weaving, there should be at least one adult to assist two children.

- Paint with watercolors on paper.

- Ahead of time, press coffee filters flat by placing them under a stack of books. Children can draw a simple design on a coffee filter using two or three colors of washable markers. Place the decorated coffee filter on absorbent paper and spray lightly with water. The colors blend beautifully!

- Print some blank calendar pages. Display the calendar the class made at CIRCLE TIME for the upcoming month. The children can make their own calendar page to take home. Be sure to add a pretty picture at the top like other calendars.

- Make an apple with a "pony bead" worm. Trace apples on red, yellow, or green craft foam. Instruct the children to cut out the apple. Punch two holes in the apple to string the worm. Use a 12-inch piece of yarn and tape the tip of one end (like a shoelace) to make it easier to string the beads. Bring the yarn through one hole from the back of the apple and string on enough beads to be a worm, then through the second hole to the back. Tie the yarn in a knot and trim the ends.

Notes & Evaluations

	Circle Time	Table Work	Free Choice Play	Crafts
Monday	Beginning: Ending:			
	Story:			
Tuesday	Beginning: Ending:			
	Story:			
Wednesday	Beginning: Ending:			
	Story:			
Thursday	Beginning: Ending:			
	Story:			
Friday	Beginning: Ending:			
	Story:			

Ee WEEK

Elephants

Earth

Entomology (study of bugs)

Estimate

Dramatic Play

Zoo Hospital

A variety of stuffed zoo animals with doctor instruments and lots of bandages

Learning Objectives

Physical and Motor

- Balances or hops on one foot
- Runs with ease and stops quickly
- Uses small muscles in hands to color, cut, paste, and paint

Cognitive

- Draws basic shapes and expressive art
- Matches objects

Communication and Language

- Tells stories without prompting
- Understands the meaning of most preschool words (semantics)

Social and Emotional

- Shows independence
- Shares

Approaches to Learning

- Creates stories, imagining and describing things or situations that do not exist

Listening Activities and Songs

- Song: "Do Your Ears Hang Low?" (Traditional)
- Chant: "We're Going on a Bear Hunt" (Echo the leader)
- "Elephant" poem (adapted from "Five Little Monkeys Swinging in a Tree")

"Elephant" poem

Five little monkeys swinging in a tree

Teasing Mr. Elephant, "You can't catch me, you can't catch me!"

Along came Mr. Elephant, quiet as can be *(speak very quietly)*

He s-t-r-e-t-c-h-e-d his trunk *(children stretch out one arm)*

And he snatched that monkey right out of that tree!

Stories

- *We're Going on a Bear Hunt* by Michael Rosen
- *We're Going on a Lion Hunt* adapted by Margery Cuyler
- *April Foolishness* by Teresa Bateman
- *The Grouchy Ladybug* by Eric Carle
- *The Elephants' Ears* by Catherine Chambers
- *Horton Hears a Who* by Dr. Seuss
- "The Curious Elephant's Child" in *Tell It Again! 2* by Rebecca Isbell and Shirley C. Raines
- *The Elves and the Shoemaker* by The Brothers Grimm
- *The Emperor's New Clothes* by Demi
- *The Empty Pot* by Demi

TIP To make bandages for the zoo animals, buy a yard of medium-weight interfacing at the fabric store (plain, not iron-on). Cut into 1–2-inch strips. Use scotch tape to secure the bandages.

CIRCLE TIME

Interactive Charts and Props

- Purchase a number chart 1–100 and make a sentence strip with the word *estimate* to hang above the chart. Place a jar of items for children to estimate with small papers and pencils for their guesses near the chart.

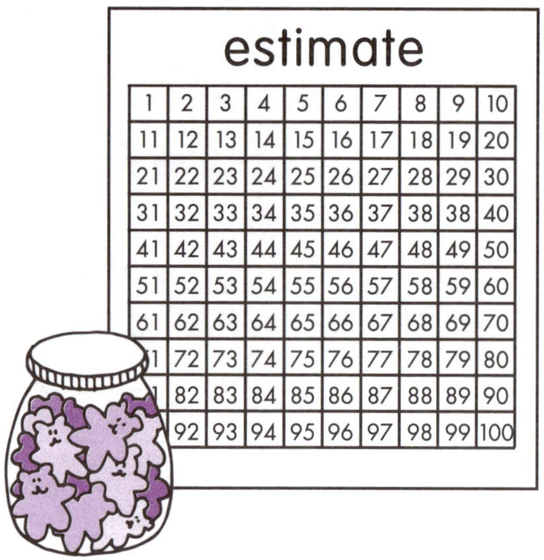

- ***Shelly Goes to the Zoo*** by Kentrell Martin
- Globe (keep it out from *Ww* Week)

Circle Time Activities

- Introduce the letter *Ee*.
- Ask the children, "Have you ever been to the zoo?" Discuss what they know about the zoo. Describe how most animals are in their natural habitat instead of cages, how the zoo helps endangered animals, etc. Talk about the DRAMATIC PLAY and how the zoo needs veterinarians to care for baby animals and sick animals.
- Have the children help make a list of all the animals that could live in a zoo. Show any pictures you have collected. Teach the children to play the game **Sequence for Kids** by Jax. Name all the zoo animals on the game board.

TIP This discussion will help the children think of what animal they want to draw at TABLE WORK.

- Sing **"Do Your Ears Hang Low?"** Sing the second verse too—"Do your ears stand high?" Ask the children to think about animals that they see at the zoo. Do the animal's ears hang low or do they stand high?
- Fill a clear glass jar with a small manipulative—like the color bears used for the game in Color Week. Place the jar in the center of the circle and ask each child to guess how many bears are in the jar. Record the guesses. Tell the children they just **estimated** how many bears were in the jar! Empty the jar and separate the bears by colors. Count each color and add them all together. Which was the closest guess? Tell the children, "Estimation is just a good guess—and you get better with practice!"

TIP Let the children try estimating again. Fill the jar with something else and put out slips of paper to write their guesses during FREE CHOICE PLAY.

- Teach the children simple facts about bugs. Tell them the study of bugs is called *entomology*. Display real or plastic bugs as a part of the DRAMATIC PLAY. Live ladybugs can be ordered and are easy to care for (www.insectlore.com). And the bugs can be released when the zoo hospital is put away.
- Teach the children to play the game **Snug as a Bug in a Rug** by Peaceable Kingdom.
- Use the book ***Shelly Goes to the Zoo*** by Kentrell Martin to teach the children American Sign Language for animals. After the children have practiced, take turns playing guess the animal game.
- Talk about telling the truth. Along with the children, retell the story of Pinocchio. On the same day read ***The Empty Pot*** by Demi at STORY TIME.
- Review how important it is to always be truthful. Explain the difference between a practical joke and being hurtful toward someone. Tell the children about April Fool's Day. Read the story ***April Foolishness*** by Teresa Bateman. Show the children the April

TABLE WORK

Fool's cup of hot chocolate they will make at FREE CHOICE PLAY (see CRAFTS on page 166 for instructions). Because it takes a few weeks to dry completely, this project needs to be made a long time before April 1. Look at a calendar and count how many days the project will stay at school to dry. Then the children can take it home to play an April Fool's joke on their families!

TIP The April Fool's cup of hot chocolate can also be done together at TABLE WORK.

- Look at the globe. Point out the blue water and the green land. Show them the map they will color and glue in their journals.

- Another word that begins with *Ee* is *energy*. Recycling has been discussed as a way to save energy, but see if the children can think of things they can do to save energy: turn off lights, close the refrigerator door, turn the faucet off, shallow water in the bathtub, cook two things at one time in the oven, *and* if children help with chores, other family members will save energy and time!

- Read the Hernando or Harriet story. Pass the puppet on to the next child.

- Practice writing the letter of the week. Practice writing the letter *Ee*.

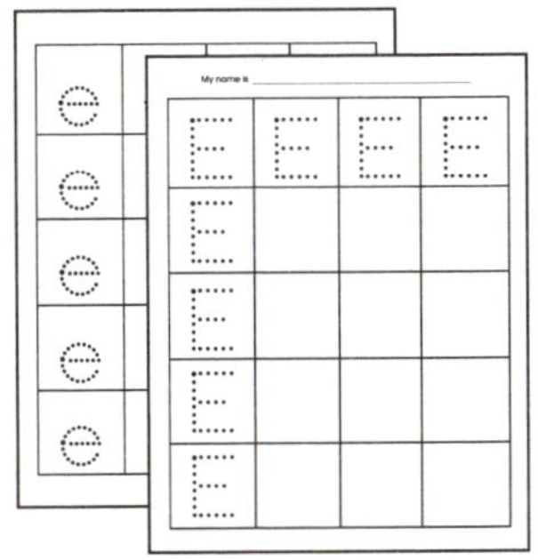

*

- Draw a zoo animal for a bulletin board display.

- Estimating and Counting Reproducible

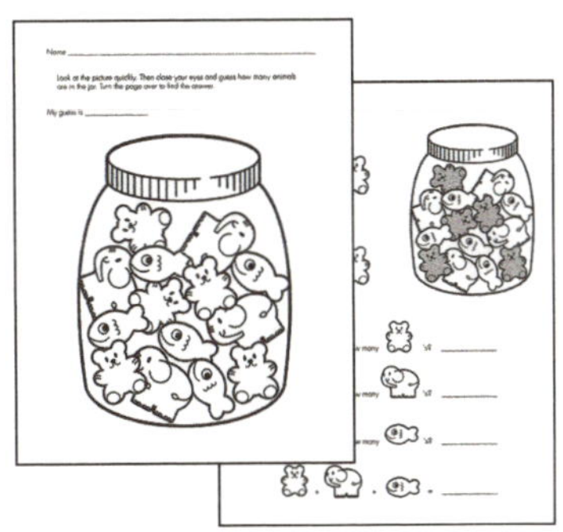

*

- First and Last Name Practice (mention that their last name is their family name).

*

- **Journal** Write *We live on the earth*. Color the water blue and the land green on the picture of the earth, then cut it out and glue in each child's journal.

FREE CHOICE PLAY

Writing Center

Alphabet Stamps

Board Games

- Sequence for Kids by Jax
- Snug as a Bug in a Rug by Peaceable Kingdom
- Elephant's Trunk by Gamewright

Sensory Table

Each child needs to make a name necklace. Purchase letter beads and tipped yarn at the craft or hobby store. Make a name card for each child to help him know what letters to find and in what order to string them. Spread the letters out in the sensory table to make them easy to find. Have children gather the letters needed, then sit down at a table with their name card and put the letters in order. String them carefully, one at a time, from the first letter to the last.

TIP When all necklaces are finished, add more beads so the children can make necklaces for themselves, friends, or siblings.

Workbench

Play **Swat the Bug!** You will need two flyswatters. Use the cards from any color, shape, or number lotto. Find a simple drawing of a bug and copy it as many times as you have cards from the lotto game. Make a copy of each card and glue all the colors, shapes, or numbers, one on each bug. These are the bugs to swat. Lay all the bugs on the surface of the workbench. Three players are needed—two to swat the bugs and one to use the lotto cards to call out which bug to swat. Whoever swats the correct bug first takes the card. The game continues until all the cards are swatted. The winner plays the card caller. This game is definitely a favorite!

Easel Art

After the children have drawn a zoo animal at TABLE WORK, place markers at the easel so they can draw more zoo animals to take home. Create a cover page so they can make a Zoo Book.

Crafts

- Trace a large circle on fingerpaint paper. Children cut out the circle. Fingerpaint the entire circle with blue and green paint. Immediately, while the paint is still wet, fold the circle in half and press. The two colors of paint will blend and the circle will look surprisingly like the earth.
- Make the April Fool's joke "a spilled cup of hot chocolate." The supplies needed are waxed paper, paper hot/cold cup, white glue, chocolate powder, plastic spoon, and marshmallows. Pour ½ inch of glue in the bottom of the cup, add 1 Tablespoon of chocolate powder, and stir with the plastic spoon. Tip the cup onto waxed paper and let the "chocolate glue" slowly spill a little

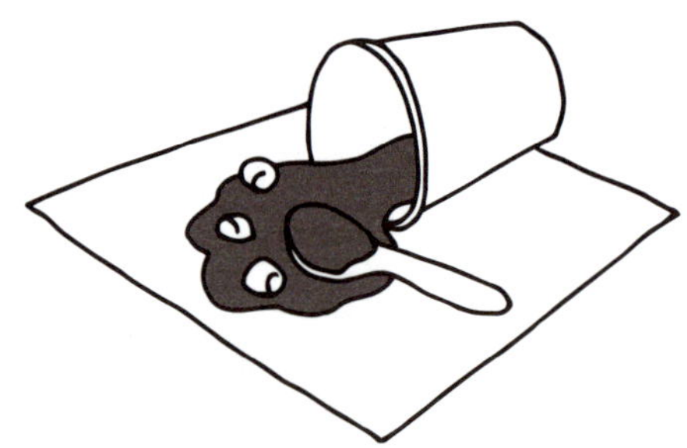

puddle. Leave the spoon just inside the cup and drop three marshmallows in the puddle (small, thick puddles are best). Carefully lift the cup and spill by the waxed paper and place it on a tray to dry.

TIP The April Fool's cup of hot chocolate can also be done together at TABLE WORK.

- Make stand-up elephants. Trace body and ears on folded gray construction paper, and trace tusks on white construction paper. Instruct the children to cut and assemble. (Remind them not to cut the fold so the elephant will stand up.) Tusks are taped behind the front legs and stick out in front of the trunk. Draw an eye on each side with a marker.

- Put out zoo animal stamps, stamp pads, and stencils for the children to use creatively. One fun idea is to have three-inch strips of green construction paper for the children to make tall grass for their animals to hide in. Tell the children to snip, snip, snip the green paper to make the grass. Glue along the bottom edge of their jungle drawing.

- Make a cage template and laminate it so it can be easily wiped clean. Children can cut pictures of zoo animals from old magazines. Glue them on drawing paper. Lay the template on top of each animal picture. Using gray or silver paint, fill in the template so it looks like the animals are in a cage.

- Make ears to go with the song: **"Do Your Ears Hang Low?"** Trace long oval ears on felt. Children will cut out the two ears and staple them to a headband.

Notes & Evaluations

	Circle Time	Table Work	Free Choice Play	Crafts
Monday	Beginning: Ending:			
	Story:			
Tuesday	Beginning: Ending:			
	Story:			
Wednesday	Beginning: Ending:			
	Story:			
Thursday	Beginning: Ending:			
	Story:			
Friday	Beginning: Ending:			
	Story:			

Zz WEEK

Zoo

Zebras

Sequencing and Ordinal Numbers

Dramatic Play

Zoo Hospital continued

Learning Objectives

Physical and Motor

- Makes marks or strokes with drawing tools
- Uses scissors

Cognitive

- Draws basic shapes and expressive art
- Expresses interest in creative movement

Communication and Language

- Understands the meaning of most preschool words (semantics)
- Makes up stories

Social and Emotional

- Takes turns
- Role-plays

Approaches to Learning

- Reflects on past experiences and applies information to new situations

Listening Activities and Songs

- Song: "There's a Hole in the Bucket" (Traditional)
- Song: "Going to the Zoo" by Tom Paxton (song with music is in the back of the book *Going to the Zoo* by Tom Paxton)
- Song: "Our City Has a Zoo E – I – E – I – O" (to the tune of "Old MacDonald")

"Our City Has A Zoo
E – I – E – I – O"
(to the tune of "Old MacDonald")

Our city has a zoo, E – I – E – I – O

And in our zoo there is a/an *[name an animal]*, E – I – E – I – O

With a *[ASL Sign for the animal]* here and a *[ASL Sign]* there, etc.

(use the animal signs learned last week in the book *Shelly Goes to the Zoo* by Kentrell Martin)

Adapted by Susan Ehrhardt

Stories

- *Zero the Hero* by Joan Holub
- *Owen & Mzee: The True Story of a Remarkable Friendship* by Isabella Hatkoff, Craig Hatkoff, and Dr. Paula Kahumbu
- *If Anything Ever Goes Wrong at the Zoo* by Mary Jean Hendrick
- *Zoomer* by Ned Young
- *Zero* by Kathryn Otoshi
- *Going to the Zoo* by Tom Paxton
- "Lazy Jack" in *Tell It Again! 2* by Rebecca Isbell and Shirley C. Raines
- *The Napping House* by Audrey Wood
- *Animal Strike at the Zoo. It's True!* by Karma Wilson

CIRCLE TIME

Interactive Charts and Props

- Create your own Our Family Went to the Zoo interactive chart

  Our family went to the zoo.
  We looked at lots of animals.
  What animal is looking at you?

  (pictures of zoo animals with a printed card for each animal)

- Make sentence strips for each verse of the song **"There's a Hole in the Bucket."** (Find or draw a picture to identify each sentence strip. Put magnets on the back so they can stick to the whiteboard.)

- Show-and-tell bags

Circle Time Activities

- Show-and-tell this week. Remind the children of the rules. Use the show-and-tell schedule and have each group of children give their presentation on the appropriate day.

- Introduce the letter *Zz*.

- Use the interactive chart **Our Family Went to the Zoo.** Be sure to give each child a turn.

- Teach the children what groups of animals are called, for example, a *pride* of lions, a *tower* of giraffes, a *crash* of rhinos, a *school* of jellyfish, a *troop* of monkeys, a *pod* of whales, and so forth.

- Read the book ***Going to the Zoo*** by Tom Paxton and sing the song at the end of the book.

- Show the children how to construct three paper plate zoo animals (see EASEL ART and CRAFTS on page 172 for explanation). Tell the children it is a two-day project. Carefully explain and label which pattern pieces go with each animal.

TIP Flat paper plates are much easier to work with. Just set some heavy books on stacks of a few plates overnight.

TABLE WORK

- Using a set of sequence cards, explain to the children how ordinal numbers are used to put the cards in order—for example, to set a table, you first lay the placemat, second the plate, third the napkin, fourth the silverware, and finally the glass. Now read ***The Napping House*** by Audrey Wood, and put the characters to bed in the correct order. Use ordinal number language to describe the sequence of the story.

- Review the animals learned from the book ***Shelly Goes to the Zoo*** by Kentrell Martin. Sing the song **"Our City Has a Zoo E – I – E – I – O."**

- Use the sentence strips made for the song **"There's a Hole in the Bucket"** to show the funny sequence.

- Read the Hernando or Harriet story. Pass the puppet on to the next child.

- Practice writing the letter of the week. Practice writing the letter *Zz*.

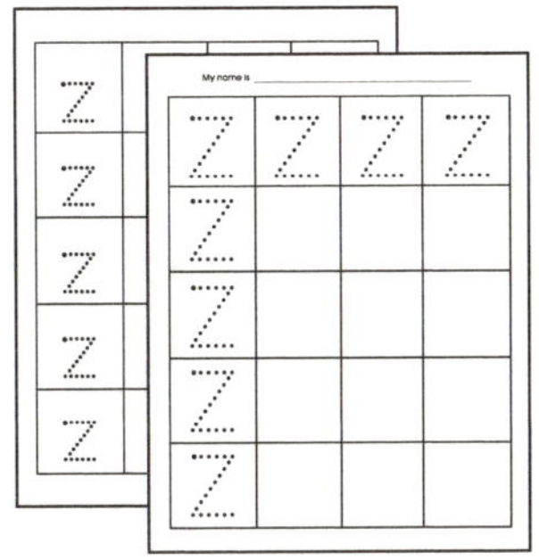

- Phonics Sheet for the letter *Zz*

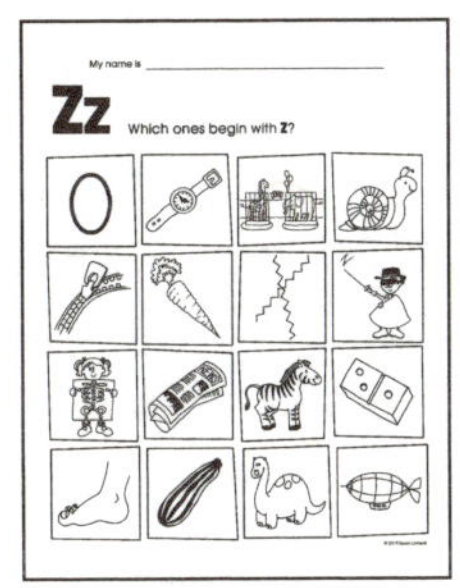

- Zoo Cage Slide with Elephant/Alligator Insert. To make the cages ahead of time, use the elephant/alligator page as a template to staple the cage bar strips in place. Be sure to staple the strips very close to the edge so the animal page slides freely when inserted.

TIP Explain to the children they are coloring two animals so they should choose a different color for each animal. Tell them to color very carefully!

- **Journal** Write *Zebras live at the zoo*. Using the book ***Ed Emberley's Big Green Drawing Book***, demonstrate step-by-step how to draw a zebra for the children on the whiteboard so they can look at each step while they are drawing in their journals. (Use the Prata Ponies illustration on pages 10 and 11 of the drawing book, and add stripes for a zebra.)

FREE CHOICE PLAY

Writing Center

Alphabet Stamps

Board Games

- Sequence for Kids by Jax
- Zimbbos! by Blue Orange
- Elephant's Trunk by Gamewright

Sensory Table

Make a habitat for small rubber zoo animals using homemade moon sand (see *Dd* Week for the recipe). Add rocks and small tree branches like a real zoo does. The children can collect these during outside time.

Workbench

Make cages using shoe boxes. Cut a rectangular opening in the top of the box. Punch holes along the top and bottom of the cut edge. Use yarn to string the bars of the cage, taping at the beginning and end. Cut out or draw pictures of animals to put on the back (bottom of the shoe box) of the cage. The children could also use the shoe box cages to play with some of the small rubber animals from the SENSORY TABLE. Label the cages with what kind of animal is inside.

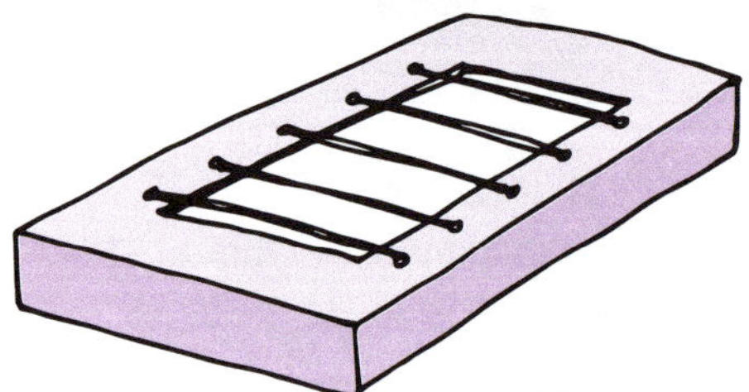

Inside view of box lid

Easel Art

Painting the paper plate on **Day 1** is the first step in making the paper plate zoo animals. Paint a plate brown for the bear, orange for the tiger, and black stripes for the zebra. Paint the plates completely and allow them to dry overnight.

TIP To assemble the animals on **Day 2,** see the instructions in CRAFTS.

Crafts

- Leave out magazines and art supplies to make zoo books this week.
- Move the letter beads from the SENSORY TABLE to the craft shelf. Add more types of beads so children can make necklaces and bracelets for themselves, friends, and siblings.
- Leave out ***Ed Emberley's Big Green Drawing Book*** so children can draw more animals.
- Add zigzag scissors for cutting and rickrack for decorating their artwork.

- Find coloring pages of zoo animals to color. Then cut them into a few pieces to make a puzzle. You could also cut them into pieces, mix them up, and glue them together to make "funny zoo animals."

- To construct the paper plate zoo animals on **Day 2**, follow the instructions for each animal. Have the construction paper pieces traced ahead of time (see the illustration for what is needed).

  Bear: Cut out the tan face circle and ears, then glue on the brown painted plate as shown. Cut out the black eyes, nose, and mouth, then glue to complete the bear.

  Tiger: A black pipe cleaner cut in thirds is needed for the tiger's whiskers. Pinch the three cut pipe cleaners together and staple in the center. Bend them apart to look like whiskers. Cut the orange ears, then glue as shown. Cut the black eyes and stripes, then glue to complete the tiger.

  Zebra: Cut out the black eyes, ears, nose, and mane. Clip the top of one black triangle as shown, so it looks like the zebra's mane. Glue the pieces in place to complete the zebra.

Notes & Evaluations

	Circle Time	Table Work	Free Choice Play	Crafts
Monday	Beginning: Ending:			
	Story:			
Tuesday	Beginning: Ending:			
	Story:			
Wednesday	Beginning: Ending:			
	Story:			
Thursday	Beginning: Ending:			
	Story:			
Friday	Beginning: Ending:			
	Story:			

Ii WEEK

Imagination

Ice Cream

Illusion/Magic

Musical Instruments

Dramatic Play

Ice Cream Parlor

Make or buy very large white, brown, and pink pom-poms for ice cream.

Learning Objectives

Physical and Motor

- Balances well
- Uses small muscles in hands to color, cut, paste, and paint

Cognitive

- Matches objects
- Develops elaborate play themes

Communication and Language

- Uses language to say what they feel, want, and need
- Answers questions about familiar stories

Social and Emotional

- Plays with peers sharing ideas and toys
- Plays simple games with rules

Approaches to Learning

- Reflects on past experiences and applies information to new situations

Listening Activities and Songs

- Song: "If You're Happy and You Know It" (Traditional)
  . . . tap the drum . . . ring the bell . . . shake the maraca . . . etc.
- Song: "The Busy Family Song" (to the tune of "A-Hunting We Will Go"—see *Mm* Week)

TIP This is a long song that takes some time to learn. Begin practicing the song this week. The words can be found at the end of *Mm* Week under **Magic Show** on page 191.

Stories

- *Christina Katerina & the Box* by Patricia Lee Gauch
- *A Box Can Be Many Things* by Dana Meachen Rau
- *Not A Box* by Antoinette Portis
- *Regards to the Man in the Moon* by Ezra Jack Keats
- *Oh, the Thinks You Can Think!* by Dr. Seuss
- *Duck! Rabbit!* by Amy Krouse Rosenthal and Tom Lichtenheld
- *Inch by Inch* by Leo Lionni
- *The Little Engine That Could* by Watty Piper
- *Ira Sleeps Over* by Bernard Waber
- *My Imagination Kit* by Jeffrey Fulmer
- *Harold and the Purple Crayon* by Crockett Johnson

TIP If the children enjoy this story, let the them vote on which of the following Harold stories they would like to hear the next day.

- *Harold's ABC* by Crockett Johnson
- *Harold's Fairy Tale* by Crockett Johnson
- *A Box Story* by Kenneth Kit Lamug
- *Big Box for Ben* by Deborah Bruss
- *Milk to Ice Cream* by Lisa M. Harrington

CIRCLE TIME

Interactive Charts and Props

- Music bulletin board set from a school supply store (see list of instruments, this page)
- A variety of musical instruments that the children can play
- Tell-A-Story Game by Ravensburger
- Magic tricks reference books & kits:

  — *Magic Box* by Katie Cleminson

  — *Children's Book of Magic: 30 Magic Tricks for Young Wizards* by Konrad Modzelewski

  — *Kids' Magic Secrets: Simple Magic Tricks & Why They Work* by Loris Bree

  — Box of Magic Tricks: "Amazingly Easy Tricks for Children" by Educational Insights

The musical instruments in the bulletin board display:

String Instruments
bass, cello, harp, violin, viola

Woodwind Instruments
bass clarinet, bassoon, clarinet, double bassoon, English horn, flute, oboe, piccolo, saxophone

Brass Instruments
French horn, trombone, trumpet, tuba

Percussion Instruments
bass drum, celesta, chimes, cymbals, gong, piano, sleigh bells, snare drum, tambourine, timpani, triangle, xylophone

- Play orchestra music and listen for the **brass, percussion, string,** and **woodwind instruments.**

TIP Play classical music very softly or on headphones during FREE CHOICE PLAY so the children can listen and hear for themselves the various instruments.

Circle Time Activities

- Introduce the letter *Ii*.
- Teach the children to use the **Ice Cream Parlor Order Form.** The Order Form will be at the WRITING CENTER this week, instead of copying words in the journal that begin with the Letter *Ii*.

*

- Use the book ***Milk to Ice Cream*** by Lisa M. Herrington. Follow how ice cream is made from the book. This shows the children the steps in a process. It will also add to their knowledge for play in the ice cream parlor.
- Explain the word *Illusion*. Demonstrate a few magic tricks each day so the children learn how to do the trick and are careful with the magic supplies. The children will have a **Magic Show** for their families during *Mm* Week. Tell them to practice the tricks during FREE CHOICE PLAY because they will get to perform a magic trick for the show. It takes a lot of practice to be a magician, and a magician never tells her secrets!
- Learn and practice singing **"The Busy Family Song"** (see *Mm* Week on page 191).

TABLE WORK

Ii
WEEK

- Read the story ***My Imagination Kit*** by Jeffrey Fulmer. Discuss *Imagination*. Use the **Tell-A-Story Game** by Ravensburger. Have the children use their imaginations to tell a story.

- Introduce as many **musical instruments** as you have on hand. Listen to each sound the instruments make. Sing the song **"If You're Happy and You Know It"** (tap the drum, ring the bell, shake the maraca, etc.). Have enough instruments for each child to have one, even if there are duplicates.

- Look at the **Music Bulletin Board Set**. Group the musical instruments into brass, percussion, string, and woodwind instruments. Listen to a piece of music and identify with the children the different groups of instruments you recognize.

- Read the book ***The Little Engine That Could*** by Watty Piper. Tell the children they are growing up and can do many things. Go around the circle and have each child say something they can do. Write their statements on a piece of paper. At TABLE WORK on journal day, the children will write "I can . . ." on two cards, along with their names (see TABLE WORK for further instructions).

- Talk about ice and icebergs. Ask the children which animals live where it is cold. Look at the world globe to find the North and South Pole. Show them why it is colder there than at the equator.

- Read the Hernando or Harriet story. Pass the puppet on to the next child.

- Practice writing the letter of the week. Practice writing the letter *Ii*.

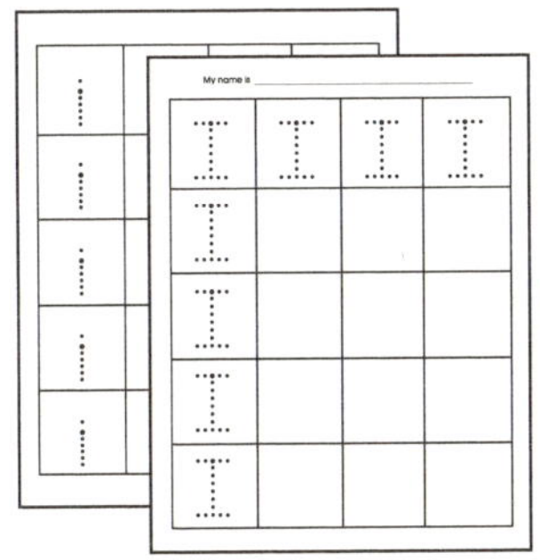

- Fill in the blanks on a flower poem for mom (save it for *Mm* Week).

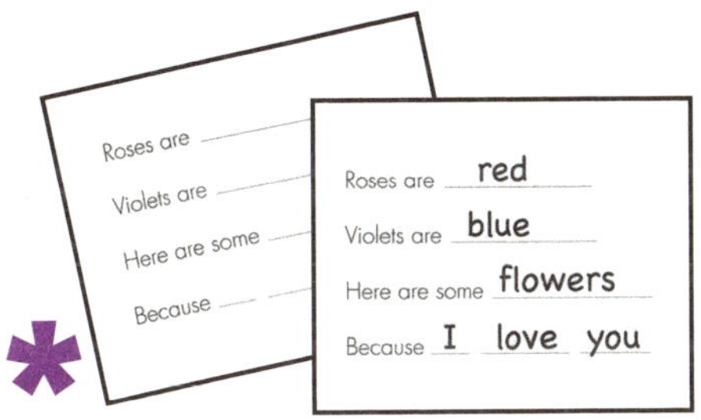

- Explain how to play the **Initial Game**. Each child should write his initials a few times to practice. Have the children choose a partner and play the game for 5–10 minutes. When time is called, count how many boxes each child has claimed. The one with the most is the winner.

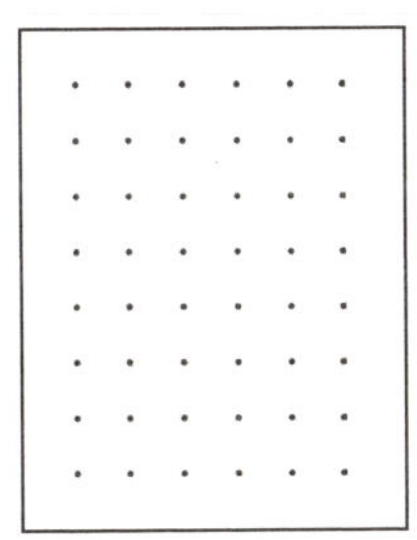

- **Journal** Write *I can smile.*
Have children draw a smile face with crayons in their journals. Also ask children to write "*I can . . .*" on two index cards. You have one answer from each child at CIRCLE TIME. Ask each child to tell you one more thing they can do. The answers from CIRCLE TIME can be copied later to save time. Make an "I can . . ." jar. Have the children put their cards in the jar.

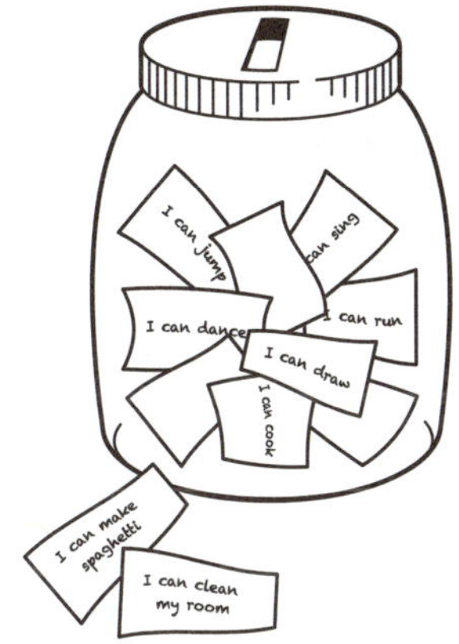

HOW TO: Play the Initial Game

Use paper dotted in a grid pattern. Players take turns drawing a line between two dots. The lines must be vertical or horizontal, not diagonal. Whoever draws the last line to form a box puts their initials in the box. When a set amount of time is up or all the boxes are made that can be made, each player counts how many boxes have their initials. Whoever has the most initialed boxes wins!

FREE CHOICE PLAY

Writing Center

Use the table to fill in **Ice Cream Parlor Order Forms**. Display two cards that say "cone" and "dish" and make a sentence strip with the numerals 1 through 5 so the children can fill in how many scoops are ordered. Also, display a picture of a scoop of ice cream with the words *vanilla* (white), *chocolate* (brown), and *strawberry* (pink) so they can mark the flavor.

Board Games

- Pegs in the Park by Jax
- I Spy Eagle Eye by Scholastic
- Mystery Garden: I See Something That You Don't See by Ravensburger
- Tell-A-Story Game by Ravensburger

Sensory Table

Use the sensory table in the DRAMATIC PLAY area to wash, drain, and dry dishes. Use a small amount of sudsy water in a dishpan and a drainer in the table. Tell the children to dry dishes very well before putting them back on the shelf.

Workbench

Become an inventor this week. Put out little parts, pieces, and so forth. Some suggestions include nuts, bolts, hooks, mini paper cups, empty thread spools, and little boxes. Be sure to include tools such as glue, tape, scissors, and string. Let the children make whatever they can imagine!

OR

After reading one of the stories about creating something from a box, make the **Magic Show** table using a variety of boxes. Cover the boxes with whimsical fabric, decorated easel paper, or even foil.

Easel Art

Try invisible art. Draw a picture with a yellow crayon on manila paper. Paint over the crayon drawing with watercolor. The invisible drawing will become visible. It is called a *resist*!

Crafts

- Make an ice cream cone puzzle. Use a simple picture, and color and cut out the pieces.
- Trace cones and make a few ice cream ball patterns the children can use to trace. Have a variety of colors of construction paper so the children can trace scoops of ice cream. Be sure to have tiny pieces of dark brown for chips. Children cut out cones and as many scoops as they want. Glue one scoop on top of the other. Children enjoy making very tall ice cream cones!

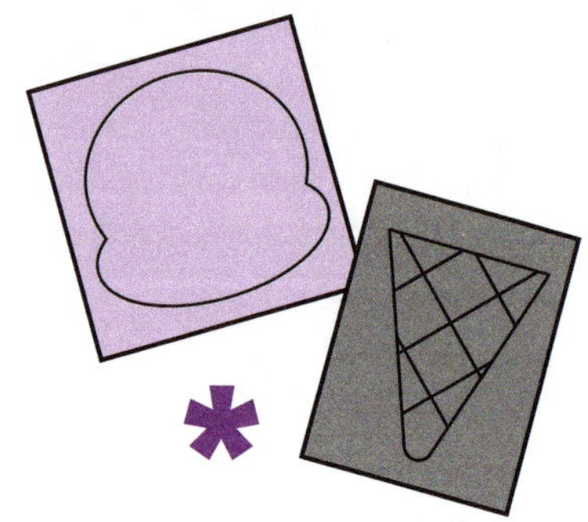

- Trace a variety of flowers for the children to cut and decorate. Put out green pipe cleaners for stems. The children can either take the flowers home or save them and make a bouquet to give to their moms (or special person) along with the poem done at TABLE WORK.
- Make extra papers for the **Initial Game** so the children can play again during FREE CHOICE PLAY.

TIP There are not too many crafts during FREE CHOICE PLAY this week so the children can take time to play and practice with the magic tricks. Next week they will have to choose which one they will perform for the **Magic Show.**

HOW TO: Make Homemade Ice Cream in a Bag

Use any homemade ice cream recipe. For safety reasons, if there is an egg in the recipe, it should be cooked thoroughly. Cut down the recipe or divide the ice cream mixture into individual portions, or children can work with a partner. Then each portion should be two servings.

To make the ice cream in a bag, you will need snap-and-seal sandwich bags, snap-and-seal gallon-sized bags, rock salt, and ice. Place the liquid mixture in the small plastic bag and seal it well. Place four parts ice to one part salt in the gallon-sized bag, leaving enough room for the bag of liquid ice cream. Put the small bag inside the large bag and seal it well. Spread out a bath towel on the floor. Two children can work together and roll the bag or gently pass the bag back and forth, keeping the bag in motion for ten minutes. Then, carefully open the big bag—just a little—and pour off the water. Add more ice and salt and continue moving the bag until the ice cream thickens. This process can be long and tiring for the children, but the ice cream treat is a great reward!

TIP Have the children bring gloves or mittens to wear. Bring a few extra pairs because the children need to wear them to protect their hands.

Notes & Evaluations

	Circle Time	Table Work	Free Choice Play	Crafts
Monday	Beginning: Ending:			
	Story:			
Tuesday	Beginning: Ending:			
	Story:			
Wednesday	Beginning: Ending:			
	Story:			
Thursday	Beginning: Ending:			
	Story:			
Friday	Beginning: Ending:			
	Story:			

Five Senses WEEK

See

Hear

Smell

Taste

Touch

Dramatic Play

Ice Cream Parlor

Display an activity for each of the five senses.

Learning Objectives

Physical and Motor

- Runs consistently without falling
- Uses left or right hand predominantly

Cognitive

- Can stay with the same activity for five-to-ten minutes
- Makes comparisons between objects after observation

Communication and Language

- Asks questions and seeks answers
- Listens for details

Social and Emotional

- Shares
- Shows independence

Approaches to Learning

- Approaches new situations with increasing flexibility

TIP A good placement for The Five Senses Week is before *Mm* Week or incorporated into both *Ii* and *Mm* Weeks. The Five Senses activities can be displayed in the classroom for the visitors coming to see the **Magic Show**.

Listening Activities and Songs

- Song: Continue to practice "The Busy Family Song" (see *Mm* Week for the words on page 191).
- Song: "Row, Row, Row Your Boat" (Traditional)
- Songs from the book *Songs in Sign* by S. Harold Collins, Kathy Kifer, and Dahna Solar

TIP When using ASL to sign a song it is acceptable to only sign the important words.

- Song: "Twinkle, Twinkle Little Star" (Traditional)
- Song: "Rock-A-Bye Baby" (Traditional)

This unit on the five senses can either be used as a themed week on its own, incorporated into an existing week, or spread out over two consecutive weeks—whatever suits the schedule.

Stories

- *The 5 Senses* by Nuria Roca
- *The Red Book* by Barbara Lehman
- *I Will Never Not Ever Eat a Tomato* by Lauren Child
- *Too Much Noise* by Ann McGovern
- *Cows in the House* by Beverly Lewis
- *Moses Goes to a Concert* by Isaac Millman
- *Skunkdog* by Emily Jenkins
- *Gladys Goes Out to Lunch* by Derek Anderson
- *The Listening Walk* by Paul Showers
- *The Girl Who Heard Colors* by Marie Harris
- *My Five Senses* by Aliki
- *Look, Listen, Taste, Touch, and Smell* by Pamela Hill Nettleton
- *Sign Language: My First 100 Words* by Michiyo Nelson

TIP This week after reading each story, ask the children a few questions to see if they are really listening. This is also a good way to evaluate each child's comprehension.

CIRCLE TIME

Interactive Charts and Props

- A variety of musical instruments and a corrugated cardboard privacy shield
- Five senses poster or cards to identify each display of one of the five senses
- Create your own Five Senses interactive chart.

TIP Use the five senses cards, then enlarge and use the pictures from the Five Senses Reproducibles as answer cards for the chart.

- Ingredients for lemonade (see CIRCLE TIME)
- Air freshner
- Three to four white flowers (carnations work well)
- Photos of the children

Circle Time Activities

- Discuss all of the five senses in general. The children should be able to name them and give examples for each. Use the **Five Senses interactive chart.** Help the children understand that many of the answer cards for the chart can be a match for more than one of the senses. For example, popsicles taste good and feel cold.

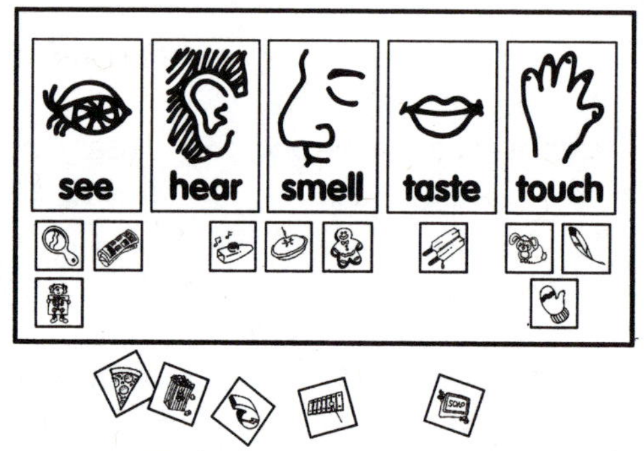

- Explain the Class Cookbook Project. Look at some cookbooks and notice the two parts of a recipe—the ingredients and the instructions—two words that begin with the letter *Ii*. Ask the children what food they like to eat at home. Tell the children you will talk with them individually at FREE CHOICE PLAY, and you will ask what ingredients are used and the instructions for preparing the food—so they should be thinking about it. If the children mention a food, make a note of it on an index card, keeping in mind that children tend to all say the same food if you ask them in a group setting. Write the food each child tells you on an index card and save the card for journal day at TABLE WORK.

- During this CIRCLE TIME, concentrate on the sense of **smell.** Before the children arrive, put out an air freshner. Don't mention it and see if they notice. Soak a few cotton balls with peppermint, orange, and vanilla extract. Another spice that children may recognize is oregano—they will say it smells like pizza! Place the different smells in small plastic butter bowls with holes punched in the lid. Pass the bowls around the circle and have the children smell and guess. Also, show the children the Gingerbread Boy craft with the cinnamon cotton ball inside. He smells good!

- During this CIRCLE TIME, discuss the sense of **taste** and make a graph of the children's favorite flavor of ice cream. Pass a pair of scissors to each child. As children tell you what flavor, trace a circle on an appropriate color of construction paper from the scrap box. Have the children cut out the circles. Cut a cone for every different flavor and glue them on the graph chart. Glue the ice cream circle in place and talk about the results.

Having discussed **smell** and **taste**, tell the children those two sense are connected. Say, "Think about when you have a cold and your nose is stuffy and food doesn't taste like it usually does. And, do you sometimes smell a new food before you try it?"

- Before the children come into the room, hide a ticking kitchen timer somewhere in the classroom, preferably away from the circle area. Set the timer for plenty of time so it doesn't ring before you play a game to be very quiet and listen for the ticking to find the timer. Before playing, discuss **hearing.** Ask the children if they know the word *lullaby*. When we sing softly to babies it calms them. Softly sing **"Rock-A-Bye Baby"** and **"Twinkle, Twinkle Little Star."** Now, ask the children to be very quiet . . . and listen . . . can they hear the ticking? Tell them to remain very quiet while they search for the kitchen timer.

- For another **listening** activity, gather as many different **musical instruments** as you have on hand. Listen to each sound the instruments make. Hide the instrument behind a **corrugated cardboard privacy shield,** sound the instrument, and ask the children if they can identify it. Explain that those with impaired hearing also enjoy music. Often they feel the vibrations of the music and can sing songs in sign language. Use the book ***Songs in Sign*** by S. Harold Collins, Kathy Kifer, and Dahna Solar. Learn to sign some of the songs.

- Discuss **seeing.** Have the children look around and name something they see. Lead the discussion toward the fact that color is one of the first things we notice. Prepare four cards with the color words *red*, *blue*, *green*, and *yellow*. However, color the words incorrectly. For example, color the word *red* blue and the word *blue* yellow. This trick of the eye may not be as effective because most of the children cannot read, but they are beginning to recognize some sight words, so it is fun to try. Moreover, the children will want to trick their family at home. So, at FREE CHOICE PLAY for one of the CRAFTS, tell the children you have made forms with the color words. Remind them to color the word using an incorrect color!

- Another activity for the sense of **sight** is to have the children observe the change when a **flower** is placed in vase of colored water. Flowers that work well are white—Queen Anne's lace or carnations. Add plenty of food coloring to the water and trim the stems for better absorption. Don't forget to place one flower in water with no color for comparison. Each day have the children look at the flowers and record what they see. Children can even use a magnifying glass to observe closely. Briefly discuss that some people who wear glasses need magnification just like what they are using.

- Find duplicates of items that the children can identify by sense of **touch.** Put one of each pair in a cloth bag and place all the duplicates in the center of the circle. Pass the cloth bag around the circle. Each child makes a guess before taking his hand out of the bag by pointing out the item in the circle. Another fun activity is to place an item on sun-sensitive paper. Follow the instructions, put it in the sun, and the shape will appear on the paper. Let children take one of the items from the circle or the cloth bag if two want the same item.

TIP If you don't have duplicate items, make a set of sun-sensitive prints to be matches for items in the cloth bag.

- For a special treat, prepare freshly squeezed lemonade with the class. The ingredients are a lemon for every two children, sugar, water, and ice. Give every two children a lemon. Tell them to take turns pushing and rolling the lemon to make it juicy. Cut each lemon in half and let each child take a turn squeezing. Pour the juice in a 2-quart pitcher and pass around the squeezed lemon for the children to smell and even touch and taste if they wish. When all the lemons are squeezed, add water to fill the pitcher. Tell the children, "I am just going to pour each of you a little juice. Let's wait and taste it together. Okay, 1, 2, 3 . . . taste!" Then you say, **"Oh, no! I forgot to add sugar!"** The children just tasted sour. Add approximately one cup of sugar, then taste. Enjoy the sweet-tasting lemonade!

- Read the Hernando or Harriet story. Pass the puppet on to the next child.

TABLE WORK

- Demonstrate with the Taste Sheet how to cut the squares out of the Answer Page and glue on the five correct squares that are examples of taste. Give the children the Answer Page for Hear and See, then the sheet on which to glue them.

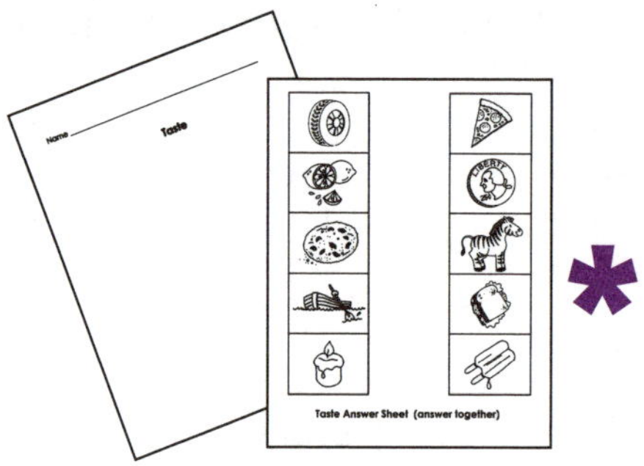

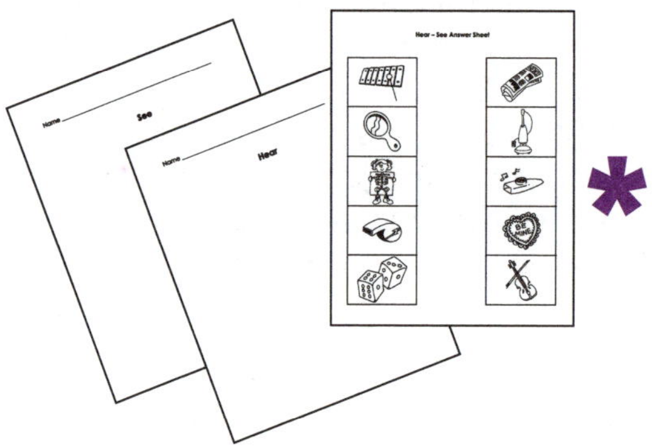

- Give the children the Answer Page for Touch and Smell, then the sheet on which to glue them.

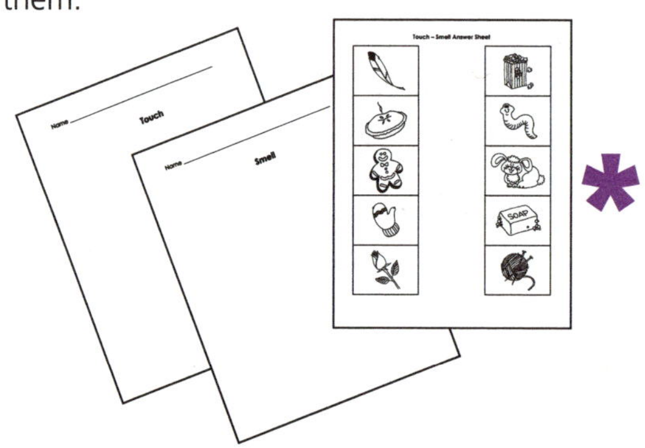

- Evaluate the children's listening skills with a Color the Shapes Reproducible.

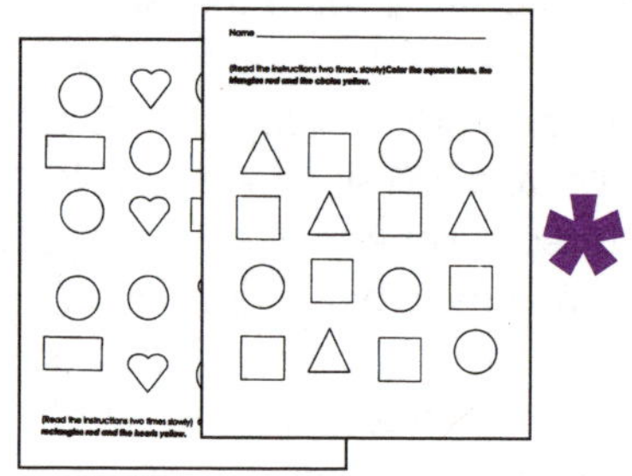

- Color the cover for the Class Cookbook.

- **Journal** Write: __________ *taste good.* (Give each child the card that has the name of the food she likes her family to prepare. If she has another food in mind, just write it on the back of the index card.) Have the children draw a picture of the food with crayons in their journals.

FREE CHOICE PLAY

- During FREE CHOICE PLAY this week, take dictation individually from each child for the Class Cookbook. First ask, "What food do you like that your family prepares?" Then, ask each child two questions: "What ingredients are used? How is it prepared?" Print a page for each child, compile the book, and place each child's cover on his cookbook.

- Remind the children to continue practicing for the **Magic Show.** At the end of the week, have them pick which trick they want to perform so the class can begin to practice for the show next week.

Writing Center

Continue to use the table to write on the Ice Cream Parlor Order Forms.
OR The space can be used for taking dictation from each child for the Class Cookbook.

Board Games

Keep the same games from *Ii* Week.

Sensory Table

Use the sensory table in the DRAMATIC PLAY area to wash, drain, and dry dishes. Use a small amount of sudsy water in a dishpan and a drainer in the table. Tell the children to dry the dishes well before putting them back on the shelf.

Workbench

Use the workbench to set up any magic trick that uses liquid or any trick that is best kept separate from the others.

Easel Art

Add menthol shaving cream to easel paint. The paint will smell good, it will be light and fluffy, and it looks like ice cream!

Crafts

- Have collage supplies so the children can make a picture with texture.
- Trace two gingerbread people on brown construction paper. Have a bowl of cinnamon and cotton balls. Children will decorate, then cut out the two gingerbread people. Roll a cotton ball in the cinnamon. Glue the two gingerbread people together with the cinnamon cotton ball in between.

- Forms with the color words. Remind the children to color the word using an incorrect color to trick their family!

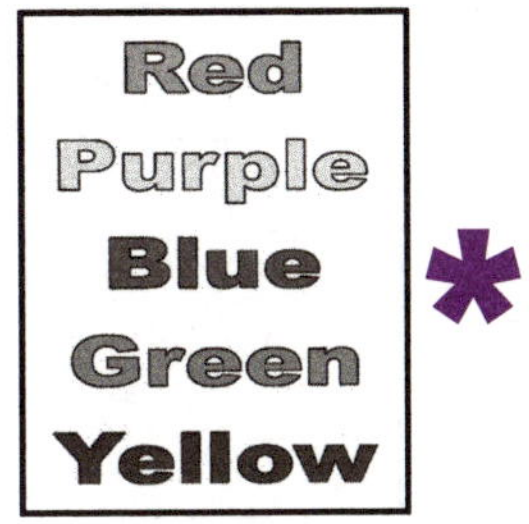

- Take a **photo of each child** and print a 5-by-7-inch picture. Use the photo to cut into pieces and make a funny photo collage.

Notes & Evaluations

	Circle Time	Table Work	Free Choice Play	Crafts
Monday	Beginning: Ending:			
	Story:			
Tuesday	Beginning: Ending:			
	Story:			
Wednesday	Beginning: Ending:			
	Story:			
Thursday	Beginning: Ending:			
	Story:			
Friday	Beginning: Ending:			
	Story:			

Mm WEEK

Moms

Measuring

Money

Magnets

Dramatic Play

Ice Cream Parlor—add play money

Display the five senses.

Learning Objectives

Physical and Motor

- Copies and draws simple shapes and letters
- Dresses with little assistance

Cognitive

- Knows some names of coins and bills (money)
- Uses measurement terms

Communication and Language

- Converses easily with adults
- Has an expanding vocabulary, up to 6,000 words

Social and Emotional

- Is sensitive to the feelings of others
- Seeks attention and approval

Approaches to Learning

- Creates stories, imagining and describing things or situations that do not exist

Listening Activities and Songs

- Song: "The Busy Family Song" (to the tune of "A-Hunting We Will Go")
- Listen to music by Mozart with headphones.
- Chant: "Five Little Monkeys"

"Five Little Monkeys"

Five little monkeys swinging in a tree

Teasing Mr. Alligator, "You can't catch me, you can't catch me!"

Along came Mr. Alligator, quiet as can be *(speak very quietly)*

And he snatched that monkey right out of that tree! *(open arms and clap them shut)*

(four little monkeys . . . 3 . . . 2 . . . 1 . . .)

TIP Use the book ***Shelly Goes to the Zoo*** by Kentrell Martin to do the gestures for Mr. Alligator, Mrs. Elephant, and so forth.

Stories

- *Five Minutes' Peace* by Jill Murphy
- *Hero Mom* by Melinda Hardin (*Hero Dad* is also an option if any child has a mom or dad in the military)
- *Lily Learns about Wants and Needs* by Lisa Bullard
- *Johnny's Decision* by Jeff Felardo
- *Those Shoes* by Maribeth Boelts
- *Coat of Many Colors* by Dolly Parton
- *The Berenstain Bears' Trouble with Money* by Stan and Jan Berenstain
- *A Chair for My Mother* by Vera B. Williams
- *Me and the Measure of Things* by Joan Sweeney
- *Hazel's Amazing Mother* by Rosemary Wells
- *Measuring Penny* by Loreen Leedy
- *Milo's Hat Trick* by Jon Agee
- *Go Away, Big Green Monster!* by Ed Emberley
- *What Makes A Magnet?* by Franklyn M. Branley

CIRCLE TIME

Interactive Charts and Props

- Props for **"The Busy Family Song"** (suggestions are listed with the words of the song at the end of this week on page 191).
- Six Listening Containers (see CIRCLE TIME)

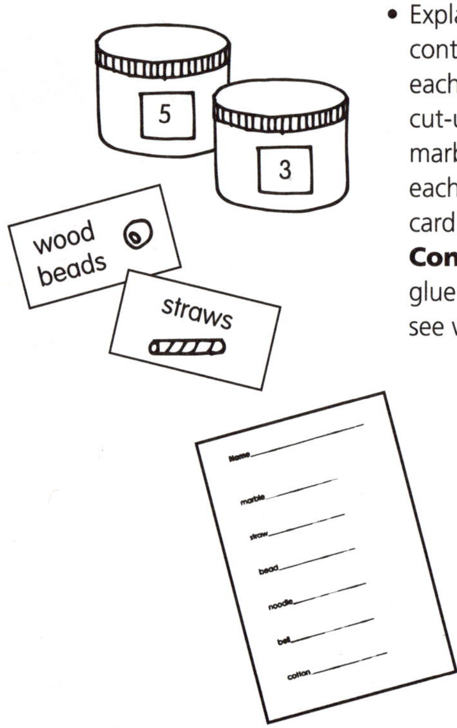

Circle Time Activities

- Introduce the letter *Mm*.
- Talk with the children about practicing the **Magic Show** and **"The Busy Family Song"** with props each day.
- Read the book ***What Makes A Magnet?*** by Franklyn M. Branley to help with the discussion of the properties of magnets. Set up the jar of water with magnets. Ask the children, "Do you remember what else water does with the objects in the jar?" Water magnifies them! Set up a magnet display at the WORKBENCH.
- Explain the **Listening Containers.** Fill six containers with different items hidden inside each container (jingle bells, wood beads, cut-up straws, cotton balls, dry pasta, and marbles are good choices). Write a number on each of the containers. Then make an index card for each item placed in the **Listening Containers**. For example, write *bead* and glue a bead on the card so the children can see what they are hearing.
- Teach the children to measure using a ruler. Practice until the children are competent. Do this on the day they do the I Can Measure Sheet at TABLE WORK.
- Set up a large mirror in the block area. Put the children's name tags nearby. Show the children a book in the mirror, now show them their name tags—they appear to be backwards! Explain that a mirror has a thin coat of silver on the back so light bounces back and forth and it reflects an image. But if the name tag is held behind a pane of clear glass it does not look backwards because the light goes straight through. Discuss where mirrors are used in our home and cars—even a periscope uses mirrors to see around a corner. (Purchase a child's periscope if funds are available.)
- Play "What's Missing?" or "What Letter is Missing?" Place at least ten items or letters on a tray. Children look at the items for fifteen seconds; take one away and see if the children can guess which one is missing.
- Read the story ***Go Away, Big Green Monster!*** by Ed Emberley. Tell the children to use their imaginations and any supplies on the art shelf to make their own monster.

TABLE WORK

- Review manners with the children for the **Magic Show**—they will be serving and eating ice cream.
- Read the Hernando or Harriet story. Pass the puppet on to the next child.
- On the day of the **Magic Show,** tell the children your expectations. They will be touring their guests, so review the five senses and the displays in the classroom. Practice **"The Busy Family Song"** using the props.

- Practice writing the letter of the week. Practice writing the letter *Mm*.

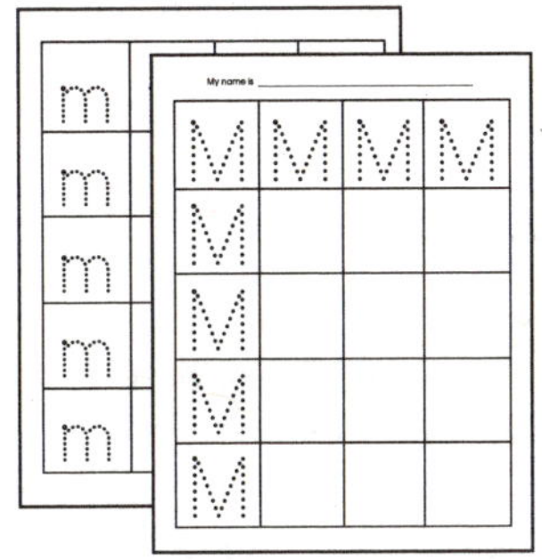

- Phonics Sheet for the letter *Mm*

- I Can Measure Reproducible
  Place numerous items on tables in the classroom with an index card identifying each. The child chooses an object, writes it on her paper and then measures it and writes the number that it measures. Have more items than needed so the children have choices and the activity flows smoothly.

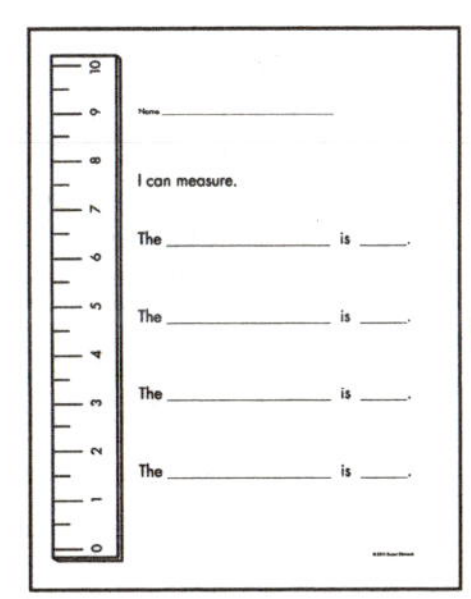

- **Journal** Write: *This is mosaic art.*
  Cut construction paper squares for the children to create a design to glue in their journals.

FREE CHOICE PLAY

Writing Center

Alphabet Stamps

Board Games

- Five Little Monkeys Jumping on the Bed by Briarpatch
- Loose Change by MindWare
- Maisy's Hide and Seek Adventure Game by International Playthings
- Old maid cards
- Labyrinth Jr. by Ravensburger

Sensory Table

(Take the sensory table out of the DRAMATIC PLAY area.)

Put Marbleworks by Discovery Toys in a dry table. On the last day of the week, add about an inch of water for variety.

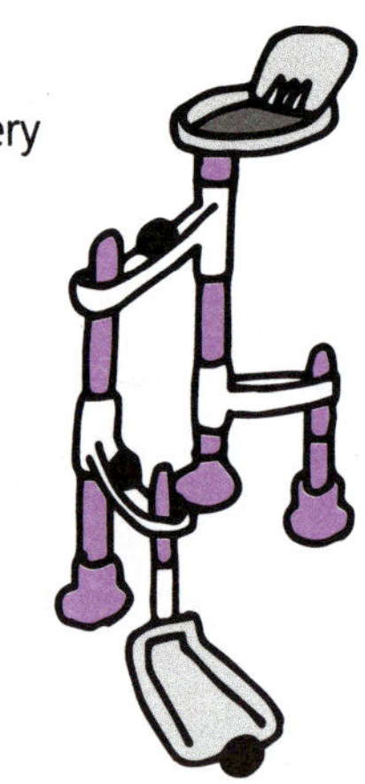

Workbench

Magnet activities set up at CIRCLE TIME

Easel Art

Put the easel away and marble paint with magnets. Use both sides of a box so two children can paint at one time. Have them sit on the floor and place a piece of paper in the box with two magnetic marbles. Squirt a *small amount* of one or two colors on the paper. Show the children how to hold the box with one hand and use a bingo magnet wand to slide around under the box, dragging the marble. As the marble moves back and forth across the paper and through the paint, the masterpiece just gets better and better!

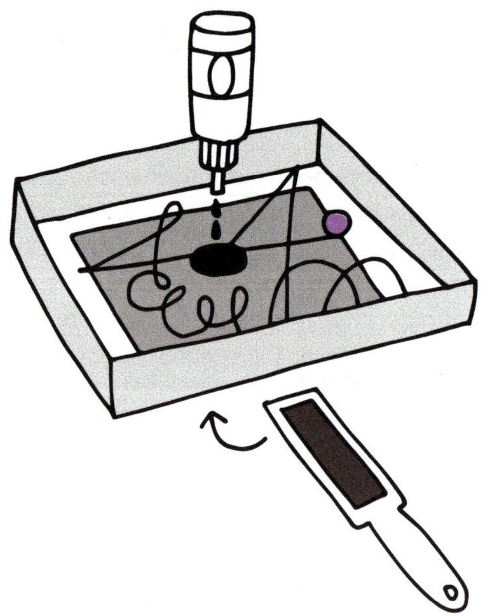

Crafts

- Use pages of mazes from the book ***Alphabet Mazes*** by Fran Newman-D'Amico
- Make a card for Mom (or any special person). Either let the children use their imaginations or provide a few samples for ideas.
- After reading the story ***Go Away, Big Green Monster!*** by Ed Emberley, the children can use any supplies on the art shelf to make their own monster.
- Move any leftover mosaic squares from the journal activity to the craft area.
- Leave out the flower-making craft materials for any child who wants to make flowers or add more flowers to their bouquet.
- Also leave out any craft materials for projects from the Five Senses Week.

Notes & Evaluations

Mm WEEK

"The Busy Family Song"
(to the tune of "A-Hunting We Will Go")

A-washing we will go, a-washing we will go.
The clothes get clean in the washing machine.
And then we say, "There's more!"
(prop suggestion: laundry detergent and fabric softener)

A-shopping we will go, a-shopping we will go.
We'll buy some socks then ask for a box.
And then we say, "There's more!"
(prop suggestion: socks and box)

A-scrubbing we will go . . .
We'll take our mop, it goes flip-flop . . .
(prop suggestion: mop that flip-flops)

A-walking we will go . . .
We'll wear our sweater to mail a letter . . .
(prop suggestion: sweater and letter)

A-cooking we will go . . .
We'll all make dinner and it's a winner . . .
(prop suggestion: cookbook and paper plate with pictures of food cut from magazines)

A-sporting we will go . . .
We'll kick the ball; it goes over the wall . . .
(prop suggestion: soccer ball)

A-traveling we will go . . .
We'll go on a plane, once to Maine . . .
(prop suggestion: toy airplane and USA map to point to Maine)

A-sweeping we will go . . .
We'll use a broom to clean our rooms . . .
(prop suggestion: broom)

A-driving we will go . . .
We'll go here, and we'll go there . . .
(prop suggestion: poster-board steering wheel and sunglasses)

A-napping we will go . . .
We go to bed to rest our heads.
And then we say, "We're done!"
(prop suggestion: pillow)

NOTES FOR THE MAGIC SHOW

List the five senses that are displayed in the classroom so the children can show the guests.

SEE: Look at the flowers that have absorbed the colored water. Look at the children's funny photo collage, their journals, and any other work displayed in the classroom.

HEAR: Play with the Listening Jars. Try to guess what is in each one.

SMELL: Test the guests' senses of smell with the butter bowls with cotton balls of scents in each. The gingerbread person craft with cinnamon inside can be displayed.

TASTE: Taste the ice cream after the Magic Show. The Class Cookbook can also be on display.

TOUCH: Watch as the children perform the tricks in the Magic Show. The children have touched and practiced, so you will be amazed!

Use this page to list the tricks for the Magic Show and which child is performing each trick. Also note what props are needed for each trick.

Notes & Evaluations

- Children show their guests around the classroom.
- Perform the **Magic Show**.

- Set the table. Using their best manners, the children serve ice cream. Then they serve themselves. Together, everyone eats ice cream.
- Sing **"The Busy Family Song"** with props.
- Thank the guests for coming.

	Circle Time	Table Work	Free Choice Play	Crafts
Monday	Beginning: Ending:			
	Story:			
Tuesday	Beginning: Ending:			
	Story:			
Wednesday	Beginning: Ending:			
	Story:			
Thursday	Beginning: Ending:			
	Story:			
Friday	Beginning: Ending:			
	Story:			

Dramatic Play

Traveling

Dress-up props, suitcases, tickets, and maps

Learning Objectives

Physical and Motor

- Runs with ease and stops quickly
- Manages zippers, snaps, and buttons

Cognitive

- Recognizes own name in print
- Shows an interest in numbers and names of numbers

Communication and Language

- Likes to learn new words
- Sings simple, repetitive songs

Social and Emotional

- Plays alone
- Likes to be silly and make others laugh

Approaches to Learning

- Purposefully explores new things or ideas

Listening Activities and Songs

- Song: "Let's Go Fly a Kite" by Richard M. Sherman and Robert B. Sherman (from the film *Mary Poppins*)
- Song: "I've Been Working on the Railroad" (American folksong)
- Poem: Thank You Poem (see *Nn* Week for words on page 85).

This is a good week for a library field trip or a visitor from the public library. The children have been practicing writing their first and last names so they can sign their own library card applications. Make sure all library card applications are back and the children have signed their first and last names.

Stories

- *Rookie Read-About Science: North, South, East, and West* by Allan Fowler
- *Katie No-Pocket* by Emmy Payne
- *Transportation* by Alain Grée
- *There's a Map on My Lap! All About Maps* by Tish Rabe
- *Me on the Map* by Joan Sweeney
- *Sweet Clara and the Freedom Quilt* by Deborah Hopkinson
- *Kimmy's Marvelous Wind-Catching Wonder* by Linda Glaser
- *King Bidgood's in the Bathtub* by Audrey Wood
- *Library Mouse* by Daniel Kirk
- *Library Lion* by Michelle Knudsen

Kk WEEK

Transportation

Cartography

Addresses

Kites

Kaleidoscopes

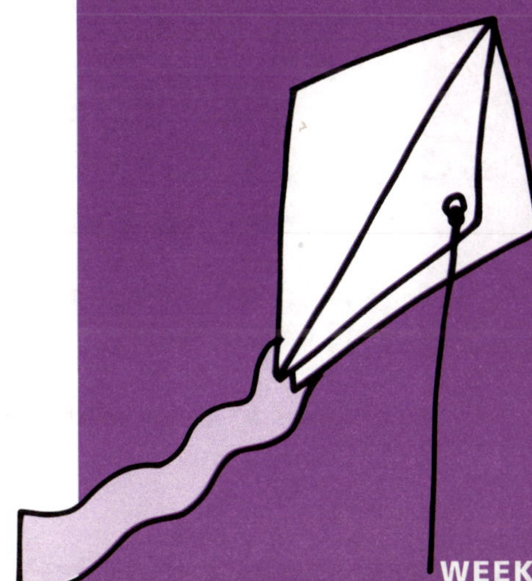

CIRCLE TIME

Interactive Charts and Props

- Make an envelope with house numbers and street names for each child.

- A world map and a United States map
- The Neighborhood Walk Map from the book ***Rookie Read-About Science: North, South, East, and West*** by Allan Fowler, or the one shown below

- ***How to Make a Kite*** by Colleen Hord
- ***Kids' Paper Airplane Book*** by Ken Blackburn and Jeff Lammers
- ***Signs in My Neighborhood*** by Shelly Lyons

Circle Time Activities

- Introduce the letter *Kk*.
- Discuss all the different forms of transportation the children can think of. Make a list of them—don't forget hot air balloon, motorcycle, etc. Go down the list and, by a show of hands, graph how many forms of transportation each child has experienced. Ask them, "Which forms of transportation would you like to try?" Sing **"I've Been Working on the Railroad."**
- Sing **"Let's Go Fly a Kite,"** composed by Richard M. Sherman and Robert B. Sherman. Demonstrate how to make a kite that really flies. Use the book ***How to Make a Kite*** by Colleen Hord. If there is a space to fly kites, have all the children make a kite. Ask for some extra adult supervision and plan a day to go outside and fly the kites. It will need to be at least somewhat windy to get those kites off the ground! Otherwise, the kite can be an optional CRAFT and the children can take their kite home. It is helpful to send home instructions on how to fly a kite.
- Have a vacation discussion. Ask the children, "Where has your family gone on vacation?" or "Where would you like to go on vacation?" Make a list of all the places the children said. Point out the places on a **USA** or **world map.**
- To further the vacation discussion, ask the children, "What would you pack in your suitcase to take on your vacation?" Go around the circle once and let the children answer. Next, play the "Pack the Suitcase" memory game. The first child says, "I'm going on vacation, so in my suitcase I will pack my bathing suit." The next child says, "I'm going on vacation so in my suitcase I will pack my bathing suit and my pillow." Every child adds another item, continuing around the circle. If memory fails, the other children can help.
- Pass out a **Neighborhood Walk Map** to each child. Children can use their fingers to follow your directions to go places on the map. If possible, make a map of the area in which you are located so the children can really see where you are taking them. Maybe even go outside so they can see the buildings and streets!
- To review addresses, use the **house numbers and street name envelopes.** First, you say the house number and a child finds her envelope and says the street name. For the second and more challenging way, you pick an envelope and say the street name, then the child claims the envelope and says her house number.
- Teach the children to play the **Take a Walk Game.** See FREE CHOICE PLAY section for how to play.

TABLE WORK

- Talk with the children about the field trip or the visitor from the public library and the responsibility of having their own library card.
- Look at many different kinds of kaleidoscopes. Take a kaleidoscope apart so the children can see how it works.

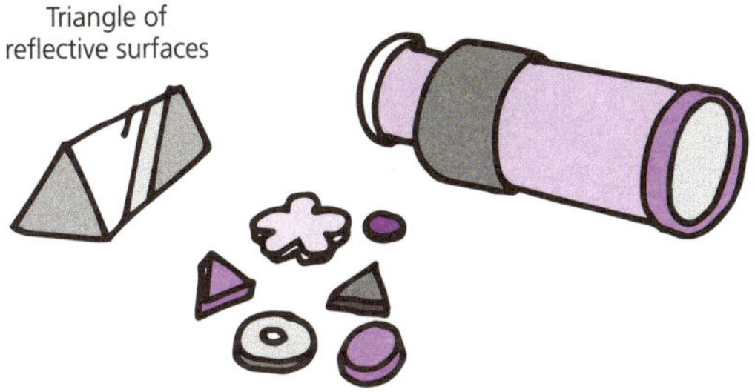

- Hop like a kangaroo. Ask the children to count as they hop. Have a long jump competition. Use a tape measure to measure how far each child can jump.
- For an indoor large-muscle activity, kick a sponge soccer ball and have each child stand where their ball first bounces. Be careful not to hit your friends with the ball!
- Read the Hernando or Harriet story. Pass the puppet on to the next child.

- Practice writing the letter of the week. Practice writing the letter *Kk*.

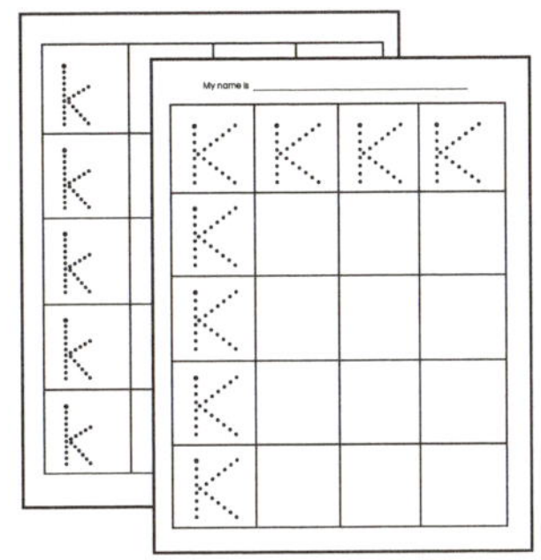

- Phonics Sheet for the letter *Kk*

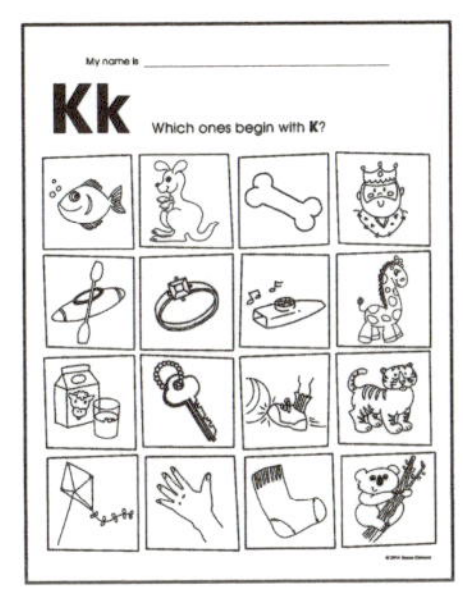

- Practice tracing the boy flying his kite.

- Give each child the envelope with his house number and street name from the **house numbers and street name envelopes.** On a paper, have the children write their address and then draw the front of their house or apartment. Tell them to think about these questions: Where is the front door? How many windows are there? Is the garage door in the front of the house? Is the house brick or wood or something else? What colors can you see?
- **Journal** Write: *I can fly a kite.* Draw yourself flying a kite. Teach children to draw a kite (diamond) by drawing a cross and connecting the ends.

TIP Tracing on the line is one way to evaluate eye-hand coordination. It is a long enough activity to also see how a child holds their pencil and their small muscle strength.

FREE CHOICE PLAY

Writing Center

Alphabet Stamps

TIP If there are any children unable to write their first and last name from memory, have them practice at the writing center this week during FREE CHOICE PLAY.

Board Games

- Rivers, Roads, and Rails by Ravensburger
- Race to the Treasure! by Peaceable Kingdom

Sensory Table

Put water in the table to create a large swimming pool. Make rafts and floats using art foam for play people in the water. Place an open shelf near the table with a dollhouse and outdoor furniture so the area becomes a vacation resort hotel with a pool. Just be sure all items are water safe!

Workbench

Provide constructable vehicles such as Motor Blocks Vehicles by TOMY. With the kit, a child can build a race car, plane, train, or helicopter by following the instructions.

Easel Art

Feather paint paper with light blue or gray for the sky. Trace airplanes on construction paper. Children cut out the airplanes and glue them in the painted sky. Finish by sponge painting white clouds for fun!

Crafts

- Make kites that really fly! For step-by-step instructions, use the book ***How to Make a Kite*** by Colleen Hord. Trace the kite on wallpaper and use a plastic drinking straw for the spar.

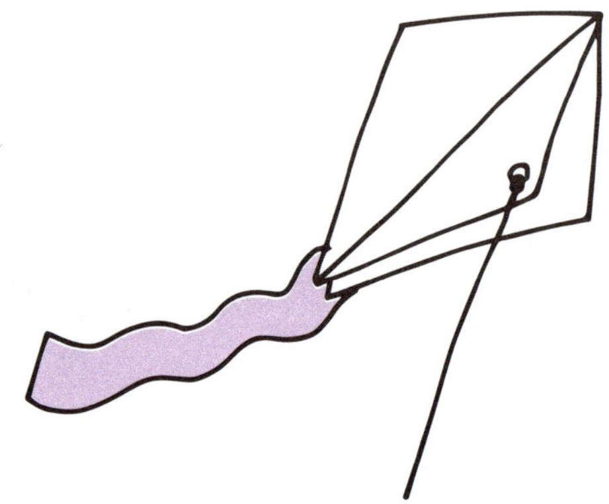

- Help the children make paper airplanes. Use the book ***Kids' Paper Airplane Book*** by Ken Blackburn and Jeff Lammers.
- Purchase transportation stencils or make patterns for the children to trace, color, or cut.
- Put the book ***Signs in My Neighborhood*** by Shelly Lyons out for children to use as a reference. They can draw the signs and even make a book of street signs.
- Provide reproducibles with large empty blocks so the children can draw their own neighborhood map.

- Hang up a **USA map** near the CRAFT AREA. Cut plastic canvas into USA shapes. Children can sew a "road map" all over the USA with different colored yarn, showing where they would like to travel.

- Trace footprints to make the **Take a Walk Game** (see instructions below).

HOW TO: Play the Take a Walk Game

You will need the following:
- A box with four flaps labeled *north*, *south*, *east*, and *west*
- 20 each of four different color footprints (children can cut out the footprints during FREE CHOICE PLAY)
- Dice
- Tape measure

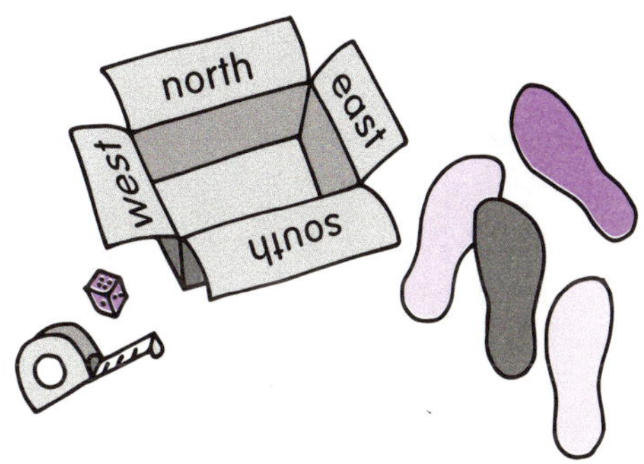

To play
The first player chooses a direction, for example, "east." The child chooses a color of footprint, for example, "blue." Roll the dice and place that many footprints walking east, beginning at the "east" flap on the shoe box.

The second player chooses a direction and *a different color footprint* and rolls the dice. The second player can
1. Add his footprints to the first player's footprints if east is the direction chosen.
2. If north, south, or west is the direction the player wishes to walk, then the footprints will start a new path at the shoe box.

A third and fourth player can also take a turn. There can be only four walking paths: north, south, east, and west. Each player uses different colored footprints. On each turn, footprints can be added to any *one* direction.

To end the game
The first player to use all 20 of her footprints says, **"I'm tired! We've walked far enough!"** Using a tape measure, see how far each walk went. Hold the tape measure from the shoebox to the last footprint of the walk.

There are no winners or losers, just measuring to see how far the players walked!

Notes & Evaluations

	Circle Time	Table Work	Free Choice Play	Crafts
Monday	Beginning: Ending:			
	Story:			
Tuesday	Beginning: Ending:			
	Story:			
Wednesday	Beginning: Ending:			
	Story:			
Thursday	Beginning: Ending:			
	Story:			
Friday	Beginning: Ending:			
	Story:			

Uu WEEK

Explore the Universe

Rain

Umbrellas

Rainforest

Opposites

Dramatic Play

Add Space Travel to *Kk* Week's Vacation Travel theme

Learning Objectives

Physical and Motor

- Jumps into the air with both feet
- Builds and stacks several small blocks

Cognitive

- Uses props to symbolize real objects
- Has increasing memory

Communication and Language

- Enjoys books
- Uses language socially (pragmatics)

Social and Emotional

- Is self-directed
- Role-plays

Approaches to Learning

- Works at tasks despite distractions and interruptions

Listening Activities and Songs

- Song: "It's Raining, It's Pouring" (Traditional)
- Song: "R-A-I-N-Y" (to the tune of "B-I-N-G-O")
- Repeat the activity Making the Sound of a Thunderstorm. Add the sound of a drum for thunder. (See *Tt* Week for step-by-step instructions on page 37.)

"R-A-I-N-Y"
(to the tune of B-I-N-G-O)

I put my raincoat on today
'Cause outside it was rainy.
R-A-I-N-Y, R-A-I-N-Y, R-A-I-N-Y
'Cause outside it was rainy.

The following verses can be added:

And I brought my new umbrella
'Cause outside it was rainy . . .

I looked and looked then found my
boots
'Cause outside it was rainy . . .

[Take one letter away at each verse—snap fingers instead of clap.]

Stories

- My *Yellow Umbrella* by Chris Robertson
- *The Umbrella* by Jan Brett
- *The Great Kapok Tree: A Tale of the Amazon Rain Forest* by Lynne Cherry
- *The Ugly Duckling* by Hans Christian Andersen
- *The Scrambled States of America* by Laurie Keller
- *National Geographic Kids: Little Kids First Big Book of Space* by Catherine D. Hughes
- *Tops and Bottoms* by Janet Stevens
- *Opposites* by Sandra Boynton
- *Silly Sally* by Audrey Wood
- *Round Trip* by Ann Jonas
- *Mitchell on the Moon* by R.W. Alley
- *Hello, World! Solar System* by Jill McDonald
- *National Geographic Kids: Rain Forest Colors* by Janet Lawler
- *Me And My Place In Space* by Joan Sweeney
- *Our Stars* by Anne Rockwell

CIRCLE TIME

Interactive Charts and Props

- Keep the United States and world maps from *Kk* Week.
- Bulletin board set: Planets—Our Solar System by Frank Schaffer
- Streamers or floating scarves (enough for each child)
- Drum for "Making the Sound of a Thunderstorm" activity
- An umbrella to open and turn upside-down while reading the story ***The Umbrella*** by Jan Brett

Circle Time Activities

- Introduce the letter *Uu*.
- Ask the children, "How can the traveling DRAMATIC PLAY be extended to space travel?" Tell them to use their imaginations. Ask what they will need—boxes, paper grocery bags to make space helmets, jumpsuits, space maps, keyboards, etc. Ask them, "How could you make a utility belt?" As a large-motor activity, take the children on a pretend space adventure. Make up a story and echo chant, just like "Going on a Bear Hunt."
- Review opposites. To evaluate, have each child give an example of opposite words. Because it is *Uu* Week, explain that adding "un-" to the beginning of many words will create the opposite. Together with the children, make a list of words that apply.
- Explain the sink and float activity in the SENSORY TABLE (see SENSORY TABLE for details). Test a few objects and explain how to record their findings.
- Teach the children to play **Uno Card Game** by University Games.
- Read the book ***Me And My Place In Space*** by Joan Sweeney to introduce the children to the topic of space. At the end of the book is a list of words to learn. Teach the children facts about our sun, the stars, and planets. A fun way to learn is to purchase planet balls (add a star and a yellow ball for the sun). Create index cards with facts about the sun, stars, and each planet ball. Put the planets, star, and sun in a cloth bag. Pass the bag around the circle and then read the facts and see if the child can match the fact to the space prop. There will probably be a few children without a prop. Allow those children to make another guess when a child gives an incorrect answer.

TIP This activity can be done a few times. The children will learn quickly with repetition!

- Practice with the children until they can count backwards from ten to one. Use their countdown to launch a balloon rocket. To make a balloon rocket you will need a length of yarn long enough to reach across the classroom, a plastic straw, masking tape, and a balloon. Slip the plastic straw onto the yarn and connect the yarn across the classroom,

TABLE WORK

up high, so all the children can see. Slide the straw all the way to one side. Blow up the balloon and pinch the end so the air does not escape. Tape the balloon flat against the straw. Count down ten, nine, eight . . . BLASTOFF! Let go of the balloon rocket and it will fly across the room along the yarn. The children will want to do this over and over, so place yourself up high so you can blow up the balloon again without taking it off the straw. Have the children countdown from twenty the second time!

- Show the children examples of constellations. Tell them, "It's like dot-to-dot with the stars in the night sky." Explain the craft activity: making shape and animal constellations with little star stickers (see CRAFTS).

- Sing: **"It's Raining, It's Pouring"** (Traditional)

- Sing: **"R-a-i-n-y"** (to the tune of B-I-N-G-O)

- Read the story ***Silly Sally*** by Audrey Wood on journal day. Explain the journal writing activity (see TABLE WORK).

- Read the Hernando or Harriet story. Pass the puppet on to the next child.

- Practice writing the letter of the week. Practice writing the letter *Uu*.

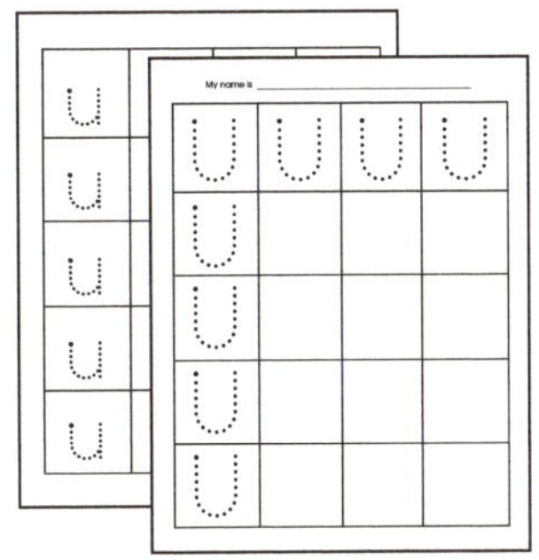

- Rocket of Shapes Reproducible: Count how many of each shape is found in the rocket drawing. Write the number on the line beside the shape. Color the rocket.

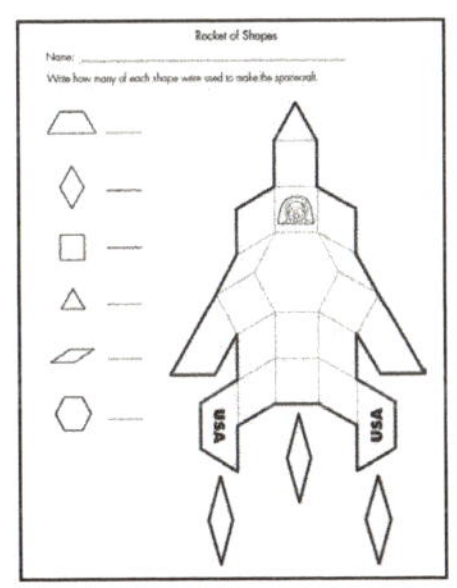

TIP Color each shape a different color to make it easier to count.

- Opposite Reproducible

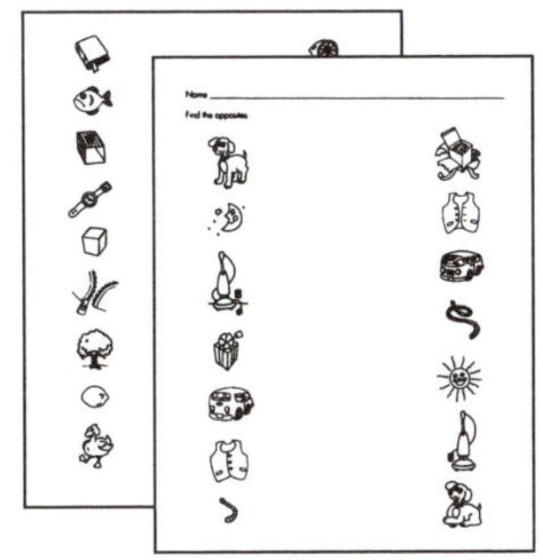

- **Journal** Write *I am upside-down*. Next, turn the journal book upside down and have the children simply draw a picture of themselves right side up. Tell them, "When you turn your journal book back, you are upside down!"

FREE CHOICE PLAY

Writing Center

Alphabet Stamps

Board Games

- Great States Junior by International Playthings
- Carmen San Diego USA Junior Edition by University Games
- Uno Card Game by International Games

Sensory Table

Use the sensory table for a sink and float experiment. A table is needed nearby to enable children to record their results. Suggested items are pencil, nail, penny, eraser, plastic cup, wood block, metal spoon, wood bead, marble, paper clip, magnifying glass, cotton ball, etc. List the items with a short line next to each item. The children should write either an *S* or *F* on the line next to each item.

Workbench

Make a pierced star suncatcher. Trace large stars on construction paper. Lay indoor/outdoor carpet on the workbench. Using a corn cob holder, punch holes in the star. Next, cut out the star and attach a ribbon to hang the suncatcher in a window.

Easel Art

Free paint

If the easel has two sides, planet stamps can be added on one side.

Crafts

- Purchase sets of planet stickers. Write the words "Our Solar System" for the children to copy. Tell them to look at the planets displayed to help put them in the correct order from the sun.

- Cut a star stencil from a plastic lid. Here are three ways to use the stencil:
  1. Use the stencil to trace stars. Trace on silver paper so the stars shine!
  2. Trace the star and color with a "glitter crayon," then paint with watercolor for a resist.
  3. Use the cutout star as a rub. Rub a few stars with light-colored crayons, cut them out, and glue the stars to dark blue or black construction paper (the night sky).

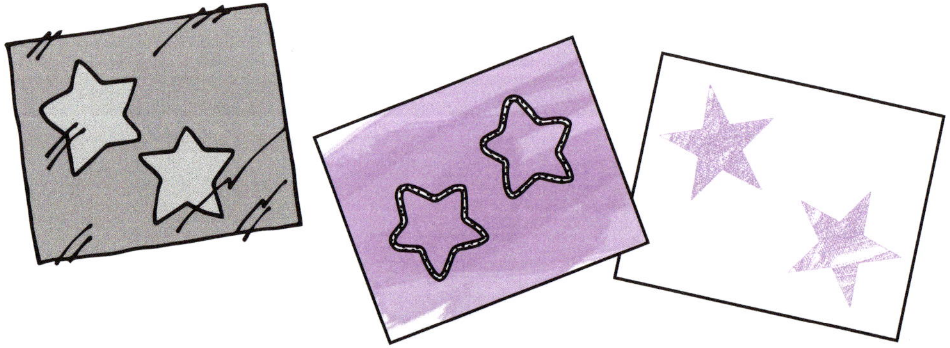

- Draw some simple shapes or animals. Tell the children to lay a piece of very thin copy paper over a picture and place small star stickers to make their own constellations. The stars can be connected lightly with a pencil and ruler to define the shape. If the stars are not connected, the picture can become a constellation guessing game.

- Trace a space drawing. For this activity, use very thin copy paper (real tracing paper can be too thin for small children). Make copies of the background. Children, trace space objects onto the space drawing. Optional: Children can color their space drawings.

- Make a sun using a paper plate. Put red and yellow paint in squirt bottles. Squirt a swish of red and a swish of yellow paint on the paper plate. Use a paintbrush to mix and paint the paper plate, which looks HOT like the sun! Print stickers with facts about the sun to stick to the back of the plate. Suggestions for facts include the following:
  1. The sun is a star. It is made of hot glowing gases.
  2. The sun is 93 million miles away from the earth.
  3. The sun is a source of light, heat, and energy.

Notes & Evaluations

	Circle Time	Table Work	Free Choice Play	Crafts
Monday	Beginning: Ending:			
	Story:			
Tuesday	Beginning: Ending:			
	Story:			
Wednesday	Beginning: Ending:			
	Story:			
Thursday	Beginning: Ending:			
	Story:			
Friday	Beginning: Ending:			
	Story:			

Spring

WEEK

Spring

Positions

Addition

Dramatic Play

Spring puzzles, games, and crafts

Learning Objectives

Physical and Motor

- Makes marks or strokes with drawing tools
- Swings arms while walking

Cognitive

- Names simple shapes
- Notices patterns

Communication and Language

- Uses sentences with seven words or more
- Knows book and print rules

Social and Emotional

- Plays with other children
- Understands others' perspectives

Approaches to Learning

- Offers ideas and suggestions

Listening Activities and Songs

- Song: "There's a Rabbit in a Box" (to the tune of "If You're Happy and You Know It")
- Poem: "Humpty Dumpty" (Traditional)

"There's a Rabbit in a Box"
(to the tune of "If You're Happy and You Know It")

There's a rabbit in a box, in a box.

There's a rabbit in a box, in a box.

There's a rabbit in a box,
he is hiding from the fox.

There's a rabbit in a box, in a box.

Stories

- *Here Comes Peter Cottontail* by Steve Nelson and Jack Rollins
- *Too Many Carrots* by Katy Hudson
- *When Spring Comes* by Kevin Henkes
- *Lola Plants a Garden* by Anna McQuinn
- *My Garden* by Kevin Henkes
- *The Best Bike Ride Ever* by James Proimos
- *Planting a Rainbow* by Lois Ehlert
- *Mud* by Mary Lyn Ray
- *And Then It's Spring* by Julie Fogliano
- *Chicken Sunday* by Patricia Polacco
- *The Very Hungry Caterpillar* by Eric Carle
- *Hermie A Common Caterpillar* by Max Lucado
- *The Tiny Seed* by Eric Carle

Spring
WEEK

CIRCLE TIME

Interactive Charts and Props

- Large basket with grass and plastic eggs for games
- Purchase eggs that look like real birds' eggs from a craft store.
- Position cards (at least one per child)

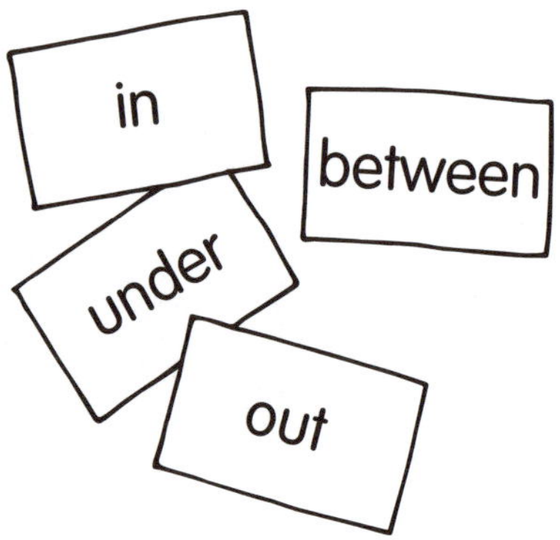

Circle Time Activities

- Use recycled scraps of construction paper to make homemade recycled paper. The paper must be torn into small pieces (approximately one-inch squares). (See Instructions for "How to Make Paper" in CRAFTS.)

TIP The tearing and sorting of paper can be done throughout the year whenever there are a few extra minutes. If some children finish work before the others, tearing paper scraps is a great time filler—and it fills the recycle scrap bins too!

- Explain the plastic egg show-and-tell. The children should take the show-and-tell note home on Monday so that they can bring their egg back at the end of the week. Role-play for the class so they know what you expect.
- Fill a glass jar with pretend bird eggs—count them. Hang up a chart numbered 1–100. Put out slips of paper and let the children estimate how many eggs are in the jar. Tell them, "There are between one and one hundred. Estimate—make a good guess and write it on a slip of paper." Tell the answer at the end of the week.

TIP Use the number chart 1–100 from *Ee* Week.

- Tell the children to name animals that hatch from an egg. Write each correct animal on an index card to be used at TABLE WORK. If the children have difficulty, tell them all birds and reptiles come from an egg.
- Play "How Many Eggs in the Basket?" Use a **large basket with grass.** Say, "I will put two eggs in the basket. Now I will add three more eggs. Tell me how many eggs are in my basket?" The eggs can be hidden under the grass so the children have to add in their heads. Then uncover the eggs and count them to check your answer. Do this activity the same day the children make math sentences with jelly beans at TABLE WORK.
- Play "Obstacle Course Egg Collecting." Build a block city. Ten children pick a **position card** and use it to place a plastic egg in the block city. Pick another child's name to collect ten eggs and hold them without dropping any. By showing the children the game at CIRCLE TIME, they can play it again at FREE CHOICE PLAY.

TIP Setting up the game by putting the eggs in the proper position is the learning part—the collecting is just fun!

- Use the song **"There's a Rabbit in a Box."** Give each child a turn to pick a **position card** and hide the rabbit.

- Say the poem **"Humpty Dumpty."** Discuss with the children that sometimes things cannot be fixed. This is a great example to explain: have the Child Helper squeeze an entire tube of toothpaste onto a paper plate. Now ask, "Can anyone put the toothpaste back in the tube?" Tell the children sometimes when hurtful words are said, they cannot be taken back. They can apologize, but the words remain. Also, if something is broken, like an egg, it cannot always be repaired.

- Teach the children how to accordion fold strips of construction paper to make pop-out eggs as a CRAFT during FREE CHOICE PLAY. Use green paper strips to practice, then let the children add them to the SENSORY TABLE.

- Play "The Disappearing Egg." Use the **large basket with grass.** Place different colored eggs in the basket. While hiding the eggs in the grass, take one away. See if the children can guess which egg has disappeared. Again, by showing the children the game at CIRCLE TIME, they can play it again at FREE CHOICE PLAY.

- Do a relay race carrying a pretend bird egg on a tablespoon. Divide the class into two, three, or four groups and do an old-fashioned relay race down a hallway, outside, or in a gym.

- Color eggs with nature. Put eggs in a pan of water to cook at the beginning of CIRCLE TIME. Simmer for 20 minutes to show the children how to make hard-cooked eggs. Ahead of time, cut pantyhose into four-inch pieces. (Cut across the leg to make four-inch tubes.) Take the children outside to find a small leaf to print on their eggs. During FREE CHOICE PLAY, give each child a turn to color an egg with nature. To color, lay the leaf on the egg and place the nylon tube tightly over the leaf to hold it in place; twist tight and rubber band the ends. Use a spoon to dip the wrapped egg into egg dye and color according to directions, *but soak the egg for four minutes.* Remove the egg with the spoon, snip the rubber band, and take off the nylon tube and leaf. Let the egg dry before touching it.

TIP Before going outside to collect leaves, show the children some examples of tiny leaves that will fit on an egg.

- Read the book ***I Can Count 100 Bunnies and So Can You!*** by Cyndy Szekeres. Count and hop one hundred times.

TABLE WORK

- Trace two eggs on white construction paper. One is printed, "A ____________ is inside ____________'s egg" and the other egg is blank.

Children cut out the two eggs. Use the index cards made at CIRCLE TIME to write an animal's name, and then the children write their own names to fill in the blanks on the appropriate egg. Next, the children must draw the animal they chose on their empty egg. Have a sample of an animal drawn on an "empty" egg. Explain to the children in the old days farmers "candled" their eggs to make sure they were safe to sell. Turn the picture of the animal to the back and hold it up to the light and they will be able to see the animal through the paper. Ask the children, "Can you guess what animal it is?" Staple the two eggs together *at one edge* with the animal's picture inside. When the egg is closed, it is as if the animal is inside the egg. The back side of the egg can be held up to the light to see the drawing inside—just like candling an egg!

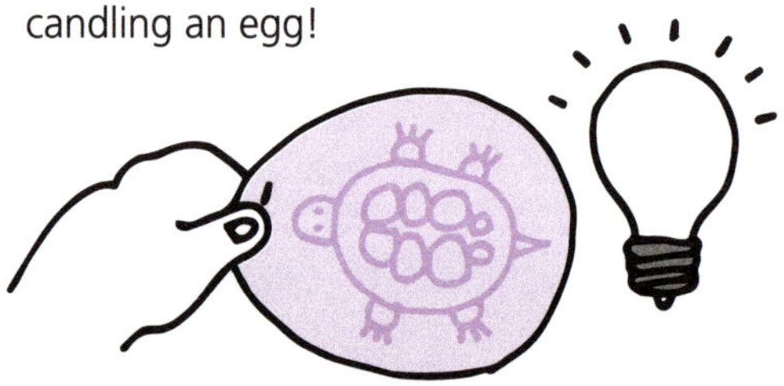

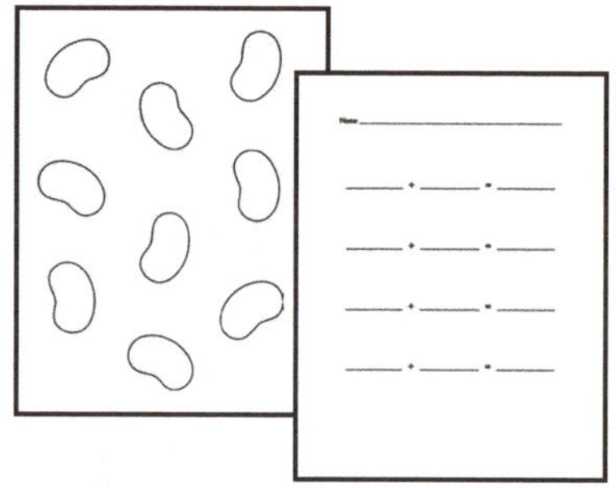

- Color with crayons the page of nine jelly beans all one color. Cut out the jelly beans. Turn them to the other side and color them a different, but all the same, color. For example, one side is all pink and the other side is all green. Give each child a paper cup to shake up his jelly beans. Dump the jelly beans onto the table and look at them; maybe two are pink and seven are green. Teach the children to write the number sentence 2 + 7 = 9. Now have the children shake and dump their jelly beans and write three more math sentences.

- Print the rabbit puzzle pieces on pastel copy paper. Cut the pieces of the rabbit puzzle, assemble, and glue the pieces to a small paper bag.

- Use the recycled handmade paper to make a card for the family. Make paper at CIRCLE TIME or during OUTSIDE TIME early in the week so it dries completely. It is best not to fold the paper. Rather write a message on the front of the card and make a butterfly for the back. Use a wooden craft stick for the body of the butterfly. Make butterfly wing patterns for the children to trace. Use paper from the scrap box to trace the wings so it is an authentic recycled project!

- **Journal** Write: *The egg cracks. The egg opens. Hello chick.*
(Tell the children they are writing a story this week.) Cut out the two egg halves and the yellow chick. Punch a hole in the two shell pieces where marked. Join the top and bottom shells with a paper fastener so the egg opens and closes. Glue the chick to the bottom half of the shell with its head sticking up, but be sure the top shell covers it when closed. Glue *only the bottom half of the shell* in the journal. The top shell opens so the chick can say, "Hello!"

FREE CHOICE PLAY

Writing Center

Use any dot-to-dot, spring coloring pages, or spring activity pages this week.

Board Games

- Hisss by Gamewright
- Frog Pond Fractions Game by TREND Enterprises
- Hoot Owl Hoot by Peaceable Kingdom
- Let's Feed the Very Hungry Caterpillar by Briarpatch
- The Very Hungry Caterpillar Spin & Seek ABC by Briarpatch

Sensory Table

Fill the table with paper grass. Add plastic eggs, egg cartons, spoons, and a large basket. This week the children may take the items out of the sensory table to play the games taught at CIRCLE TIME.

TIP Children can make the paper grass by cutting strips of green construction paper and accordion folding the strips to make bouncy grass.

Workbench

Weave ribbon into vegetable produce baskets. Twist on a pipe cleaner for a handle.

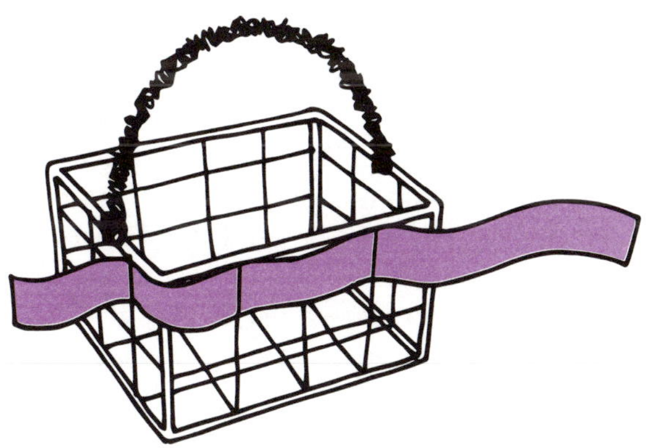

Easel Art

Add white to the easel paint to make a variety of pastel colors. Use butterfly stencils to paint.

TIP Tell every child to paint two dessert-sized paper plates completely, leaving no white spaces. Save the plates for a bulletin board display later in the year.

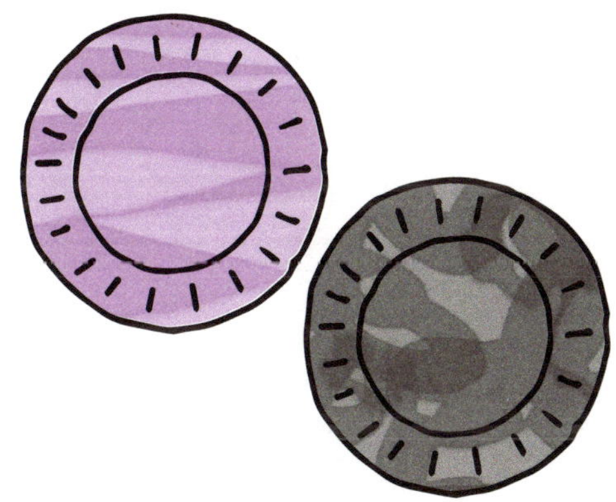

FREE CHOICE PLAY

Crafts

- Place more jelly bean pages used at TABLE WORK on the craft shelf to color. More jelly beans will make their math sentences more difficult.

- Make pop-out eggs. Trace eggs on white poster board. (Children have practiced accordion folding strips of paper.) Children will cut out the egg and punch a hole in the top to tie a ribbon to hang. Accordion fold strips and glue five to six rows on each side of the egg. Glue only at the two ends of the strip and let the middle "pop out."

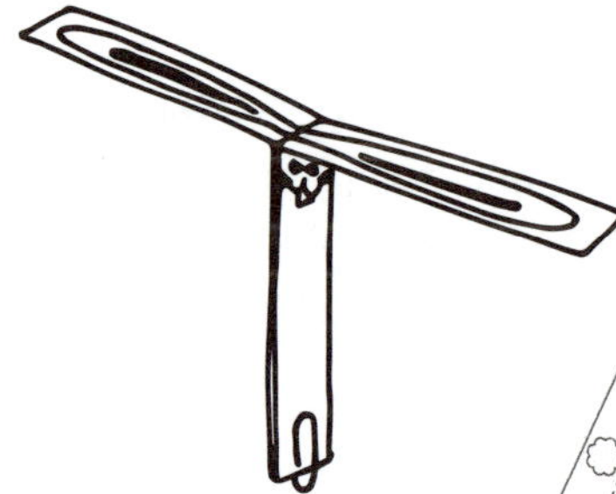

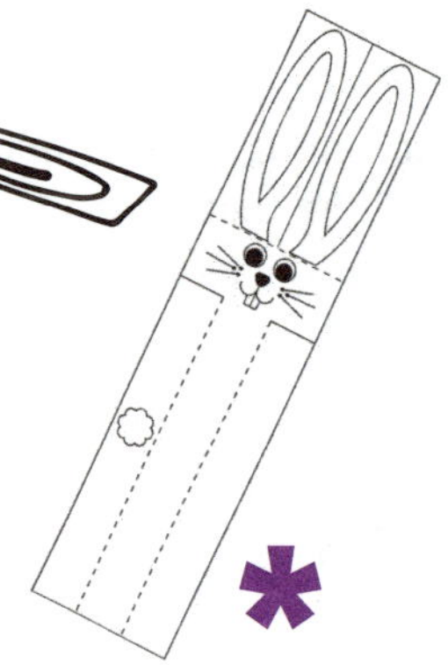

- Cut, fold, and staple a bunny twirler. It is a bunny like the helicopter made at TABLE WORK in Simple Machines Week on page 74. Cut on the solid lines, fold on the dotted lines, and staple to hold the folded body flat. Fold one ear forward and one ear backward so it spins.

- Make coffee filter butterflies. For each butterfly, color two coffee filters with markers. Spray the colored coffee filter *very* lightly with water. The colors will spread and mix. Let the coffee filter dry while preparing the "body" clothespin. Use a marker to draw a little face on the top of the clothespin. Fold a pipe cleaner in half and wrap the crease around the top, just below the face. Curl the antennae with a pencil or finger. When dry, pinch each coffee filter in half and slip into the clothespin.

- Draw an egg on manila paper. Then, draw a design on the egg using a white or yellow crayon. Paint the egg with watercolors. The design will show up because the crayon is made of wax and resists the watercolor. It's called a *resist painting*!

- Make a simple front-facing bunny pattern.

TIP Assemble the bunny puzzle used at TABLE WORK to make the pattern for tracing.

Trace the bunny on pastel-colored construction paper. Cut out the bunny. Paint the bunny lightly with glue. Set two moveable eyes and a button nose in place. Fill in the rest of the bunny with pieces of yarn to make a soft, touchable bunny.

HOW TO: **Make Recycled Handmade Paper**

1. Cut recycled construction paper scraps into one-inch squares or small pieces.

2. Place two handfuls of the cut-up paper into a blender. Fill the blender three-quarters full of warm water and blend the paper and water for two minutes on medium speed. The sloppy paper mixture is called *slurry*.

3. Set up an old window screen over a large basin, drain, or set it up outside. Pour the slurry onto the screen in the form of a rectangle. (The card can be trimmed when it is dry.) Children can press the slurry gently against the screen to squeeze out excess water.

TIP **Very important!** Bring the screen inside and out of the sun as soon as it is finished dripping (construction paper fades in the sun).

4. Let the recycled handmade paper dry completely; it may take two days.

5. Repeat the process for each child. (This may need to be a two-day activity.)

Notes & Evaluations

	Circle Time	Table Work	Free Choice Play	Crafts
Monday	Beginning: Ending:			
	Story:			
Tuesday	Beginning: Ending:			
	Story:			
Wednesday	Beginning: Ending:			
	Story:			
Thursday	Beginning: Ending:			
	Story:			
Friday	Beginning: Ending:			
	Story:			

Dramatic Play

Decorate with baseball-themed posters, games, and activities. Children can dress up in baseball caps and T-shirts. In addition, set up a bowling alley with empty water bottles and a small beach ball.

Learning Objectives

Physical and Motor

- Catches a ball when thrown or bounced
- Throws a ball to a target overhand and underhand

Cognitive

- Knows half or more letter sounds
- Sorts and organizes

Communication and Language

- Retells a story in sequence
- Refers to *yesterday* and *tomorrow* correctly

Social and Emotional

- Shows strong emotions
- Shows increasing responsibility

Approaches to Learning

- Seeks and accepts help and information

Listening Activities and Songs

- Song: "Take Me Out to the Ball Game" by Jack Norworth and Albert Von Tilzer
- Song: "Do the Hokey Pokey" by Larry LaPrise
- Play music by Ludwig van Beethoven. Set up the headphones near the easel so the children can listen to music while they draw (see EASEL ART on page 218).

This week, play T-ball during outside or gym time. For safety, use a sponge ball with a plastic bat. Stand behind the batter at home plate and direct them to the right toward first base when the ball is hit. All other children can play the field until it is their turn to bat. Play for fun and don't keep score.

Stories

- *Getting to Know the World's Greatest Composers: Ludwig Van Beethoven* by Mike Venezia
- *Take Me Out to the Ballgame* by Jack Norworth and Amiko Hirao
- *The Berenstain Bears Play T-Ball* by Stan and Jan Berenstain
- *Goodnight Baseball* by Michael Dahl
- *Here Comes the Strikeout* by Leonard Kessler
- *Pinny the Bowling Pin* by Leah Ward
- *Mitchell Goes Bowling* by Hallie Durand
- *Sally's Great Balloon Adventure* by Stephen Huneck
- *One Bean* by Anne Rockwell
- *Jack and the Beanstalk* by Parragon Books
- *Pop! A Book about Bubbles* by Kimberly Brubaker Bradley
- *Harvey Potter's Balloon Farm* by Jerdine Nolen
- *(Math Start Directions) Bug Dance* by Stuart J. Murphy

Bb WEEK

Baseball

Bowling

Blowing Bubbles

Balloons

Body Parts

CIRCLE TIME

Interactive Charts and Props

- Parts of the Body chart (see Week 1 for the chart on page 14)
- Create your own Baseball Diamond interactive chart.
- Create your own Baseball Card Matching Chart.

TIP You can use any baseball cards or photos as long as you have a duplicate set.

Circle Time Activities

- Introduce the letter *Bb*.
- Sing **"Take Me Out to the Ball Game."** Use the **Baseball Diamond interactive chart** to teach the children the basic rules of baseball. Make a die from a cube and label it *Single*, *Double*, *Triple*, *Home Run*, and *Strike* on two sides. Make two sets of game pieces in two different colors. Make enough so each child has a game piece. (Baseball hats are easy to draw and can easily be colored red and blue.) Divide the class into two teams, and take turns rolling the dice. Move around the bases to the right. Three strikes and you're out; after three outs, it's the next team's turn to roll the dice. Play baseball at CIRCLE TIME each day, keeping the same teams and adding to the score each day. Baseball is a good way to teach right and left.

- Read the book ***Getting to Know the World's Greatest Composers: Ludwig van Beethoven*** by Mike Venezia. Listen to music by Beethoven. Tell the children they can draw at the easel this week while listening to music like they did during *Cc* Week (see EASEL ART on page 218).
- Talk with the children about the SENSORY TABLE activities for the week. Give the children rules for play with each activity. Keep it simple because the activity changes each day. Discuss the first two days of bubble activities (see SENSORY TABLE on page 218).
- Read the book ***One Bean*** by Anne Rockwell. Prepare green bean seeds for planting according to the story (in the SENSORY TABLE).
- Show the children a flower bulb. Explain the difference between a bulb and a seed. Purchase an amaryllis flower bulb and plant it on the day the children plant their green bean seeds (see SENSORY TABLE on page 218). Tell the class what to expect as it grows. Ask them if they will help take care of the plant. This flower will grow very large and has a dramatic bloom. Every day, measure and record the progress of the plant.
- Teach the children to play **The Berenstain Bears Join The Team Card Game** by Briarpatch.
- Play and sing **"Do the Hokey Pokey"** to reinforce right and left and parts of the body.

TABLE WORK

Bb WEEK

- Review body parts using the **Parts of the Body chart.**

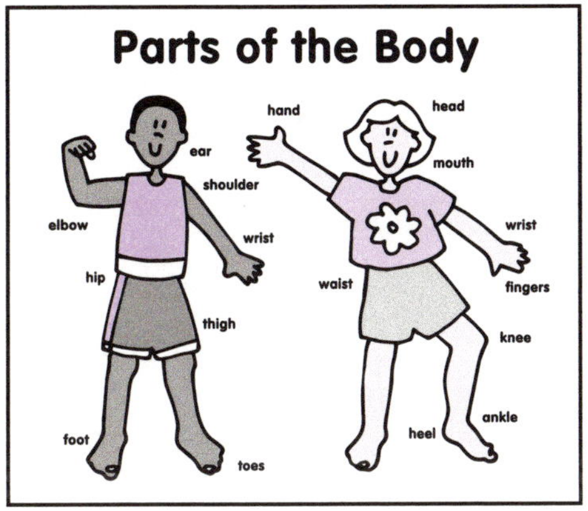

- Read the book ***Bug Dance*** by Stuart J. Murphy. Everyone stand up and dance!
- Learn about and play with balloons.

1. Create static electricity by rubbing a balloon on your head and sticking it to the wall.
2. Ask the children, "How do you pop a balloon?" Answers may be "sit on it" or "pop it with a pin." Show the children this trick: place a cross of adhesive tape on an inflated balloon. Stick a pin in the center of the tape and the balloon will not pop.
3. Blow up a balloon for each child and play "Keep the Balloon in the Air." Use a stopwatch and see how long before the last child is out. It's more fun for everyone if they try to beat the time as a class, not individually.

- Practice writing the letter of the week. Practice writing the letter *Bb*.

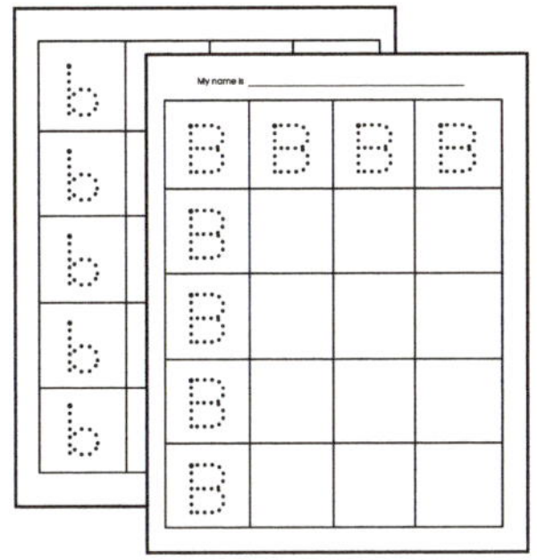

- Phonics Sheet for the letter *Bb*

- Right and Left Reproducibles

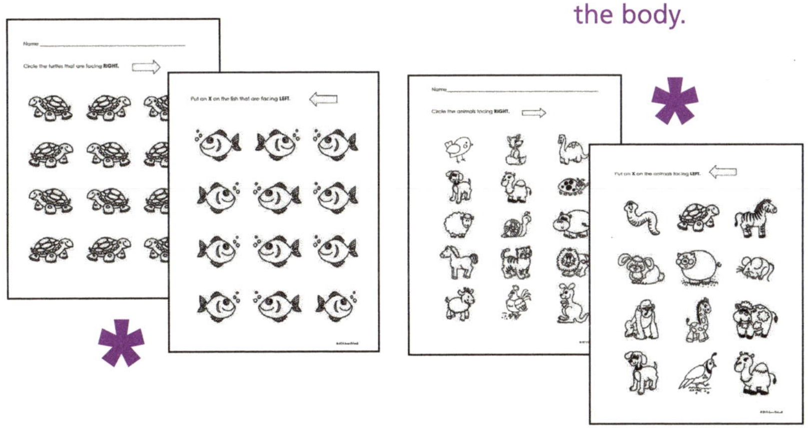

- **Journal** Write: *My body bends*. Cut out the body parts. Glue them in the journal in a bent position so the body fits on the page.

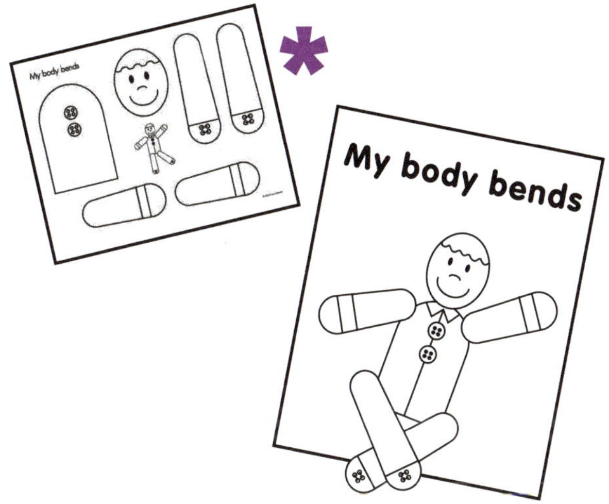

TIP Make the body parts too large to fit on the page in the journal when the body is standing straight and tall, so the children must bend the body.

FREE CHOICE PLAY

Writing Center

Alphabet Stamps

Board Games

- Boggle Jr. by Hasbro
- Berenstain Bears Join The Team Card Game by Briarpatch.

Sensory Table

Day 1. Blow bubbles. Place two dishpans of bubble solution and a variety of bubble wands and other tools that can be used to blow bubbles in the sensory table. Try using a straw to blow one bubble inside another bubble. Bubbles can be blown in the classroom if there is enough space, otherwise do this activity outside.

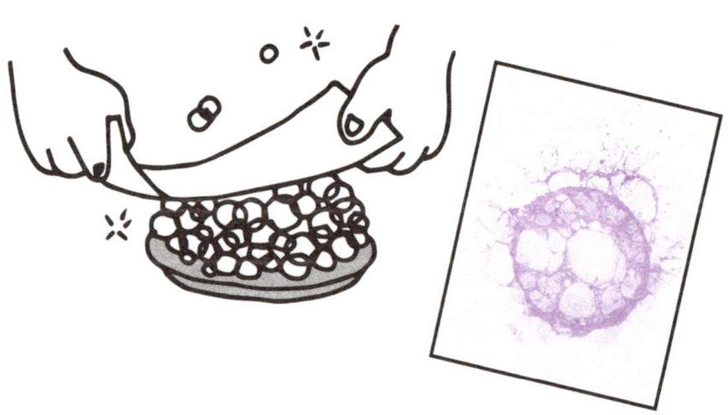

Day 2. Transfer the bubble solution left from the previous day to tin pie pans. Add a generous amount of tempera paint to the bubble solution and mix well. To make bubble prints, place a straw into the bubble solution and blow until bubbles reach the top and overflow the pie pan. Lay a piece of paper on the bubbles to make a beautiful print. Large pieces of paper can be printed to make bubble-print gift wrap.

TIP The children should wear goggles while blowing bubbles so that soap does not splash into their eyes.

Day 3. Read the book ***One Bean*** by Anne Rockwell. Use the table to prepare beans for planting.

Day 4. Plant the green bean seeds in soil. Also plant an amaryllis bulb for the class to observe and care for. As the bulb grows, measure and record each day's growth. Count the days until it blooms.

Day 5. Have children water their green bean seeds by squirting them with a spray bottle. Let them take their plants home at the end of the week. Tell them, "Put your plant in the sun and water it every day!" Continuing to care for the amaryllis bulb should remind the children to care for their bean plants.

Workbench

Make craft stick boxes. Enlarge this illustration for the children to use as a guide.

Easel Art

Use markers to draw while listening to music. Set up the headphones near the easel and just turn on the music! (This activity was also done in *Cc* Week.)

Crafts

- Use the colored bubble solution in the SENSORY TABLE to make bubble-print gift wrap (see SENSORY TABLE **Day 2**). This activity can be moved to a tray on a table in the craft area. Use the solution until it is gone.
- Copy "My Body Bends" from the journal TABLE WORK onto cardstock. Before copying, mark with a small *x* where pieces will be joined. Children cut out the pieces and punch holes wherever there is an *X*. Join the pieces with paper fasteners to make bendable children. Draw a face, hair, and clothes to decorate. Hang up the bendable children, posing them jumping, dancing, and playing!

- Provide sports stamps: baseball, bat, glove, football, soccer ball, basketball, etc. Add stamp pads and paper.

- Make beautiful birds:

1. Cut a variety of colors of construction paper lengthwise into 1½-inch-wide strips (makes six strips).

2. Take three strips and, one at a time, measure and cut one at 5 inches, one at 6 inches, and one at 7 inches.

3. Take a 5-, 6-, and 7-inch piece and staple them together at one edge. Do the same with a second set of 5-, 6-, and 7-inch pieces. One set will be the body and the other set will be the tail.

4. Take one more full-length strip and cut it into a 3-, 4-, and 5-inch piece.

5. Take the 4- and 5-inch piece and staple together for the head. (The 3-inch piece is the beak, step 9.)

6. Form the head by rolling the pieces together with the shortest strip rolled to the inside. Staple the head to the outside center of the 7-inch strip of the section that will be the body.

7. To join the body, pull the unstapled edges together and roll into a circle, with the shortest strip rolled to the inside, and staple.

8. Staple the tail strips to come out from under the body.

9. Use the last 3-inch strip to make the beak for the bird. Glue the beak in place.

TIP Cut all the strips ahead of time. Have the children gather the strips needed for their beautiful bird. Much of the assembly must be done by an adult, but allow the children to measure, cut, and staple whenever possible.

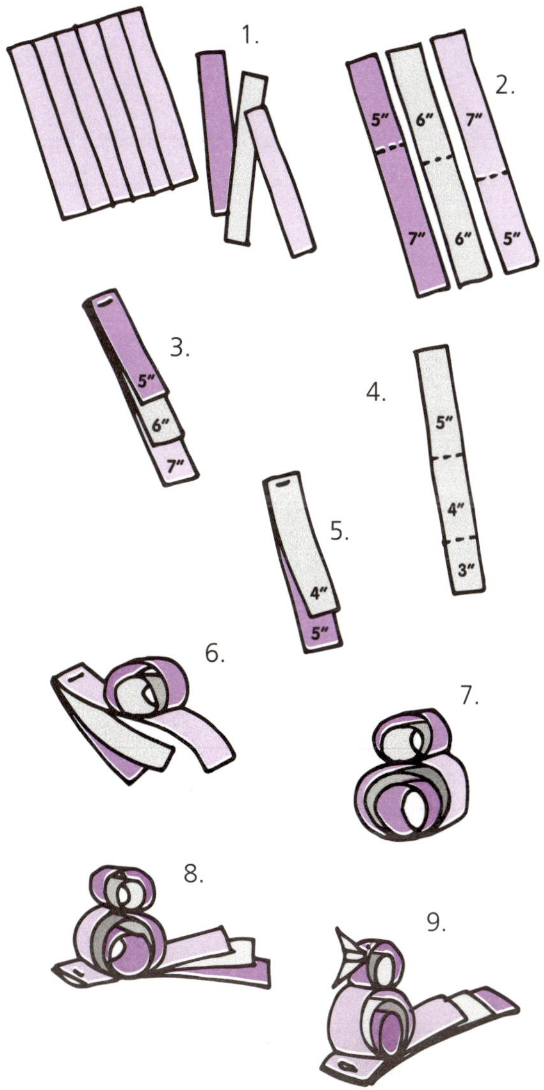

Notes & Evaluations

HOW TO: Make bead key chains

Make bead key chains. Purchase a few instruction booklets from a local craft store along with pony beads, cord, and rings. Enlarge the instruction sheet for each project. Children can cross off each row as it is completed. Keep it simple, for example, a worm, a kite, a fish.

TIP Children may need some encouragement to work on their project for a few days in order to finish.

	Circle Time	Table Work	Free Choice Play	Crafts
Monday	Beginning: Ending:			
	Story:			
Tuesday	Beginning: Ending:			
	Story:			
Wednesday	Beginning: Ending:			
	Story:			
Thursday	Beginning: Ending:			
	Story:			
Friday	Beginning: Ending:			
	Story:			

Artist WEEK

Artists and the techniques they used to create art

The artists studied are

- **Leonardo da Vinci**
- **Michelangelo**
- **Vincent van Gogh**
- **Paul Gauguin**
- **Georges Seurat**
- **Henri Matisse**
- **Alexander Calder**
- **Pablo Picasso**
- **Marcel Duchamp**
- **Jackson Pollock**

Dramatic Play

Set up areas to use age-appropriate methods to explore each artist and his techniques.

Learning Objectives

Physical and Motor

- Uses scissors
- Uses small muscles in hands to color, cut, paste, and paint

Cognitive

- Can stay with the same activity for five to ten minutes (increasing concentration)
- Uses prepositional terms (*under*, *over*, *through*, *next*)

Communication and Language

- Uses language to control and give directions
- Follows two-to-three-step directions

Social and Emotional

- Expresses feelings and emotions with words
- Understands others' perspectives

Approaches to Learning

- Invents new purposes for objects

Listening Activities and Songs

Play instrumental classical music softly while the children work on art pieces.

Stories

- *The Art Lesson* by Tomie dePaola
- *Ish* by Peter H. Reynolds
- *The Dot* by Peter H. Reynolds
- *Leonardo and the Flying Boy* by Laurence Anholt
- *Camille and the Sunflowers* by Laurence Anholt
- *Matisse: the King of Color* by Laurence Anholt
- *Picasso and the Girl with a Ponytail* by Laurence Anholt
- *Action Jackson* by Jan Greenberg and Sandra Jordan
- *Degas and the Little Dancer* by Laurence Anholt

A list of reference books can be found at the end of the **Artist Week** chapter.

CIRCLE TIME

Interactive Charts and Props

- Make a poster for each artist studied and place it in the area for that artist. Label the poster with the artist's name and a few examples of his work. Show a sample of how the children are to create their own masterpiece using the artist's technique.

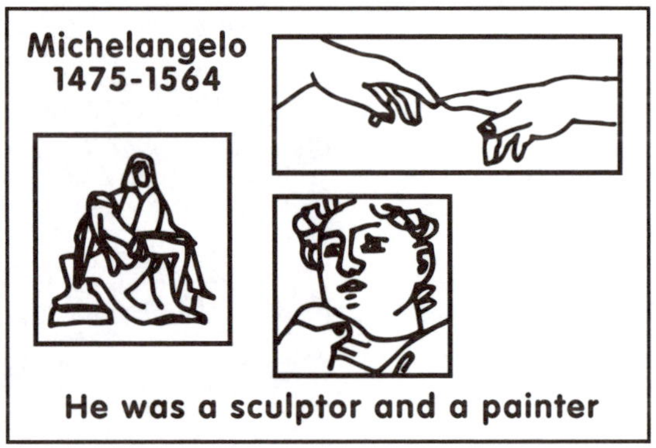

- Two paintings by different artists and paint chips to play "Artist Eyes" (see CIRCLE TIME)

Circle Time Activities

- Tell the children, "I am going to introduce you to ten famous artists this week. We cannot talk about them all at once, so we will study a few each day. Then I will let you try to draw and paint and sculpt the way they created their masterpieces. You will create masterpieces too!" Give them each a pocket folder and tell them, "You will create pieces of art for your portfolio. Then your artwork will hang in our art gallery. Everyone will see that you are artists too!" (see CRAFTS on page 226).

- Read the book ***Neo Leo: The Ageless Ideas of Leonardo da Vinci*** by Gene Barretta, or tell the children about Leonardo da Vinci using the book as a reference. Display the *Mona Lisa* and ask the children if they have ever seen the painting (many children will recognize it). Give each child a coloring page of the *Mona Lisa*. Explain the TABLE WORK activity to the children. They will color the *Mona Lisa* using crayons. Tell them it is their masterpiece, so they may color her any way they choose. For a CRAFT this week, pick out coloring pages of the famous artists studied this week. Tell the children that if they finish and have time during FREE CHOICE PLAY, they may color and assemble a book of artists to take home.

- Read ***Getting To Know The World's Greatest Artists: Michelangelo*** by Mike Venezia, or use the book as a reference and tell the children about Michelangelo in your own words. Explain the activity set up "at and under" the writing table (see WRITING CENTER for explanation on page 225). Tell the children that even though Michelangelo is famous for his painting, his favorite form of art was sculpting. Explain the sculpting activity in the SENSORY TABLE.

- Read ***The Life and Work of Alexander Calder*** by A. R. Schaefer, or tell the children about Alexander Calder. Show them a mobile. Explain the wire art at the WORKBENCH.

TIP Review the safety rules (see WORKBENCH on page 225).

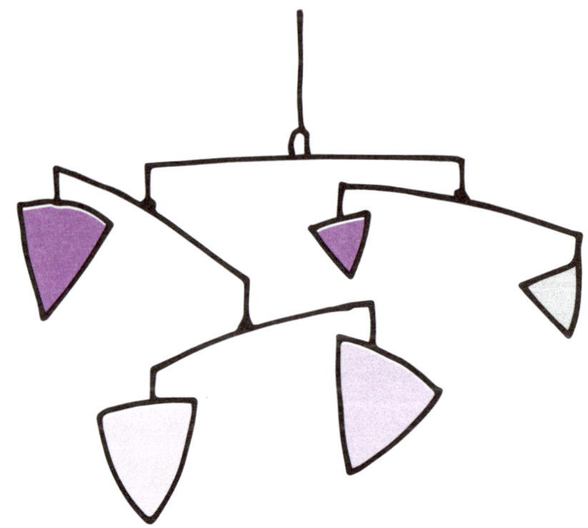

- Read ***Getting To Know The World's Greatest Artists: Vincent van Gogh*** by Mike Venezia, or tell the children about Vincent van Gogh in your own words. Explain how the children will paint flowers with thick paint like van Gogh. Have a variety of vases cut for the children to glue on a paper at TABLE WORK. Set up the activity with fingerpaint, brushes, and paper. The children can take turns at FREE CHOICE PLAY painting their art piece for the portfolio. Display the **poster about van Gogh** nearby.

- Read ***The Life and Work of Pablo Picasso*** by Leonie Bennett. Because Picasso was known for using monochromatic colors when he painted, demonstrate how black and white can be added to the easel paint to make a shade and tint of a color. Make two sets of paints to be used at the easel (see EASEL ART on page 225). Also explain how the children's art piece for their portfolio will imitate Picasso's cubism technique. They will draw using shape stencils at TABLE WORK and paint at the easel at FREE CHOICE PLAY (see TABLE WORK on page 224).

- Read ***The Life and Work of Georges Seurat*** by Paul Flux. Show the children an example of how small dots of color will mix and fool the eye—for example, many tiny dots of red and yellow will look orange when seen from far away. Explain that the children will use dot markers to "dot" their painting to imitate Seurat. They can try a small area of tiny dots using different colors; however, to make an entire art piece using this technique would take too long. Set up an area with paper and dot markers. Display the **Seurat poster** nearby.

- Use the book ***Discovering Great Artists: Hands-On Art for Children in the Styles of the Great Masters*** by MaryAnn F. Kohl and Kim Solga. Introduce the children to Marcel Duchamp and his unique art technique. Tell the children the SENSORY TABLE will be used for them to try "The Happy Accident String Drop" that imitates Marcel Duchamp. Finish this activity in one day if possible.

- Read ***The Life and Work of Paul Gauguin*** by Paul Flux. Have the children draw a picture using silly colors at TABLE WORK (see TABLE WORK on page 224).

- Read ***The Life and Work of Henri Matisse*** by Paul Flux. Explain how to "draw with scissors" to imitate Matisse. Make a Matisse art piece at TABLE WORK. Empty the box of scrap construction paper into the SENSORY TABLE so many hands can look together.

- Read: ***Getting To Know The World's Greatest Artists: Jackson Pollock*** by Mike Venzia, or ***Action Jackson*** by Jan Greenberg and Sandra Jordan. Tell the children the class will be painting like Jackson Pollock, but because he was such a messy artist, the class will paint just one large painting together. (Do this outside or on a drop cloth inside.) Allow each child to take a turn to drizzle or even "throw" the paint with a brush.

- Take time to name each child's Picasso art piece just like Picasso did.

- A favorite activity is to play "Artist Eyes." To prepare, find two prints of paintings by different artists. I use Vincent van Gogh, who paints with muted, soft colors, and Pablo Picasso, who uses bold, bright colors. Go to a paint store and find paint chips that match the colors exactly. Tape each paint chip to a craft stick so the children can hold it close to the painting and see which painting the paint chip matches. This activity demonstrates, for example, that all blues are not the same. When each child finds a color match say, "You have artist eyes!" Leave the paint chips out so the children can continue this activity during FREE CHOICE PLAY.

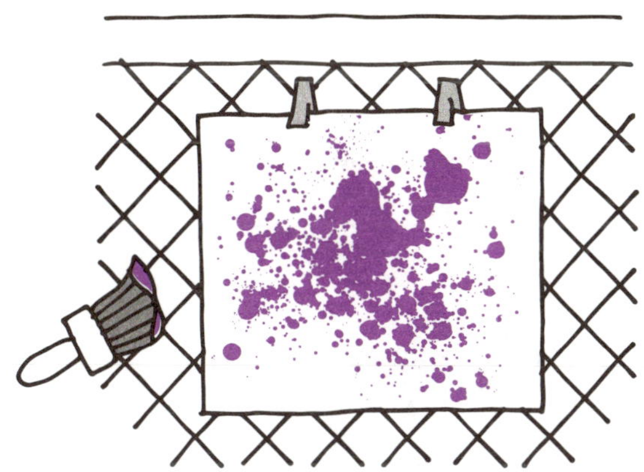

TIP For the Jackson Pollock art piece, use clothespins to hold a piece of poster board to the fence on the playground.

TABLE WORK

- Use a reproducible coloring page of the *Mona Lisa*. Have the children color the picture using crayons. Remind them to color the entire picture. Allow them to use their choice of colors, but have a print of the *Mona Lisa* by Leonardo da Vinci available for the children to see.

*

- In preparation for their van Gogh art piece, have each child trace and cut out a construction paper vase and glue it on her paper. Paint flowers with a brush using fingerpaint (thick paint) at FREE CHOICE PLAY.

- After discussing Pablo Picasso at CIRCLE TIME, make enough circle, square, and triangle patterns for the children to share at TABLE WORK. The children use the shape patterns to create a geometric drawing. The children are imitating Pablo Picasso's cubism technique. Take turns painting the art piece at the easel during FREE CHOICE PLAY.

- After discussing Paul Gauguin at CIRCLE TIME, have the children draw a picture using silly colors. For example, if they draw a dog, color it blue or color a tree trunk red with purple leaves, etc.

- After discussing Henri Matisse at CIRCLE TIME the children will "draw with scissors" to make their art pieces. Dump the scrap box in the SENSORY TABLE so there is room for lots of little hands to find scraps for their art piece.

- **No journal this week.**

Have the children check their portfolios and see if there are any art pieces that they still need to complete. Each portfolio should include the following:

1. The *Mona Lisa* by da Vinci, colored with crayons
2. Drawing of people imitating Michelangelo
3. Picture of flowers painted with fingerpaint to imitate van Gogh
4. Silly color picture to imitate Gauguin
5. A dotted art piece to imitate pointillism by Seurat
6. An art piece to imitate "drawing with scissors" by Matisse
7. The geometric drawing painted with monochromatic colors at the easel to imitate cubism by Picasso
8. "The Happy Accident String Drop" art piece to imitate Duchamp

(One Jackson Pollock art piece is done together; clay sculpting to imitate Michelangelo and wire art to imitate Alexander Calder are optional.)

FREE CHOICE PLAY

Writing Center

Use this area for the artist Michelangelo. Display the **art poster** on the tabletop with paper, masking tape, and markers. Set up for two children to work at a time. Have the children lie on their backs on a floor pillow, tape a paper on the underside of the table, and draw people using markers. Michelangelo spent four years painting the Sistine Chapel in this way.

Board Games

- Pictionary Jr. by Mattel
- Shape, Letter, and Number lotto
- You can purchase artist puzzles. These are from the *For the Young at Art Series:* "Edgar Degas—*The Dance Class*," "Paul Cezanne—*Apples and Oranges*," "Vincent van Gogh—*Vase with Twelve Flowers*," and "Georges Seurat—*A Sunday on La Grande Jatte*."

Sensory Table

- Days 1 & 2: Provide clay for the children to experience sculpting like Michelangelo. Give the children small pieces to work with to avoid waste.
- Day 3: Tell the children about Marcel Duchamp and the "Happy Accident String Drop" while the children hold the strings with tweezers and dip them in paint with glue added (so the strings stick to the art piece). Set up a step ladder and have the children climb up a few steps (with adult supervison) and drop colored strings on paper. Allow them to drop at least five strings.
- Days 4 & 5: Dump the scrap paper box in the sensory table so the children can easily find construction paper pieces to use for the Matisse art piece.

Workbench

This area will show the art of Alexander Calder. Hang a mobile in the area along with a **poster** showing his brightly colored artwork. Use the workbench for wire art. Thin, pliable wire coated with colored plastic is appealing to children. Remind the children to wear safety goggles and use wire cutters, not scissors, to cut the wire. A variety of diameters of dowel rods can be used to wrap the wire, and simple cookie cutter shapes can be used to bend the wire into shapes. The wire art can be displayed as a mobile, or you can stick the pieces into a large piece of Styrofoam wrapped with silver paper for the art gallery.

Easel Art

On each side of the easel, place three cups of paint: a tint, a shade, and the original color. For example, sky blue, navy blue, and true blue; or maroon, pink, and red. The monochromatic colors are used to paint the geometric art piece each child drew at TABLE WORK to imitate Picasso's cubism.

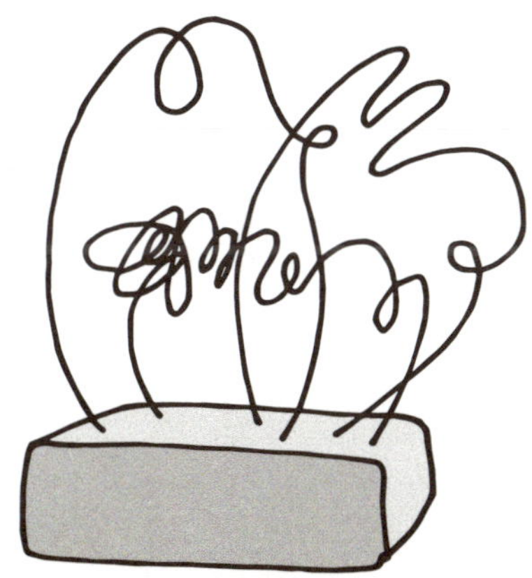

FREE CHOICE PLAY

Crafts

This week is already full of art and crafts so encourage the children to build with blocks, assemble puzzles, and play games when they finish art pieces. Also, when their portfolios are complete, allow the children to make more than one art piece imitating a favorite artist. Then have children choose their favorite one to hang in the art gallery.

Reference Books

- *Discovering Great Artists: Hands-On Art for Children in the Styles of the Great Masters* by MaryAnn F. Kohl and Kim Solga

  Author's Note: This book contains a brief biography of each artist as well as a suggested way for children to create art using a technique similar to the real artist. If you can only purchase one book, let this be the one!

- *The Children's Book of Art* by Rosie Dickins
- *The Usborne Introduction To Art* by Rosie Dickins and Mari Griffith
- *Art Is . . .* by Bob Raczka
- *Neo Leo: The Ageless Ideas of Leonardo da Vinci* by Gene Barretta
- *Getting To Know The World's Greatest Artists: Michelangelo* by Mike Venezia
- *Getting To Know The World's Greatest Artists: van Gogh* by Mike Venezia
- *The Life and Work of Paul Gauguin* by Paul Flux
- *The Life and Work of Georges Seurat* by Paul Flux
- *The Life and Work of Henri Matisse* by Paul Flux
- *The Life and Work of Alexander Calder* by A.R. Schaefer
- *Pablo Picasso: Breaking All the Rules* by True Kelley
- *Marcel Duchamp A Life in Pictures* by Jennifer Gough-Cooper and Jacques Caumont
- *Getting To Know The World's Greatest Artists: Jackson Pollock* by Mike Venzia

Notes & Evaluations

Art Gallery

When Artist Week is finished, hang the children's artwork to create an art gallery. Group all the art pieces made to imitate each artist together. For example, display all the Picasso art pieces with the **Picasso Poster.** Families will be able to see how the children learned and understood the artist's techniques. This is a wonderful example of what young children are capable of, and they will be so proud to show all their hard work!

	Circle Time	Table Work	Free Choice Play	Crafts
Monday	Beginning: Ending:			
	Story:			
Tuesday	Beginning: Ending:			
	Story:			
Wednesday	Beginning: Ending:			
	Story:			
Thursday	Beginning: Ending:			
	Story:			
Friday	Beginning: Ending:			
	Story:			

Aa WEEK

Alphabet

Addition

Apples

Ants

Dramatic Play

Gardening

Learning Objectives

Physical and Motor

- Copies and draws simple shapes and letters
- Puts puzzles together

Cognitive

- Recognizes alliterative sounds in words
- Understands concepts such as age, number, and distance

Communication and Language

- Answers questions about familiar stories
- Pronounces words and letters correctly

Social and Emotional

- Follows and makes simple rules
- Engages in group play

Approaches to Learning

- Offers ideas and suggestions

Listening Activities and Songs

- Song: "The Ants Go Marching One by One" by Robert D. Singleton
- Song: "*Alouette*" (Traditional)

Stories

- Walt Disney's *Alice in Wonderland (Little Golden Books)* by RH Disney
- *The Grasshopper and the Ants* by Jerry Pinkney
- *The Ants Go Marching* by Dan Crisp
- *Chicka Chicka Boom Boom* by Bill Martin Jr. and John Archambault
- *Johnny Appleseed* by Steven Kellogg
- *Alexander and the Terrible, Horrible, No Good, Very Bad Day* by Judith Viorst
- *Truman's Aunt Farm* by Jama Kim Rattigan
- *My Garden* by Kevin Henkes
- *Matthew A.B.C.* by Peter Catalanotto
- *Alpha Oops! The Day Z Went First* by Alethea Kontis
- *The Alphabet Tree* by Leo Lionni
- *Alphabet Adventure* by Audrey Wood
- *The Apple Orchard Riddle* by Margaret McNamara and G. Brian Karas

CIRCLE TIME

Interactive Charts and Props

- Parts of a Plant poster (used in *Ll* Week)
- Create your own sequence cards that show planting a seed step-by-step.
- Apples to cut in half crosswise to print a star pattern
- A variety of vegetable seed packets
- Vegetable cutouts that show the following:
  - Leaf of the plant: spinach, lettuce, kale, cabbage
  - Root: carrots, radishes, potato, onion, turnip
  - Stem: celery, asparagus
  - Fruit: cucumber, pumpkin, squash, tomato, green beans
  - Flower: broccoli, cauliflower
  - Seeds: peas

Circle Time Activities

- Introduce the letter *Aa*.
- Scientists that study ants are called *myrmecologists*. Read the book ***The Ants Go Marching*** by Dan Crisp. An ant farm can be purchased or set up for the children to observe.
- Sing **"The Ants Go Marching One by One"** by Robert D. Singleton.
- Talk about **apples.** Explain that there are different kinds—some are crisp for eating, some are for cooking into pies and applesauce, etc. Cut an apple to identify its parts. Cut an apple in half crosswise to find the "star." Use paint on a sponge to print the star inside the apple. Leave the **apples** and paint for printing during FREE CHOICE PLAY.
- Review the parts of a plant using the **Parts of a Plant poster.** Show the **vegetable cutouts.** Sort them into what part of the plant we eat: the leaf, root, stem, fruit, flower, or seed of a plant. Draw a line on the whiteboard to represent the soil. Pass out the **vegetable cutouts.** The children will take turns placing the vegetables above the ground or below the ground according to how they grow.
- Ask the children to help make a creative alphabet bulletin board. Use TREND Enterprises' 4-inch Casual Black Letters. Give each child a letter to take home, use their imagination and decorate. Hang up each letter as the children return them. Two of my favorite examples are when a child glues a photo on the letter—for instance, Natalie chooses the *N* and glues a photo of herself on the letter. Another child glued green grass on the letter *G*.

TABLE WORK

- Explain the craft in which children cut out flowers and circle centers to make a set of upper and lower case alphabet letters for matching. Have a set of flowers and centers made and play "match the capital and lower case letters" to create interest in the activity (see CRAFTS on page 232).
- Sing: **"Alouette"** (Traditional)
- Practice the concept of addition. After making a math sentence at TABLE WORK, show the children how to use seeds to make more math sentences.
- After children have explored and sorted seeds at the WORKBENCH for a few days, ask them to guess which seeds match the vegetable packets that are displayed.
- Ask the children their favorite activity done in class this school year. Use their answers as a page in the End-of-the-Year Memory Book (see details in the box at the end of FREE CHOICE PLAY on page 233).
- Practice writing the letter of the week. Practice writing the letter *Aa*.

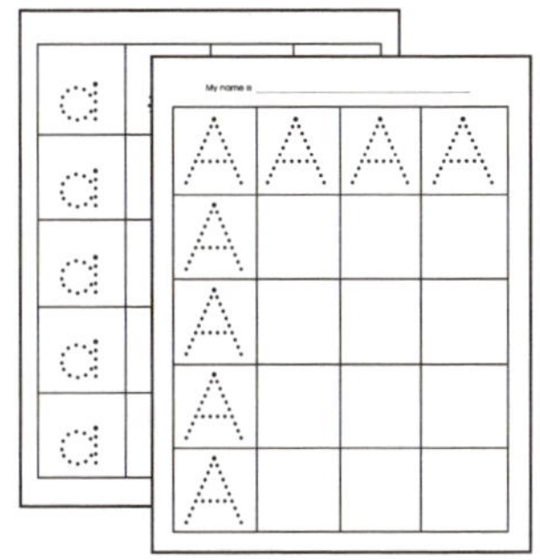

- Have each child draw a self-portrait to be copied for the memory book (see details in the box at the end of FREE CHOICE PLAY).
- Make the autograph page for the End-of-the-Year Memory Book (see details in the box at the end of FREE CHOICE PLAY).

  1. Set out an autograph page for each child in a large circle on the tables.
  2. Children write their names on the paper in front of them.
  3. Children move one space to the right and sign the paper that is now in front of them.
  4. Continue until the children have signed all the autograph pages.
  5. Save the autograph pages for the memory book.

- Use the Apple Math Reproducible. Give each child ten apple stickers. Make a math sentence on a half-sheet of construction paper with the apple stickers (see below). Then write the math sentence in the tree using the corresponding numerals. Tape the two parts together.

- **Journal** Write: *I do like apples* **OR** *I do not like apples* (give the children a choice). Make copies of the apple reproducible with lines for the children to use. Make samples for the children to copy. Tell the children to follow the sample and use the lines to guide their writing. Children can cut out the apple and glue it in their journals.

FREE CHOICE PLAY

Writing Center

Alphabet Stamps

Board Games

- ABC Match and Learn Game by Scholastic
- Sequence Letters by Jax
- Scrabble Junior by Hasbro
- Chip-O! by TREND Enterprises

Sensory Table

Provide modeling sand **OR** dough with alphabet letter molds (recipe for homemade modeling sand in *Dd* Week).

Workbench

Place a variety of vegetable seeds in a bowl. Using tweezers, children sort the seeds into a divided tray, like an ice cube tray or egg carton. Display the **seed packets** near the workbench. After sorting, have children guess which seeds match each vegetable.

Easel Art

Purchase a large set of ABC stencils. Fill in the ABC stencils with dot markers **OR** free paint.

Crafts

- Finish any remaining artwork from Artist Week until all portfolios are complete.
- ABC stamps and stamp pads
- Cut apples in half crosswise to stamp "stars."

TIP To experiment, try cutting an apple in half from top to bottom to see the print.

- When the WORKBENCH activity of sorting seeds is exhausted, glue vegetable seeds to create art.
- Trace flowers and circles for the center of the flower. Children cut out the flowers and circle centers to make a set of upper and lower case alphabet letters for matching. When twenty-six flowers and twenty-six centers are cut, stamp or print a capital letter on the flower and the lower case letter on the circle center. Play with a set at CIRCLE TIME. Children can help make a few sets if they enjoy the activity.

Notes & Evaluations

- Make flower rings using pipe cleaners, felt or art foam, circles, and buttons.

- Trace an alligator for the children to cut out. Use a paper fastener to make the mouth open and close.

- Make a paper plate angel. Draw two lines on the plate, dividing the plate into fourths. In one section, trace a 2½-inch diameter circle close to the center. Draw a cutting line along the ridges of that same section, which will become the arm. Staple the angel's dress, one piece on top of the other. Staple the head and arm on the top. Draw a face on the angel. Punch a hole and tie a ribbon to hang.

End of Year Memory Book

Give each child a memory book at the end of the year. Pages can include the following:

- A letter from you (their teacher)
- One or two poems or short stories of encouragement
- A page listing all the children's birthdays
- The children's answer to the question "What was your favorite activity done in class during the school year?"
- Autograph page (TABLE WORK Activity)
- A class photo
- Have all the children draw a picture of themselves with their name clearly written. Print copies so each child has a picture of all their friends (TABLE WORK Activity).
- A thank-you letter to the families

	Circle Time	Table Work	Free Choice Play	Crafts
Monday	Beginning: Ending:			
	Story:			
Tuesday	Beginning: Ending:			
	Story:			
Wednesday	Beginning: Ending:			
	Story:			
Thursday	Beginning: Ending:			
	Story:			
Friday	Beginning: Ending:			
	Story:			

Ready for Kindergarten

End-of-the-Year Activities

Open House

Class Play

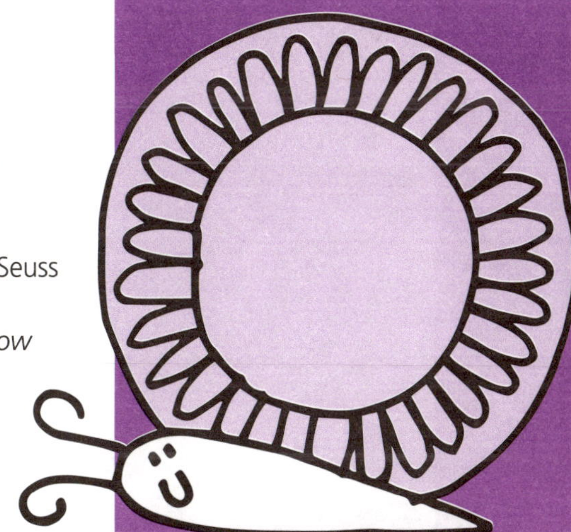

Dramatic Play

Create scenery and props for the play.

Learning Objectives

Physical and Motor

- Walks on a balance beam or line
- Uses large muscles to throw, climb, skip, hop, jump, catch, turn somersaults, and bounce

Cognitive

- Has a vocabulary of 2,000 to 6,000 words
- Counts twenty or more objects with accuracy

Communication and Language

- Sings songs, fingerplays, and rhymes with increasing accuracy
- Listens for details

Social and Emotional

- Is sensitive to the feelings of others
- Plays with peers, sharing ideas and toys

Approaches to Learning

- Reflects on past experiences and applies information to new situations

Listening Activities and Songs

- Review the songs learned throughout the year to see which ones could be used in the class play.

Stories

- *This Is the Way We Go to School: A Book about Children around the World* by Edith Baer
- *Off to Class: Incredible and Unusual Schools Around the World* by Susan Hughes
- *Hooray for You! A Celebration of "You-ness"* by Marianne Richmond
- *You Are Special* by Max Lucado
- *Rain School* by James Rumford
- *Miss Bindergarten Gets Ready for Kindergarten* by Joseph Slate
- *School Around the World* by Casey Null Petersen
- *The Night Before Kindergarten* by Natasha Wing
- *Happy Birthday To You!* by Dr. Seuss
- *It's Hard to be Five: Learning How to Work My Control Panel* by Jamie Lee Curtis
- *Armando and the Blue Tarp School* by Edith Hope Fine and Judith Pinkerton Josephson

CIRCLE TIME

Interactive Charts and Props

Sock puppets that were made in *Pp* Week for storytelling.

Circle Time Activities

- Tell the children about the **class play.** Explain the process (see FREE CHOICE PLAY section on page 239).
- Tell the children the characters chosen. Make a list of all the characters. Group them together to give some direction to the story. Brainstorm story ideas with the children.
- Use sock puppets from *Pp* Week. To prepare, place a sticky name tag on each child's sock puppet of the character they chose the day before. Using the sock puppets, help the children see all the characters of the story and not focus just on themselves. Continue to create the story with the children. Take notes so the story can be finalized. Continue this process until the play is written.

TIP As the class writes the story and you write the script, listen to how each child expresses their lines. Children memorize their lines very quickly. Therefore, when practicing, it is best to keep the script consistent to avoid confusion.

- Each day, discuss props or scenery that will be worked on during FREE CHOICE PLAY. Explain the process so children can begin promptly with minimal assistance.
- Identify some songs, learned throughout the year, which can be adapted to fit in the storyline. Practice the songs.
- Read the play with the children. Have the characters repeat their lines.
- Block the play. Include all stage directions: when characters enter and exit, where they move, who they speak to, use of props, etc.
- Practice, practice, practice! Make it fun. Sing the songs. And the children love using the props!
- Discuss costumes. Keep it simple; however, know that what the children wear helps identify the character. Practice in full costume at least three times to be sure all children are comfortable with the costumes chosen.

TIP Try to keep CIRCLE TIME short so more time can be devoted to practice.

TABLE WORK

- Print an Invitation to the **class play.** Include the date and time. Children will draw a scene or prop from the play to decorate the invitation. Use their drawings to create the program and/or posters for the class play.

- Trace snail bodies. Each child cuts out a snail body and chooses a painted dessert plate (Spring Week). Staple the body of the snail to one side of the dessert plate. The snails are Part 1 of a bulletin board display for the **open house.** Trace the letters *SLOWLY WE HAVE GROWN . . . AND CHANGED*. Divide the letters among the children to cut out. Hang the snails on the bulletin board during FREE CHOICE PLAY so the children can see their work.

- Trace letters for any props or scenery. Have children cut them out. Review how to cut out the centers of the *O*s, *B*s, *D*s, etc.

- Give the children specific activities that will help to make the scenery and props. For example, if there is a field of flowers in the scenery, have each child cut out a few flowers and glue them in place.

- **Journal** Write: *I am a* _____________. Children draw a picture of their character in the play.

TIP Teacher, take photos of children in costumes and glue them in their journals.

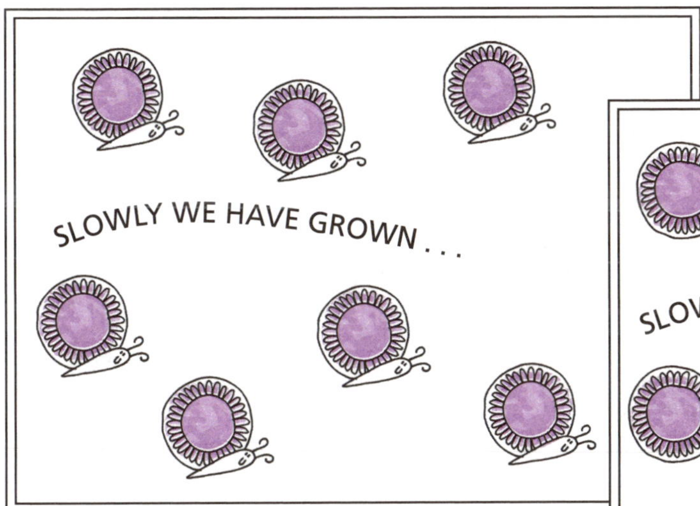

TIP Display PART 2 of the bulletin board. Change the snails to butterflies by adding a second plate to the other side of the body and add the words *AND CHANGED*.

TIP Display PART 1 of the bulletin board with the snails and the words *SLOWLY WE HAVE GROWN . . .*, then on the last day before the **Open House**, put up PART 2.

FREE CHOICE PLAY

Writing Center

Any sit-down work that needs to be done for the **class play.**

Board Games

- Tell-A-Story by Ravensburger.
- Bring out a few of the children's favorite games.

Sensory Table

Use for a messy activity to make props.

Workbench

Use the workbench to make props that need construction tools.

Easel Art

Put the easel away to create more space unless it is needed to make specific props.

Crafts

Encourage the children to help with the scenery and props rather than projects to take home. Explain that help from everyone is needed for a big project like the **class play.**

TIP Try this scenery idea if the children have chosen characters that could be part of a town—for instance, grocery clerk, pet shop owner, dentist, librarian, doctor, etc. Make doors using poster board and hang each one on a chart rack. The children can look through old wallpaper books and find appropriate designs for a "door collage." Letters can also be cut out of wallpaper to make signs to label the doors.

CLASS PLAY

HOW TO: Put on a class play with young children

1. Each child chooses the character she would like to be. Tell the children to choose a real person, not a superhero or cartoon character. Say, "Maybe think about what you would like to be when you grow up."

TIP Ask the children to tell you the character individually at FREE CHOICE PLAY. It works best if there is a variety. You might say, "Only one of each character."

2. Write the story with the children, using all the characters chosen.

TIP Unlike other plays, there are no stars; all characters have an equally important role.

3. Incorporate lessons learned during the school year in the story.
4. Teacher, write the script.
5. Add songs. (optional)
6. Create the scenery and props with the children during class time.
7. Discuss and decide on costumes for each character.
8. Photograph the children in costume and display the cast photos.
9. Make a program to give to the guests during the **class play.**
10. Teacher, write a synopsis of the **class play** so the audience can easily follow the story. Include the synopsis in the program.

TIP Here are a few ideas:

- Set the story on a farm. Make the barn into a shadow puppet stage (*Ll* Week).
- Have a construction worker pull a wagon up an INCLINED PLANE. Include a well with a PULLEY. A rancher and a cowboy play the spoons sitting around the campfire—the spoons are LEVERS (Simple Machines).
- Change the Box Race Cars (*Rr* Week) into a fire truck, police car, bulldozer, tractor, or any vehicle needed. Connect two boxes to make a limousine. Make a boat or even an airplane!
- Use a catapult to make an animal fly (*Cc* Week).
- Have a mail carrier use addresses to deliver packages (*Vv* Week).
- More lessons to use are Days of the Week (*Ww* Week), Estimating (*Ee* Week), the Five Senses (Five Senses Week), Measuring (*Mm* Week), posters of artwork done by artists studied (Artist Week).
- Even Hernando and Harriet, the little creative writing project puppets, can find their way into the play as pets of the characters!

Notes & Evaluations

PREPARING FOR OPEN HOUSE

Include in the Memory Book

- A letter from you (their teacher)
- One or two poems or short stories of encouragement
- A page listing all the children's birthdays
- The children's answer to the question "What was your favorite activity done in class during the school year?"
- Autograph page (TABLE WORK Activity in *Aa* Week)
- A class photo
- Have all the children draw a picture of themselves with their name clearly written. Print copies so each child has a picture of all their friends. (TABLE WORK Activity in *Aa* Week)
- A thank-you letter to the families

TIP Assemble the memory book in time for the **open house.**

Art Gallery

Hang the art gallery on an open wall or in the hallway.

ABC Bulletin Board

Create an ABC bulletin board made by the children (see explanation in *Aa* Week on page 230). Hang a letter created by each child.

Snails to Butterfly Bulletin Board

Create the Snails to Butterflies bulletin board with the words *SLOWLY WE HAVE GROWN… AND CHANGED*.

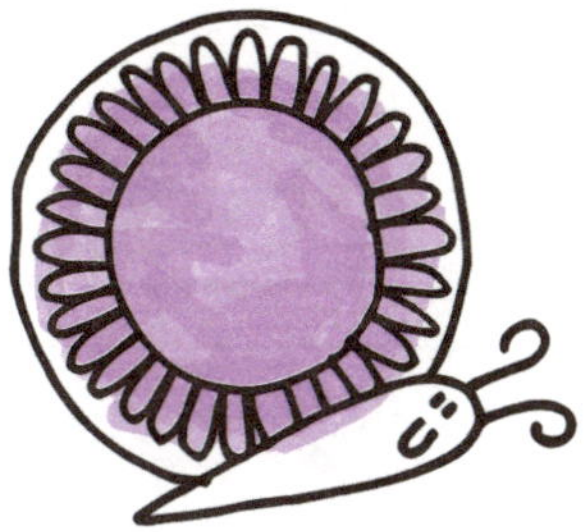

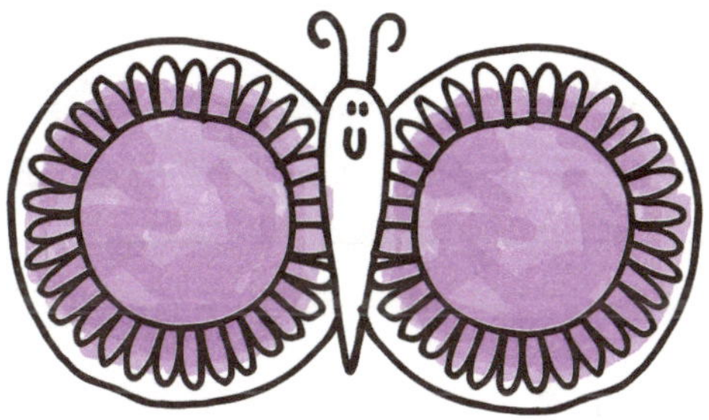

Cast Photos

Put cast photos from the **class play** on display.

Journals and Memory Books

Place journals and memory books at each child's place.

Creative Writing Puppets

Display the creative writing puppets Hernando and Harriet with the journals of the children's adventure stories.

Notes & Evaluations

	Circle Time	Table Work	Free Choice Play	Crafts
Monday	Beginning: Ending:			
	Story:			
Tuesday	Beginning: Ending:			
	Story:			
Wednesday	Beginning: Ending:			
	Story:			
Thursday	Beginning: Ending:			
	Story:			
Friday	Beginning: Ending:			
	Story:			

Observe and record each child's development to share with families

The revised edition lays out the milestones and provides space to record the dates when the child begins moving towards, achieves, and finally masters milestones. It is a valuable, easy-to-use tool to record the child's development.

The Redleaf Family Child Care Curriculum Developmental Assessment
Ten individual booklets. Age focus: 0–5.
#544168 $15.95

Includes the curriculum plus 35 children's books hand selected by the author

This set includes the complete 35-week preschool curriculum and 35 supplemental children's books suggested by the author to correspond with each week's lesson plan. Examples of the books included are *The Day the Crayons Quit, All the Colors We Are, Last Stop on Market Street,* and *Planting a Rainbow.*

Visit **RedleafPress.org/A-to-Z** for a full list of the children's books included with this set.

A to Z Ready for K: A Complete 35-Week Preschool Curriculum with Resources
Softbound, 256 pgs. Includes 35 children's books.
#545418 $399.95

Set price reflects a savings of $100 off the retail value, plus receive free shipping.

Redleaf Press®

Visit www.RedleafPress.org or call 800-423-8309 to order.